Knowledge, Language and Mind

On Wittgenstein

Edited on behalf of the
Internationale Ludwig Wittgenstein Gesellschaft e.V.
by James Conant, Wolfgang Kienzler,
Stefan Majetschak, Volker Munz, Josef G. F. Rothhaupt,
David Stern and Wilhelm Vossenkuhl

Volume 1

Knowledge, Language and Mind

Wittgenstein's Thought in Progress

Edited by
António Marques and Nuno Venturinha

DE GRUYTER

ISBN 978-3-11-048174-7
e-ISBN 978-3-11-028424-9

Library of Congress Cataloging-in-Publication data
A CIP catalog record for this book has been applied for at the Library of Congress.

Bibliographic information published by the Deutsche Nationalbibliothek
The Deutsche Nationalbibliothek lists this publication in the Deutsche Nationalbibliografie; detailed bibliographic data are available in the Internet at http://dnb.d-nb.de.

© 2012 Walter de Gruyter GmbH & Co. KG, Berlin/Boston.
Typesetting: Medien Profis GmbH, Leipzig
Printing: Hubert & Co. GmbH & Co. KG, Göttingen
∞ Printed on acid-free paper
Printed in Germany

www.degruyter.com

Contents

Abbreviations

AWL	*Wittgenstein's Lectures: Cambridge, 1932–1935*, ed. A. Ambrose, Oxford: Blackwell, 1979.
BBB	*The Blue and Brown Books*, 2nd edn, ed. R. Rhees, Oxford: Blackwell, 1969.
BEE	*Wittgenstein's Nachlass: The Bergen Electronic Edition*, Oxford: Oxford University Press, 2000. (Numbers of manuscripts (MS), typescripts (TS) and dictations (D) are according to G. H. von Wright's catalogue.)
BT	*The Big Typescript*, ed. and trans. C.G. Luckhardt and M.A.E. Aue, Oxford: Blackwell, 2005.
CE	"Cause and Effect: Intuitive Awareness", trans. P. Winch, in PO, pp. 368–426.
CV	*Culture and Value*, rev. 2nd edn (A. Pichler), ed. G. H. von Wright, trans. P. Winch, Oxford: Blackwell, 1998.
DB	*Denkbewegungen: Tagebücher 1930–1932, 1936–1937 (MS 183)*, ed. I. Somavilla, Innsbruck: Haymon, 1997.
GB	"Remarks on Frazer's *Golden Bough*", trans. J. Beversluis, in PO, pp. 115–155.
LC	*Lectures and Conversations on Aesthetics, Psychology and Religious Belief*, ed. C. Barrett, Oxford: Blackwell, 1966.
LFM	*Wittgenstein's Lectures on the Foundations of Mathematics: Cambridge 1939*, ed. C. Diamond, Ithaca, NY: Cornell University Press, 1976.
LW II	*Last Writings on the Philosophy of Psychology*, vol. II, ed. G. H. von Wright and H. Nyman, trans. C. G. Luckhardt and M. A. E. Aue, Oxford: Blackwell, 1992.
LWL	*Wittgenstein's Lectures: Cambridge, 1930–1932*, ed. D. Lee, Oxford: Blackwell, 1980.
NB	*Notebooks 1914–1916*, 2nd edn, ed. G. H. von Wright and G. E. M. Anscombe, trans. G. E. M. Anscombe, Oxford: Basil Blackwell, 1979.
OC	*On Certainty*, rev. edn, ed. G. E. M. Anscombe, trans. D. Paul and G. E. M. Anscombe, Oxford: Blackwell, 1974.
PG	*Philosophical Grammar*, ed. R. Rhees, trans. A. Kenny, Oxford: Blackwell, 1974.
PI	*Philosophical Investigations*, 2nd edn, ed. G.E.M. Anscombe and R. Rhees, trans. G. E. M. Anscombe, Oxford: Blackwell, 1958.
PIr	*Philosophical Investigations*, rev. 4th edn, ed. P. M. S. Hacker and J. Schulte, trans. G. E. M. Anscombe, P. M. S. Hacker and J. Schulte, Oxford: Blackwell, 2009.
PO	*Philosophical Occasions 1912–1951*, ed. J. C. Klagge and A. Nordmann, Indianapolis: Hackett, 1993.
PPF	"Philosophy of Psychology – A Fragment", in PIr, pp. 182–243.
PR	*Philosophical Remarks*, ed. R. Rhees, trans. R. Hargreaves and R. White, Oxford: Blackwell, 1975.
RFM	*Remarks on the Foundations of Mathematics*, 3rd edn, ed. G. H. Von Wright, R. Rhees and G. E. M. Anscombe, trans. G. E. M. Anscombe, Oxford: Blackwell, 1978.
RPP II	*Remarks on the Philosophy of Psychology*, Vol. II, ed. G. H. von Wright and H. Nyman, trans. C. G. Luckhardt and M. A. E. Aue, Oxford: Blackwell, 1980.
TLP	*Tractatus Logico-Philosophicus*, trans. C. K. Ogden, London: Routledge & Kegan Paul, 1922.
VW	*The Voices of Wittgenstein: The Vienna Circle*, ed. G. Baker, trans. G. Baker, M. Mackert, J. Connolly and V. Politis, London: Routledge, 2003.

WA   *Wiener Ausgabe*, ed. M. Nedo, Vienna: Springer Verlag, 1993ff.
WC   *Wittgenstein in Cambridge: Letters and Documents 1911–1951*, ed. B. F. McGuinness, Oxford: Blackwell Publishing, 2008.
WVC   *Wittgenstein and the Vienna Circle*, ed. B. F. McGuinness, trans. B. F. McGuinness and J. Schulte, Oxford: Blackwell, 1979.
Z   *Zettel*, 2nd edn, ed. G. E. M. Anscombe and G. H. von Wright, trans. G. E. M. Anscombe, Oxford: Blackwell, 1981.

Acknowledgments

This book was prepared within the framework of the research project *Wittgenstein's* Philosophical Investigations: *Re-Evaluating a Project*, funded by the Portuguese Foundation for Science and Technology (FCT) and hosted by the Institute for Philosophy of Language (IFL) at the Faculty of Social and Human Sciences (FCSH), New University of Lisbon (UNL). The editors would like to express their gratitude to all these institutions as well as to the authors who have contributed to this volume, the majority of whom have had the opportunity to discuss their work in Lisbon during various activities carried out under the project. We also would like to thank Carlos Pereira and Vanessa Boutefeu for their editorial assistance as well as Alberto Arruda for organizing a meeting with the editors in 2011 and for his collaboration throughout the project.

Editors' Introduction

The essays included in the present book present a multitude of topics and suggestions all relating to Wittgenstein's philosophy. Nonetheless, in most chapters (if not in all of them) it is easy to identify the problem of *method*, indeed of a new method for philosophy, as a transversal theme. It is true that the development of his post-*Tractatus* thought, the identification of processes of discontinuity, the characterization of the rupture brought about by Wittgenstein himself or the exact timing of the establishment of a new philosophy have always occupied a central place in Wittgenstein interpretation. Already the 1945 "Preface" to the *Philosophical Investigations* is itself an important piece of self-criticism and, to a certain extent, does not allow much doubt as to the moment when he first recognized "grave mistakes" in his former philosophy: "For since I began to occupy myself with philosophy again, sixteen years ago, I could not but recognize grave mistakes in what I set out in that first book".[1] The invention of new methods associated to different "Copernican revolutions" has, of course, been a recurrent procedure of philosophers throughout the history of philosophy, and always represents a kind of self-reception of their own former thought. In the case of Wittgenstein interpretation, the evaluation of more or less dramatic discontinuities is by itself a chapter of commentary on his work, namely if the line of discontinuity between a dogmatic and an undogmatic philosopher acquired a new strength with the discussion promoted by the so-called "New Wittgenstein" approach.[2]

If one takes a closer look at the different chapters, we find that Peter Hacker's essay, although not primarily centred on the methodological issue, makes an important contribution to helping clarify the "logico-grammatical" method that Wittgenstein uses to criticize the traditional (empiricist as well as rationalist) account of self-knowledge and self-ascribed experience. He does this by confronting it with Kant's doctrine of transcendental apperception, where the awareness of the subject's ownership of his representations is the basis for human experience or objective knowledge. In Wittgenstein no such requirement is necessary in order to become master of the perceptual vocabulary and concepts of perception. In Hacker's view, Wittgenstein's account of self-consciousness breaks with the Cartesian/Lockean tradition which culminates in Kant: in order to express feelings or perceptual experiences it is simply not necessary to presuppose that there be a core of *a priori* conditions to produce such expres-

---

1 All quotes are from PIr.
2 See as the most relevant starting point for this discussion, Crary and Read 2000.

sions, that is to say, transcendental apperception. This logico-grammatical (not epistemological) account of human experience is at the root of the new method, which deserves to be seen as a "Copernican revolution" in philosophy at least as fundamental as Kant's methodological revolution was in his day. What is interesting is that such methodological ruptures have a singular common aspect: they occur under the form of critical self-reception. Hacker's chapter explores in great depth the specificity and novelty of the new method of philosophy, considering it against the background of Kant's philosophy of mind and self-consciousness. The exploration of such issues and their consequences should be easily perceived by the reader: the new method is the product of a complex reflection on the paradoxes and entanglements of earlier convictions, and it must be developed not only against the background of these earlier convictions but also against the background of the great names of the philosophical tradition who also exercised similar self-criticism.

As is well known, the debate between the different positions on Wittgenstein's later criticism of his own philosophy, namely the *Tractatus Logico-Philosophicus*, starts from essentially different hermeneutic positions. In the current debate it is possible to isolate two positions: (i) the New Wittgenstein supporters who claim that both the *Tractatus* and the *Investigations* are therapeutic works or possess a central therapeutic inspiration and that both should be viewed as non-dogmatic works; (ii) the opponents of this view who claim that Wittgenstein read his *Tractatus* afterwards in a way that contradicts his later non-dogmatic interpretation. The argumentation used by opponents of the New Wittgenstein interpretation can be designated as typical contextual argumentation.[3] We could add that, according to this view, Wittgenstein is the most important critic of the *Tractatus'* dogmatism. This debate does not have a central place in the following essays although several of them bring to light a number of different, interesting questions and help to identify some of the central issues that are to be found in the discussion between the New Wittgenstein interpreters and their opponents. In the end, what is at stake are a number of points regarding Wittgenstein's self-reception and the evolution of his therapeutic semantics.

A first question can be raised with regard to the problem of an author's criticism of his own earlier work, which is the problem of the value of such retrospective self-criticism. The history of philosophy is peppered with many such cases, beginning with Plato, who in a dialogue with the great Parmenides is forced to acknowledge that in regard to "things [...] such as hair, mud, dirt, or anything else particularly vile and worthless [...] it would be quite absurd to

---

3 See Pichler forthcoming.

believe that there is an idea of them".[4] Or the case of Kant when he breaks with his Leibnizian-Wolffian phase through a rehabilitation of sensibility by giving it specific non-intellectual forms (time and space). This is also done through a form of self-reception or self-evaluation. But if an author says that he was wrong about certain central points of his earlier writings and warns the reader of that very fact, how should we behave towards the part that has been criticized by its author? This is not an irrelevant question since it has to do with the status of authorship and the consideration that, in principle, it is reasonable to assume that there must be a kind of final correct interpretation – the interpretation that the author himself gives of what he did or thought.

In point of fact, the *Tractatus*, besides its apparent dogmatic central doctrines such as logical atomism, simple objects and the representational nature of the proposition, to refer only to the most important and well known topics, also possesses clear non-dogmatic declarations and, one could even add, a therapeutic perspective. It is enough to remember the view that logical form *shows itself*, but cannot be described from a higher meta-logic, and the general insight that philosophy is not a doctrine but an activity. If this is true, then stressing only those passages in the *Investigations* where Wittgenstein criticizes Tractarian theses, or those theses that Wittgenstein himself thinks are the main theses of the *Tractatus*, is perhaps not the best way to understand the *Tractatus* itself, and consequently Wittgenstein's philosophy in general. It should be remembered that in the Preface of the *Investigations* Wittgenstein speaks of regarding the *Tractatus* as a *Gegensatz* to his new way of thinking in order to see his new thought in the right light. He does not mention a correction or a set of theses that the *Investigations* should overcome. Moreover, in § 23 of the *Investigations* he speaks of comparing (*vergleichen*) "the diversity of the tools of language and of the ways they are used, the diversity of kinds of word and sentence, with what logicians have said about the structure of language. (This includes the author of the *Tractatus Logico-Philosophicus*.)" Continuous self-reception therefore means continuous self-therapy in a selective form. What the *Investigations* aims to do is not so much to erase the potential for philosophical therapy that the *Tractatus* already contains, but rather to discover new therapeutic procedures, which of course emerge from Tractarian aims. In fact, the above quotation regarding the comparison of what logicians (including the author of the *Tractatus*) have said about language and the new way to see language, thus placing all the critical understanding of language in post-*Tractatus* works, seems to ignore what Wittgenstein himself has said about natural language in the *Tractatus* (for example,

---

4 Plato 1926, 130c–d.

in 4.002). There he recognizes the immense complexity of natural language and says nothing which leads us to think that it is not useful for mutual understanding. This problem of understanding language as a tool for mutual understanding is after all not a problem in the *Tractatus*. At this point it makes sense to remember that the framework is different.

The Wittgenstein of the *Investigations* criticizes the *Tractatus* but at the same time uses it to take his work further, which is an interesting point that generally goes unnoticed. But, on the other hand, and this is something that opponents of New Wittgenstein interpretation present as an *onus probandi* for New Wittgenstein representatives, looking at the pre-1929 Wittgenstein, how is someone entitled to say that it makes sense to speak of a therapeutic method? Was it always present but just not explained in the *Tractatus*? It would seem that New Wittgenstein interpretation opponents have a point here: the concept of therapy itself is explicitly linked by Wittgenstein to the implementation of a new method (and here the parallelism with Kant's new method or Copernican revolution is very clear). A meaningful remark about his new method is to be found in § 133 of the *Investigations*:

> We don't want to refine or complete the system of rules for the use of our words in unheard-of ways.
> For the clarity that we are aiming at is indeed *complete* clarity. But this simply means that the philosophical problems should *completely* disappear.
> The real discovery is the one that enables me to break off philosophizing when I want to. – The one that gives philosophy peace, so that it is no longer tormented by questions which bring *itself* in question. – Instead, a method is now demonstrated by examples, and the series of examples can be broken off. – Problems are solved (difficulties eliminated), not a *single* problem.
> There is not a single philosophical method, though here are indeed methods, different therapies, as it were.

However, one must recognize that the aims of "*complete* clarity" and reaching "peace" in philosophical inquiry are desiderata of philosophical reflection in general. At this point, what can be said is that Wittgenstein's work certainly develops self-criticism, and perhaps in a more dramatic way than in other philosophers' work, and if that feature is to be linked to a so-called therapeutic approach, then that characteristic can be found throughout his writings.

It is precisely this characteristic of self-criticism that promotes new insights into the same issues. Perhaps it was this attitude that did not allow Wittgenstein himself to publish his *Investigations*, in particular the so-called "new direction" (von Wright and Schulte) of his thought. After the last redaction (*Spätfassung*) of Part I of the *Investigations*, the writings written between 1945–46 and 1949 mostly on the philosophy of psychology express other therapeutic methods. Other themes that were probably induced by new therapeutic motivations emerge. A well known case which obviously deserves to be more fully demonstrated is the therapeutic of what can be seen as "understanding meaning" or to have experience of meaning. It is clear that there is a transition from a semantics of physiognomy pointed out in Part I of the *Investigations* to a semantics of *aspect changing* developed in the later period mentioned above. In what sense is this new therapy developed in the "fragment" of "Philosophy of Psychology"[5] corresponding to the so-called Part II? One answer could be that Wittgenstein did it through implementing a new figure of *übersichtliche Darstellung*, which was after all an already worked Wittgensteinian concept. At this point it represents another close link between understanding, use of language and perception, that is, a link of three elements forming a system which has its more trivial formulation in the suggestion: "now see this as ..., then see it as ...". The phenomenon of reversible figures like the Jastrow duck-rabbit very much interested Wittgenstein and through this phenomenon he describes a new approach to physiognomy and meaning. The reversible experience "now I see this as a duck head, now as a rabbit head" or from the third person "now see this as A, now as B" does not apply simply to visual perception but also to sound experiences and of course spoken language. What is important is to underline that all change of aspect is correlated to change of meaning of one perception (visual or not) which can change aspect or meaning depending on our will and according to the command "now see (hear) this as ..., then see it as ...". What is important here is that the experience of meaning, like the experience of physiognomic aspect, involves the capacity of seeing aspect changes in the same structure. *Knowledge, Language and Mind* promotes a reflection on this constellation of topics in surveying Wittgenstein's thought in progress.

As previously mentioned, the first chapter, by P. M. S. Hacker, offers a critical analysis of Kantian epistemology by exposing Wittgenstein's *linguistic revolution* in his later philosophy. According to Hacker, "despite Kant's brilliant criticisms of the Cartesian and empiricist traditions, there are four general principles, rooted in Cartesian methodology, which Kant never questioned" whereas "Wittgenstein [...] rejected them all". To begin with, the perspective adopted by Kant in dealing with the fundamental question "How are synthetic a priori judgments possible?" is, for Hacker, "steadfastly epistemological". In second place,

---

5 "Philosophy of Psychology – A Fragment" is the title for the so-called Part II of the *Philosophical Investigations* proposed by the editors (P. M. S. Hacker and Joachim Schulte) of the 4th edition (PIr).

Hacker argues, we have the egocentrism or subjectivism of his view. The third principle is the concept of consciousness inherited from Descartes, Locke and Leibniz. And the last one is Kant's implicit commitment to the logical possibility of a private language. This chapter provides a full-scale examination of the third point, engaging with the nature of consciousness and apperception. The philosophy of language and mind developed in the *Investigations* constitutes indeed a powerful answer to a tradition of thought still anchored to a metaphysical view of knowledge. What Hacker meticulously examines is the behavioural dimension of our experience, which requires a very different approach to human cognition. As he notes, Wittgenstein is interested in the "public criteria for possession of the concepts of seeing, hearing, feeling, etc.", that is to say, in what we, as speakers, "*do with words*". The passages from the *Big Typescript* and the *Investigations* discussed by Hacker allow us to better understand issues like the apperceptive "I", empirical ownership or the classic "I think", as well as why "a transcendental deduction is impossible". As Hacker notes, following Wittgenstein's pathways, the issues "are *not* epistemological, but logico-grammatical ones".

Whereas Hacker's inaugural chapter places Wittgenstein's later thought in contrast with a whole philosophical tradition that culminates in Kant, the second chapter, by João Vergílio Gallerani Cuter, takes the reader from Wittgenstein's *Tractatus* into his post-1929 philosophy. Cuter claims, challenging the standard reading, that it is somehow misleading "to associate the fall of the Tractarian project with the 'colour exclusion problem'". "Numbers", he says, "were at the centre of the crisis". Cuter's close study of the issues Wittgenstein deals with in the early 1930s reveals a decisive background for an understanding of the *Investigations*. What Cuter demonstrates is that the "five red apples" of § 1 "summarize the crisis of the Tractarian project as Wittgenstein faced it", with the *Investigations* aiming to overcome his failures in both the *Tractatus* and the work published as *Philosophical Remarks*.

In the third chapter, Jesús Padilla Gálvez invites us to reflect on the blurring conceptuality of "sentences" and "language" such as discussed by Wittgenstein in the 1933 *Big Typescript*. Revisiting Frege's and Husserl's views on concept and meaning, Padilla Gálvez shows why the Tractarian question for the general form of the proposition remains relevant to the "middle" Wittgenstein, who clarifies it by exposing the grammar of the concepts we use on his path to the *Investigations*.

The fourth chapter, by Nikolay Milkov, summarizes the various phases of Wittgenstein's methodological development from the *Tractatus* until 1936 when the preparation of the *Investigations* properly begins. Milkov initially focuses on the interpretation made by the New Wittgensteinians, especially Cora Diamond and James Conant, and tries to make clear what elucidation means in the *Tracta-*

tus. The second phase is, for Milkov, the period between 1929 and 1932, whereas the third one starts with the *Big Typescript* and ends with the *Brown Book*. It is on this third phase that Milkov centres his attention, advancing the view that in a certain sense "Wittgenstein's turn of 1933 was occasioned – if not caused – by Susan Stebbings' paper "Logical Positivism and Analysis", read to the British Academy as a Henriette Hertz lecture on 22 March 1933, and shortly afterwards published as a brochure". Taken together with Wittgenstein's famous letter of 27 May 1933 to the editor of *Mind*, in which Richard Braithwaite's 1933 paper "Philosophy" is severely criticized, Milkov's suggestion contributes to a better understanding of Wittgenstein's separation from an approach which still shared much of its motivation with the Vienna Circle. Milkov finds particular evidence for this in Wittgenstein's lectures from this period and in the revision of the *Big Typescript*, traces of which can be found in the *Philosophical Grammar* and the *Blue Book*.

The fifth chapter, by Rui Sampaio da Silva, engages with Wittgenstein's middle period but already makes the bridge to the first third part of the *Investigations*. Silva's essay does this by considering the Brandom-McDowell debate on rule-following, a key theme for the understanding of the *Investigations* but which was already under consideration in earlier reflections. Rejecting Brandom's and Kripke's readings, Silva follows McDowell and traces the complex establishment of the idea that "practices and linguistic uses are intrinsically normative" and that "rules are immanent to practices and standards of linguistic use are immanent to use".

In the sixth chapter, Nathan Hauthaler focuses on Wittgenstein's philosophy of action in a continuous dialogue with Davidson's view. Exploring the important distinction between grammars of reasons and causes of action, Hauthaler draws on some of Wittgenstein's texts from the 1930s to consider new ways of thinking about mental states and individual action. Hauthaler's essay sheds light on the discussions about these themes in the *Investigations* and also accesses recent approaches in this field.

The seventh chapter, by Alberto Arruda, continues the examination of Wittgenstein's philosophy of action and mind, concentrating on the concept of "intention" and its role in the *Investigations*. Arruda's exposition revitalizes the significance of § 25, where Wittgenstein claims that our mastering of language implies the recognition that "[g]iving orders, asking questions, telling stories, having a chat, are as much a part of our natural history as walking, eating, drinking, playing". Arruda deepens our understanding of these "natural actions", as Wittgenstein also calls them in the 1930s, illuminating the way in which "acting somehow" involves epistemologico-linguistic processes that the *Investigations*, more than trying to explain, try to describe.

The eighth chapter, by Emiliano La Licata, introduces the complexity theorists into the debate, analysing in particular the close relationship between Wittgenstein's *Philosophical Investigations* and Kaufmann's *Investigations*. The explanation of meaning via use corresponds in complexity theory to "a dynamic view of semantics" and this, for Kaufmann, "produces linguistic creativity". La Licata presents Kaufmann's constructivist approach to autonomous agency as a propagation of meaning, in the midst of which semantic entropy plays a prominent role. La Licata is convinced that Kaufmann's reading of Wittgenstein's *Investigations* "opens the way for a new interpretative paradigm", one that takes Wittgenstein "as an emergentist philosopher".

In the ninth chapter, Constantine Sandis analyses a remark which has given rise to much discussion: "If a lion could talk, we wouldn't be able to understand it."[6] Sandis' thorough study of this phrase makes it evident that Wittgenstein is not interested in this particular animal species or in any other, but solely in "the nature of *understanding*, and its relation to the behaviour of those we understand". Sandis compares Wittgenstein's lion to Nagel's bat, stressing that in neither case are "any ethological facts" at stake. Like the bat, the lion is used to illustrate our problematic access to other forms of life, a question that dominates Wittgenstein's later thought.[7] A very interesting part of Sandis' chapter is the consideration of Dennett's various criticisms of the lion remark, thus placing Wittgenstein's philosophy of mind in contrast with his view of consciousness. What Sandis convincingly shows is the tendency in Wittgenstein commentary to portray the speaking lion as having many of our own characteristics when the problem lies in the fundamental gap between human conceptualization and all that goes beyond *humanity*. Wittgenstein, as Sandis puts it, "is probing for *limiting cases* of resemblances associated with knowledge and understanding" in such a way that "the supposed lion [may] be intended to be as nonsensical as a private language".

The tenth chapter, by Maria Filomena Molder, the last in the volume, deals with diary notes and other remarks written down by Wittgenstein from the 1930s up to his death in 1951 and aims to trace the dynamism of Wittgenstein's mature philosophy. Molder shows why it has resisted a unified interpretation, impregnated as it is with a personal attitude towards life and the world that can only be grasped intuitively. When Wittgenstein struggles with knowledge, language and mind, he is seeking clarity about himself, not theoretical results. This is well

---

6 PPF § 327.
7 On how to interpret Wittgenstein's notion of "form of life", see Marques and Venturinha 2010.

documented by Molder when she analyses many of the thoughts published in *On Certainty* as direct continuations of the reflections we find in the *Investigations* as posthumously published. Making reference to what he himself says in the Preface to that work, Molder writes that "[w]hat Wittgenstein does in philosophy could be described as 'observations' [...], a fact related to a way of abstaining from the pretensions characteristic of most modern philosophers, namely the determination of principles from which consequences are deduced, the establishment of a method, the demand for universality". Wittgenstein's intellectual development is exactly a way to liberation from all possible forms of opacity, including those presupposed by the *Tractatus* and its immediate successors. As Molder remarks apropos of the materials collected in *On Certainty*, "he can be seen to be making an effort, which never stabilizes into a thesis, not to allow himself to be bewitched by the word knowledge". It is indeed a project of clarification of the human mind that lies at the bottom of the *Investigations*, one for which Wittgenstein's continuous attempts to *express* the correct view on the multiple subjects that constitute our experience are only the first steps towards an entirely new and much needed philosophy.

António Marques
Nuno Venturinha

P. M. S. Hacker
Kant's Transcendental Deduction – a Wittgensteinian Critique

1 Kant and Wittgenstein

Although Wittgenstein read at least parts of the *Critique of Pure Reason*, he never wrote about it. His comments on Kant and Kant's philosophy are few and brief.[1] There are interesting convergences between their respective philosophies, but also deep differences. Despite Kant's brilliant criticisms of the Cartesian and empiricist traditions, there are four very general principles, rooted in Cartesian methodology, which Kant never questioned. Wittgenstein, by contrast rejected them all.

First, Kant's approach to the resolution of his master-problem: "How are synthetic a priori judgements possible?" is steadfastly epistemological. He seeks to explain the possibility of synthetic a priori *knowledge* by reference to the a priori conditions of the possibility of experience – understood as objectively valid perception, i.e. *knowledge* of nature.

Secondly, his approach is unwaveringly, if abstractly, subjective. "In transcendental science everything must be derived from the subject"[2] – and that abstract subject is I, not He. Kant's primary inquiry is not into the conditions of the possibility of other-ascription of experience, but into the *bare form of consciousness*, conceived as the framework for the possibility of empirical self-consciousness.

Thirdly, the concept of consciousness that he deploys in his investigations into the conditions of the possibility of (a subject's own) experience is the heir to the concept of consciousness introduced into philosophy by Descartes, developed by Locke and refined into the concept of apperception by Leibniz. Although he advances powerful criticisms of Descartes's use of the concept to prove his nature as a thinking substance, Kant never challenges the fundamental features of the concept of consciousness that he inherited. On the contrary, what he does is to investigate the a priori conditions of the possibility of self-consciousness thus conceived.

---

1 For their itemization, see Hacker forthcoming A.
2 Kant 2005, 5058.

Finally, in conformity with the Cartesian and empiricist traditions, Kant held that the possibility of conceiving of experience as one's own was *logically independent* of the possibility of other-ascription of experience. For he held that experiences are ascribable to others on the basis of analogy with one's own case.

> I cannot have the least representation of a thinking being through an external experience, but only through self-consciousness. Thus such objects are nothing further than the transference of this consciousness of mine to other things, which can be represented as thinking beings only in this way.[3]

> It is obvious that if one wishes to represent a thinking being, one must put oneself in its place, and thus substitute one's own subject for the object one wants to consider (which is not the case in any other species of investigation).[4]

We have no grounds for conceiving of experiences as our own. So Kant did not think that the concepts of experience thus groundlessly self-ascribed are logically bound up with behaviour.[5] Consequently, he implicitly committed himself to the possibility of mastering the use of such concepts in self-ascription of experience independently of mastering their use in other-ascription of experience. For if such concepts are not partly determined by reference to constitutive behavioural grounds for their other-ascription, then they must be determined in inner sense. But if they are determined in inner sense, there is no way for them to be determined other than by private ostensive definition employing a representation as a defining sample. So Kant implicitly committed himself to the logical possibility of a private language. (This will not be discussed here.)

In the following essay, I shall be concerned with the third issue: the nature of consciousness and apperception. These concepts are pivotal for Kant's enterprise in the "Transcendental Deduction of the Categories". That chapter lies at the very heart of transcendental philosophy. It is, I think, possible to bring Wittgenstein's thought to bear directly upon Kant's account of the unity of apperception and the conditions of the possibility of experience. This will shed critical light on Kant's conceptions of consciousness and self-consciousness. I believe it will show that while Kant effectively destroyed the Cartesian/empiricist framework of philosophical thought, he was still entrapped in the rubble.

---

3 A 347/B 405.
4 A 353.
5 The term "self-ascription" may seem too weighty. I employ it to do no weightier service than to indicate a first-person present tense sentence with an experiential predicate.

2 Kant's Transcendental Deduction

Kant's master problem was "How are synthetic a priori judgements possible?" The answer to this question will also answer the question of whether *metaphysics as a science* is possible[6] We know synthetic a priori propositions of geometry and arithmetic. We also know, Kant thought, synthetic a priori propositions of pure natural science. Metaphysics lays claim to knowledge of the truth of synthetic a priori judgements: for example, that every event must have a cause, that substance must persist throughout change, that objects must stand in reciprocal causal relations. But how *can* we know such truths? They are not derived from experience, since experience can yield only contingent truths. They are not projections of associative habits (as Hume had argued). They are known a priori, and are both universal and necessary. But how is such knowledge possible, if is neither analytic nor empirical? Kant's critical step was his so called Copernican Revolution – the thought that our knowledge of such synthetic a priori truths does not have to conform to objects, but that objects, in so far as we have synthetic a priori knowledge of them, have to conform to the a priori conditions of our sensible and cognitive capacities. So his aim is to show that the truth of synthetic a priori judgements is an a priori condition of the very possibility of experience (cognition that arises out of perception).

Synthetic a priori knowledge is ampliative. So the possibility of such knowledge cannot be explained by reference to apprehension of direct (analytic) links between concepts (e. g. as with the concepts of *body* and *divisibility*). Rather the concepts (e. g. of *cause* and *event*) associated in a synthetic a priori judgement (viz. that every event has a cause) must be shown to be linked by some third thing. The link is forged by the *possibility of experience*.[7] To show that such a connection of categorial concepts is a condition of any possible experience (and hence, in Kant's view, of the objects of experience) is to give a transcendental proof of a principle: a synthetic a priori judgement concerning experience that is both universal and necessary. It is by means of such transcendental proofs that we can attain transcendental knowledge, i. e. "All knowledge which is occupied not so much with objects as with the mode of our knowledge of objects in so far as this mode of knowledge is to be possible *a priori*".[8]

---

6 Kant 2002, 256ff., 365–371.
7 A 783/B 811.
8 A 12; B25.

The pivot upon which the arguments turn is the "Transcendental Deduction of the Categories". In it Kant argued that appearances "must stand under conditions of the necessary unity of apperception".[9] Experience, he averred, requires a twofold unity. First, the unity of the object of experience. What is given in intuition is a manifold of sensory data in different sensory modalities at successive times. If this is to constitute experience, it has to be synthesized into the perception of a unified object. Secondly, the unity of consciousness of the subject of experience. Experience must be such as to be self-ascribable to a single persisting subject of experience – it must be conceived by its subject to be the experience *of* a single persisting subject.[10] Otherwise it could not constitute anyone's *knowledge* of appearances. With remarkable ingenuity, Kant argues that "inner experience [...] is possible only under the presupposition of outer experience".[11] And it is in this necessary co-ordination of the possibility of subjective judgements and the possibility of objectively valid judgements that the possibility of synthetic a priori knowledge of nature is rooted.

I shall sketch Kant's account. I shall then suggest that the "Transcendental Deduction" and the subsequent transcendental arguments are rooted in an array of questionable presuppositions concerning consciousness and self-consciousness that he inherited from his predecessors. I shall argue that despite his brilliantly challenging the empiricist and rationalist tradition, and shifting the parameters of the debate from ideas to concepts (conceived to be "predicates of possible judgements"[12]), and from actualities to possibilities, he did not, to use a phrase of Wittgenstein's, "put the question marks deep enough down".[13]

A legal "deduction" was an argument justifying a legal right by reference to the source of its legitimacy (*quaestio juris*). A deduction of a concept, in Kant's philosophy, is an argument justifying the objective validity of a concept. A concept

9 A 110.
10 This is a purely formal condition that in itself does not provide criteria of personal identity over time. It is merely the requirement of a single persistent subject as a condition of perceptions constituting cognition (experience). Kant's brilliant criticism of the rationalist doctrine of the soul in the Third Paralogism demonstrates how the rationalist confuses the unity of perception with the perception of a unity. "The identity of the consciousness of myself at different times is [...] only a formal condition of my thoughts and their coherence, and in no way proves the numerical identity of my subject". (A 363)
11 B 275.
12 Thus anticipating, at the level of concept and judgement, Bentham's, and subsequently Frege's, context principle concerning word- and sentence-meaning.
13 CV, p. 71.

is objectively valid if and only if it applies to objects. The objective validity of empirical concepts is determined by empirical deductions by reference to actual experience. The objective validity of pure a priori concepts must be demonstrated, independently of any experience, by reference to their source in the understanding (the faculty of judgement) and its operations on intuitions (given by the faculty of sensibility). The applicability of the pure a priori concepts to objects of experience must be shown to be *a condition of any possible experience*.[14] A transcendental deduction of concepts is an explanation of how pure a priori concepts *can* relate a priori to objects.[15] If the categories (the pure a priori concepts derived from the fundamental forms of judgement in the "Metaphysical Deduction of the Categories") can be shown to be presupposed by any possible experience, then they will have been shown to be objectively valid.

Kant's argument begins from the examination of the subjective sources which form the a priori foundation of the possibility of experience.[16] Intuition (receptivity, sensibility) presents us with a synopsis of sensory data. That synopsis requires a transcendental synthesis – a unity-creating combination of the elements of a manifold. A *synthesis of representations* given in intuition is "the act of combining different representations and grasping their multiplicity in one cognition".[17] Kant distinguishes, within the synthesis of representations, three different syntheses. The first is the synthesis of *apprehension* of the manifold given in intuition, which, as it were, welds the manifold into a synchronic unity. The second is the synthesis of *reproduction* in imagination, which ensures diachronic unity of representations – that successive representations be apprehended as representations of one and the same object. The third is the synthesis of *recognition* of a representation in accordance with a concept.[18]

---

14 A 96.

15 A 85/B 117.

16 A 97.

17 A 77/B 103.

18 This conception of synthesis is the heir of the ancient misconception of a *sensus communis* (a general sense) and its function. It is also the ancestor of the contemporary cognitive neuroscientific notion of the *binding problem*. The latter is nicely exemplified in the following passage written by Francis Crick: "we can see how the visual parts of the brain take the picture (the visual field) apart, but we do not yet know how the brain puts it all together again to provide our highly organized view of the world – that is, what we see. It seems as if the brain needs to impose some global unity on certain activities in its different parts so that the attributes of a single object – its shape, colour, movement, location, and so on – are in some way brought together [...]" (Crick 1995, p. 22). To be sure, this is confused. The visual parts of the brain do not take *pictures* apart or put them together again. And what we see are neither pictures nor images – unless we are in a picture gallery. So the binding problem thus conceived

Before proceeding further, some words are needed to clarify the concept of apperception. The term originates in Leibniz's *Nouveaux Essaies* (written in 1703–5, publ. 1765), replacing Pierre Coste's *s'apercevoir de* (*awareness*), by which Coste, Locke's French translator, had rendered Locke's "perceiving one's perception". According to Locke, "Consciousness is the perception of what passes in a Man's own mind".[19] According to Leibniz, *perception* is "the transitory state which enfolds and represents a multiplicity in a unity".[20] It is "the inner state of the monad representing external things". *Apperception* is "consciousness or the reflective knowledge of this inner state".[21] It should be noted that this notion of consciousness has as its object not the perceived objects in reality that we apprehend by the use of our senses (e.g. the visible room in which I am sitting), but rather *their alleged subjective reproduction in the mind* (as it were, the "visual room" I have). According to Locke, it is "impossible for anyone to perceive, without perceiving that he does perceive".[22] Leibniz disagreed, holding that there are indefinitely many "*petites perceptions*" or "insensible (minute) perceptions" which are not apperceived (i.e. of which we are not aware). The term "apperception" was picked up by Wolff and through his writings transmitted to Kant. Pure apperception, according to Kant, is distinct from inner sense or empirical apperception. It is, Kant wrote in *Anthropology from a Pragmatic Point of View*, §24, "a consciousness of what the human being *does*" [in transcendental synthesis (see below)] and "belongs to the faculty of thinking", whereas inner sense "is a consciousness of what he *undergoes*, in so far as he is affected by the play of his

---

is a muddle. There are neural analogues of the misconceived tale of transcendental synthesis, and there are neuroscientific analogues of the dubious science of transcendental psychology. For it is a task of cognitive neuroscience to discover how in detail the diverse neural inputs from the sense-organs are processed by the brain to *make it possible for a perceiver to perceive a unified object*. That, however, is not a synthesis of intuitions. Nor is it the bogus "binding problem" – for the question is *not* how the brain manages to construct a unified *picture* or *image* of anything. Neural processes make perception of objects possible, but (pace Crick) they do not make the objects of perception, and the objects of perception are not internal representations. Nor are they external representations.

19 *Essay Concerning Human Understanding*, II-i-19.
20 *Monadology*, §14.
21 Leibniz, "The Principles of Nature and Grace, based on Reason" (1714), §4. Reid was critical of Leibniz's idea of unconscious perceptions (Reid 2002, orig. publ. 1785, pp. 190ff.), and equally critical of Locke's and Leibniz's assimilation of consciousness and reflection (ibid., pp. 42, 421).
22 *Essay* II-xxvii-9.

own thoughts. It rests on inner intuition, and consequently on the relations of ideas in time".[23]

The transcendental unity of apperception is "the supreme [principle] in the whole of human cognition".[24] It requires the satisfaction of three a priori conditions. If a manifold given in intuition is to amount to anything for a subject of experience – even merely to enter the sphere of consciousness as representations, not only must it be unified, it must be apprehended *as belonging to a subject* (the (formal) ownership condition). The data of sense are only *data* if they are given to one and the same persistent subject at different times (the (formal) persistence condition). Contrary to Hume, representations (Humean impressions) are not a field upon which one can apply a principle of differentiation to distinguish those that are mine from those that are not. That all the intuitions that I "encounter" (that I "have") are *mine* is not something derived from the character of the intuitions. It is, in Kant's jargon, "original" or "underived" – a transcendental condition of the possibility of experience (the immediacy condition).

> All intuitions are nothing for us and do not in the least concern us if they cannot be taken up into consciousness. [...] We are conscious *a priori* of the thoroughgoing identity of ourselves with regard to all representations that can ever belong to our cognition, as a necessary condition of the possibility of all representations (since the latter represent something in me only in so far as they belong with all the others to one consciousness [...]) This principle holds *a priori* [...][25]

So, Kant argues, it must be *possible* for the "I think" to accompany all my representations.[26] Why the modal qualification? Apperception, *pace* Locke, is not universally necessary – I do not have to be conscious of *all* my perceptions. Kant accepted Leibniz's conception of minute perceptions of which I am not conscious. But, *pace* Leibniz, it must be *possible* for me to be conscious of them. Otherwise I could have a sensible experience (a representation) without being able to conceive of it (to represent it to myself) as *mine*. If so, Kant says, it "would be nothing to me". So, the manifold given in an intuition would not constitute *my* representations if they did not belong to one persistent self-consciousness.[27]

---

23 Kant 2007, 7:161.

24 B 135.

25 A 116.

26 B 131.

27 B 132.

> As *my* representations (even if I am not conscious of them as such) they must yet necessarily accord with the condition under which alone they *can* stand together in a universal [i.e. general] self-consciousness, because otherwise they would not throughout belong to me.[28]

This *analytic* unity of consciousness itself presupposes a *synthetic* unity. For it does not suffice that each representation be accompanied (or be capable of being accompanied) by consciousness. For then I would merely have "as multi-coloured, diverse a self as I have representations of which I am conscious".[29] The ultimate condition of the transcendental unity of self-consciousness is that *I* synthesize the manifold given me in intuition, and *am conscious* of so doing.

> this thoroughgoing identity of the apperception of a manifold given in intuition contains a synthesis of representations and is possible only through the consciousness of this synthesis. [...] [It] does not yet come about by my accompanying each representation with consciousness, but by my *adding* one representation to the other and being conscious of their synthesis. Therefore it is only because I can combine a manifold of given representations *in one consciousness*, that it is possible for me to represent the *identity of the consciousness in these representations* itself [...] The thought that the representations given in intuition all together belong *to me* means accordingly the same as that I unite them in one self-consciousness, or at least can unite them therein; and although it is itself not yet the consciousness of the *synthesis* of the representations, it presupposes the possibility of the latter, i.e., only because I can comprehend their manifold in a consciousness, do I call them all together *my* representations.[30]

The synthesis of the manifold of intuitions is the ground of the unity of apperception, which antecedes all determinate experience. But our understanding "is able to bring about the unity of apperception a priori *only by means of the categories*".[31] The categories are held to be derivable from the general forms of judgement, and are implicit in every act of judging. So the conditions of the possibility of self-consciousness are precisely the synthesis of intuitions and their subsumption under the categories that are the pure a priori concepts of an object in general. So "The a priori conditions of a possible experience in general are at the same time the conditions of the possibility of objects of experience".[32] For representations to satisfy the conditions of the unity of apperception, they must

---

28 B 133.
29 B 134.
30 B 133–134.
31 B 145, emphasis added.
32 A 111. This quotation comes from the A-deduction, whereas the previous one is from the B-deduction. But on this point at least they concur.

have such a character as renders them in general experiences of an objective spatio-temporally unified realm of nature.

We must note Kant's unclarity regarding the "I think" that must be able to accompany all my representations. It is itself a representation, but not an intuition.[33] For it is an act of spontaneity and so cannot be regarded as belonging to sensibility. Kant equivocates between characterizing the "I think" as a *concept* (although not a concept signifying a thinking being in general),[34] and characterizing it as a *judgement* (although by itself it has no content). It is not a category, but it belongs to the table of categories in as much as it is the "vehicle of all concepts" – serving only "to introduce all our thought as belonging to consciousness".[35] It is "a representation that another representation is within me". Unlike the categories, it is not a condition of the possibility of the knowledge of objects, but rather "the form of apperception, which belongs to and precedes every experience".[36] So it is both *form* and *possible accompaniment*. But although it is merely a *form*, it is Kant holds, a *necessary form*. And although it is merely an *accompaniment*, it is *necessary* that it be a (possible) accompaniment. Finally, it is a *representation* that must be capable of accompanying all other representations (intuitions), but cannot itself be accompanied by any further representation.[37] (Roughly speaking, any appearance that "Things are thus-and-so" can be accompanied by an "It sensibly seems to me that ...". But it cannot sensibly seem to me that it sensibly seems to me that ...").

The "Transcendental Deduction" provides the background for Kant's transcendental arguments in the "Refutation of Idealism" and in the "Analogies of Experience". In the former, he attempts to show that "the mere, but empirically determined, consciousness of my own existence proves the existence of objects in space outside me". The consciousness of my own existence, he argues, "is at the same time an immediate consciousness of the existence of other things outside me",[38] for "inner experience in general is possible only through outer experience in general".[39] Inner sense involves consciousness of successive perceptions; but all determination of succession in time requires something permanent in perception; there is nothing permanent in inner sense; so my awareness of myself as existing in time presupposes something permanent outside me (and

---

33 B 132.
34 A 354.
35 A 341/B 400.
36 A 354. A Leibnizean "minute perception" would not count as an experience.
37 B 132.
38 B 276.
39 B 278.

not merely a representation of a thing outside me).[40] In the "Analogies of Experience", Kant attempts to validate such synthetic a priori propositions as the law of causality and the permanence of substance from the contrasts between the possible temporal order of experiences and the determinate temporal order of its objects. In both texts he argues from the temporal nature of apperception to the existence, permanence and causally determined character of nature, which is presupposed by the very possibility of apperception. He argues from the necessary character of conscious experience to how the objects of such experience must be in order for it to be possible that experience should have such a character.

Let me try to summarize Kant's achievement in respect of our concerns. He realised that the Cartesian/Lockean conception of empirical (perceptual) knowledge is radically mistaken. Our perceptual knowledge of objects is not *derived* from subjective knowledge of impressions, and our perceptual knowledge of how things in nature actually are is not derived from our knowledge of how things subjectively seem to us to be. On the contrary, outer sense is immediate or direct, not mediated by inner sense. Kant realised that self-ascribability of subjective experiences does not imply knowledge of a persistent *thinking substance* that is the subject of experience. The Cartesian arguments for the indivisibility, persistence, and bodily-independence of the soul, and hence for its immortality, are paralogisms. Kant saw that the Humean question "What makes an experience my experience?" is incoherent. He realised that Hume's quest for the principle of unity of experience in empirical relations between experiences (causation and similarity) is likewise incoherent. He saw clearly that Hume's quest for a self in inner sense was a bogus quest. And he realised that inner sense – what he thought of as knowledge of how things subjectively are with one – is possible only on the condition of the possibility of outer sense. For such inner sense is temporally ordered, and temporal ordering presupposes something permanent throughout change, which is not given in inner but only in outer sense. These insights were momentous in the history of modern philosophy. They shattered the house that Descartes and Locke had built. But Kant was unable to clear the ground of the rubble or to find a way out of it. That was a task left for Wittgenstein.

---

40 B 275.

3 Kant and Wittgenstein: Divergent Pathways Through the Jungle

Wittgenstein would agree with Kant that self-ascription of experience is ground-less, or, as Kant put it, "original" (the underived condition). But where Kant asks what are the a priori conditions of the possibility of apperception (of the "I think" that must be capable of accompanying all my representations), we might imagine Wittgenstein asking what is presupposed by the possibility of ground-less self-ascription of predicates of perception (of the "I perceive" that must be capable of accompanying all my perceptions, as Kant did not put it). While Kant answers his question in terms of the threefold synthesis and the subsumption of intuitions under the categories, Wittgenstein would answer his in terms of public criteria for possession of the concepts of seeing, hearing, feeling, etc. What, logically speaking, must a speaker *already be able to do with words*, if he is to be able groundlessly to avow or aver a sensible experience?

Kant's transcendental idealism and his transcendental arguments are delib-erately crafted to answer the master-question "How is synthetic a priori knowl-edge of nature possible?" How can we *know, independently of experience*, that substance in nature must persist; or that objects must stand in reciprocal causal relations; or that every event must have a cause. His explanation of the possibil-ity of such meta-physical knowledge is by reference to what he conceived to be the a priori conditions of the possibility of experience. As long as one thinks of these judgements as describing necessities in nature that are known in advance of experience, Kant's strategy of linking our *knowledge* of them to the conditions of the possibility of experience and hence to transcendental apperception will seem not only ingenious, but profoundly compelling. Wittgenstein's account of what seem to be natural necessities ("*Naturnotwendigkeit*",[41] i.e. metaphysical necessities in nature) is utterly different. What *appear* to be necessary and uni-versal truths about the world are *norms of representation*. They are not expres-sions of knowledge of necessities constitutive of the realm of nature, but rather rules for the use of words in the guise of descriptions. They are not rules for nature, but rules for the *description* of nature. They are *grammatical proposi-tions*. Wittgenstein's account of the nature of such propositions is wholly inde-pendent of his account of the conditions of the possibility of self-ascription of

---

41 PIr § 372.

experiential predicates (or, more accurately, of avowals of experience).[42] This is of capital importance.

So, Kant and Wittgenstein take different paths through the conceptual jungle. To be sure, that does not show that Kant got lost. But if Wittgenstein's arguments are correct, then Kant's path can never emerge from the jungle. The source of Kant's troubles lies in his taking the questionable conception of apperception as a reliable compass with which to find his way. To put things epigrammatically:

The "I say" that must be capable of accompanying all my representations is not an "I think".

Or, more perspicuously:

Kant confuses a fictitious form of self-consciousness with the ability to say what one perceives and that one perceives it – and, occasionally, to hedge one's bets.

Let me explain.

One can be conscious of objects in one's field of perception. Perceptual consciousness is a mode of non-voluntary attention.[43] It is a form of *cognitive receptivity* – a reception, rather than attainment or achievement, of knowledge. That is why one can order someone to observe something, but not to become or be conscious of something observed. One can try to discover something, but one cannot try to be conscious of something. One can succeed in detecting something, but one cannot succeed in becoming or being conscious of something. Because it is a form of cognitive receptivity, *being conscious* is a cousin of *noticing, realizing, recognizing* and *being aware*. Unlike its cousins, however, perceptual consciousness is limited to what catches and then holds one's attention. One may become and then be conscious of the ticking of the clock, or become and then be conscious of the smell of dinner wafting in from the kitchen. The

42 Wittgenstein (like Kant) would not speak of "self-ascription" of experience – and with good reason. But for present purposes, I hope that it may be allowed as a shorthand facilitating comparison between the two modes of philosophical thought.
43 See White 1964, chap. IV. For elaboration of the different forms of consciousness, see Bennett and Hacker 2003, chaps. 9–12. Consciousness is not an Aristotelian focal concept, it is a multi-focal concept. It has a number of different, but connected, centres of variation (see Hacker forthcoming B, chap. 1). For the analysis of another multi-focal concept, see the analysis of causation in Hacker 2007, chap. 3.

objects of perceptual consciousness are not one's perceivings but the objects of one's perceivings (typically, but not only, objects of peripheral perception). The moot point is whether one can be conscious of one's perceiving what one perceives. This is not an empirical question to be resolved by examining what goes on while we perceive.[44] Rather, we must investigate what, *if anything*, could be *meant* by phrases of the general form: "being conscious of one's sensible experiences"? In short, is there any such thing as *apperception*?

One perceives things in one's immediate environment by the use of one's senses. So, Wittgenstein queries, "Do I observe myself, then, and perceive that I am seeing [...] ?".[45] That is, presumably, absurd – and it was no part of Kant's tale to construe either pure apperception or the empirical apperception of inner sense as *perceiving* that one perceives. But – according to Kant – "I think" *must* be capable of accompanying all my representations. For only when it does do they amount to what he calls "perceptions" (representations with consciousness). So, we might imagine Wittgenstein going on to ask, "Am I then my own *witness* that I am perceiving something?".[46] Kant's answer seems clear: for me to have a perception I must be conscious, or at least capable of being conscious, of it *as my perception* – as the sensible experience I have (the Humean worry that it might be another's cannot arise). How might Wittgenstein respond?

In a remarkable passage that can be viewed as a challenge to the whole Kantian conception, Wittgenstein noted the temptation to claim that when one sees objects, one *has* something – the current experience, the contents of which are subsumed under the very same concepts as the objects perceived:

> You want to look about you and say: "At any rate only *I* have got THIS." – What are these words for? They serve no purpose. – Indeed, can't one add: "There is here no question of a 'seeing' – and therefore none of a 'having' – nor of a subject, nor therefore of the I either"? Couldn't I ask: In what sense have you *got* what you are talking about and saying that only you have got it? Do you possess it? You do not even *see* it. Don't you really have to say that no one has got it? And indeed it's clear: if you logically exclude other people's having something, it loses its sense to say that you have it.

> But what are you then talking about? It's true I said that I knew deep down what you meant. But that meant that I knew how one thinks to conceive this object, to see it, to gesture at it, as it were, by looking and pointing. I know how one stares ahead and looks about one in this case – and the rest. I think one can say: you are talking (if, for example, you are sitting

---

44 Cf. PIr § 316.
45 PIr § 417.
46 PIr § 416.

in a room) of the 'visual room'. That which has no owner is the 'visual room'. I can as little own it as I can walk about it, or look at it, or point at it. In so far as it cannot belong to anyone else, it doesn't belong to me either. Or again: in so far as I want to apply the same form of expression to it as to the material room in which I sit, it doesn't belong to me. The description of the latter need not mention an owner. Indeed, it need not have an owner. But then the visual room *cannot* have an owner. "For" – one might say – "it has no master outside it, and none inside it either".[47]

Clearly, the "visual room" consists of subjective experience – one's visual experience of things being thus-and-so (shorn of its factivity). The "material room" consists of the public objects of experience: things being thus-and-so. Both are described in terms of concepts of objects subordinate to the a priori categories of experience. Kant and Wittgenstein agree that the visual room *could* contain no owner – that nothing in one's perceptual experience could warrant its ascription to a subject. (That is why Hume's search for himself among his fleeting perceptions was a bogus search.) But Kant thinks that the visual room *must be owned* (the ownership condition of transcendental and empirical self-consciousness). For any sensible experience to be mine, *I must be able to conceive of it formally as mine.* For any series of sensible experiences to be mine, I must be able to conceive of them as *belonging to a persistent subject of experience* – to my "transcendental self" so conceived (the formal persistence condition). To be conscious of my experiences as mine is to *know* that I am having those experiences – for consciousness is a form of cognition (the subjective cognitive condition). The condition of the possibility of this self-consciousness, according to Kant, is precisely awareness or the possibility of awareness of the synthesis of the manifold given in intuition and its subsumption under the categories, which are a priori concepts of an object in general. Only then can the visual room I have also be (for the most part) the visible room I perceive.

Wittgenstein's response to this might be imagined to be fourfold. First, he would agree that the first person pronoun, the "I" of apperception, is formal. It belongs to our form of representation, not to its matter. But it is *merely* formal, and precisely because it is merely formal, it is *unnecessary*. It is unnecessary in the following sense: We can readily envisage alternative forms of representation that dispense with it. Instead of "I have a pain", a speaker S would say "There is a pain" (after all, even in our existing form of representation, we say "It hurts"), whereupon others would say "S is in pain". Instead of "I see …", S would say "There is a visual perception of things being thus-and-so", and others would say "S sees that …". And instead of "It sensibly seems to me that …", S would say

---

"There is a sensible seeming that ..." and others would say "It sensibly seems to S that ...".[48] In short, self-ascribability of experience, irrespective of whether it is objective perception, or subjective seeming-to-perceive, or even mere sensation, is *merely* a formal feature of a possible verbal expression or report of experience. The role of the personal pronoun is to *signal* the subject of experience – the speaker.[49] Or, to put it slightly differently, the role of the pronoun "I" is to *index* the experience – like the point of origin on Cartesian co-ordinates.[50] But the "I" is dispensable for the fulfilment of that role, since the speech-act itself fulfils it. In this new form of representation, the apprehension of the unity of the manifold is exhibited in the description of the object of experience and in the behaviour appropriate in the context to the object perceived.[51] The unity of the subject *qua* subject of experience is exhibited in the behaviour, including the utterances, of the perceiver. But no "I" need accompany anyone's own representations. On the other hand, "he", "she" or "it" *must* be capable of accompanying all representations. For there can be no representings without representers.

---

48 One might object: if, in this imaginary form of representation, the subject says "There is pain", does this not disconnect pain from the sentient creature that is the subject of pain? Might one not then ask "There is a pain around, but whose is it?" No – this is to conflate two distinct forms of representation. S's *saying* "There is pain" is what connects pain to a sufferer, and it is what licenses others to say "S is in pain". Instead of "I" indexing the utterance, the speaker's saying "There is pain" (like "It hurts" in our current form of representation) does so. To the question "Who is in pain?" the answer is: "S is in pain'" But if one hears S say "There is pain", one can no more intelligibly ask "Who is in pain?" than when someone who says "Do it *now*", one can ask "Do it when?". One already knows!

49 Of course, its role in silent speech "in the imagination" is not to *signal* anything. Rather it *would* signal the subject, were he to express what he is saying to himself.

50 Cf. BT, p. 523.

51 One of the many reasons why one *cannot* extrapolate from Kantian considerations of transcendental synthesis to cognitive neuroscience is that patients suffering from agnosia, for example from agnosia for movement, do not perceive a stationary car *and* a dissociated sense of motion – they cannot perceive motion at all. The various forms of agnosia do not exhibit failure to integrate a given intuition of a certain kind together with other synthesized intuitions, but *absence* of intuitions of that kind. This may be because of lack of neural signals (in the case of blindness) or inability of the brain (due to lesions) to process neural signals so as to enable the subject to perceive normally. Blindsight does not consist in failure to synthesize an intuition of a dot in the scotoma, but lack of any such intuition. The possibility of producing an intimation or hunch under prodding does not betoken an unconscious intuition or Leibnizian "petite perception", precisely because it *cannot* be accompanied by an "I think", an "I am conscious of" or an "it sensibly seems to me".

Secondly, Wittgenstein would emphasize that the possessive "to have" is likewise purely formal. "To have a pain" is simply to be in pain, "to have a visual perception" is just to see. We *represent* experience in the possessive form – but that is all the ownership of experience amounts to. *It is merely a representational form*. Its dispensability is evident if we represent experience (as above) in the form of "there is" (or our being in pain in the form "It hurts"). For example, instead of S saying "I have a visual experience of...", he would say "There is a visual experience of...", and others would say "He (S) sees ...". Instead of saying "I have a pain", S would say "There is a pain", and others would then say "He (S) is in pain". Nothing would be lost by the impersonal non-possessive form, and its third-person correlate would not be in the possessive form.

Of course, we are deeply tempted to think that *only* the subject of experience can *have* the experience he has. You can't have my pain, Frege wrote, and I can't have your sympathy. Another's pain is another pain.[52] *Having* experiences, Strawson argued in a similar vein, is a form of *logically non-transferable ownership*.[53] But that is quite mistaken. Ownership is a relation between an owner and the item owned. But to have a sensible experience is not to stand in any *relation* to anything (other than to an object perceived). In particular, it is not to stand in a relation of ownership *to the perceiving*. Perceiving is something one does or something that happens to one, not something one possesses. Moreover, while ownership may be legally or morally inalienable, it cannot be *logically* inalienable. For logical inalienability *excludes* ownership of *any* kind: "if it can't belong to anyone else", Wittgenstein remarked, "then it can't belong to me either".[54] Of course, two people may indeed have the same experience, just as two objects may have the same colour. Being A's is not a criterion of identity of a colour; or of an experience. If someone asserts "You can't have my experience", the correct response is the query "Your experience! What experience is that?".[55] And if the answer is "Listening to *Tosca* at Covent Gardens", one may well respond "Yes – I was there too" – in which case we enjoyed the same experience.[56]

---

52 Frege, "The Thought", in Frege 1984, p. 361.
53 Strawson 1959, pp. 97ff. Strawson's failure to see the error in the doctrine of logically non-transferable ownership of experience does, I think, vitiate his attempted analytic reconstruction of Kant's transcendental deduction in *The Bounds of Sense*.
54 PIr § 398 *supra*.
55 Cf. PIr § 253.
56 For detailed exposition and defence of Wittgenstein's account of the misconception of private ownership of experience, see Hacker 1993, "Part I – the Essays", pp. 19–25.

Thirdly, not only are "I" and "have" misconstrued, so too is the "think" of the "I think" that must be able to accompany all my representations. *I think* is neither a *form* of consciousness of anything, nor is it an *object* of consciousness, i.e. something one is conscious *of*. Or, to give the dove some air-resistance in which to fly: to think I see something or for it visually to seem to me that things are thus-and-so, is *neither* to be conscious of seeing, nor is it to be conscious of things being thus-and-so. It is not anything I could be conscious of *or* not conscious of. This denial may seem counter intuitive. – So it should, otherwise three and a half centuries of thinkers would not have been persuaded by the Cartesian/Lockean prestidigitations and their Kantian refinements. Let me explain the flight of the dove.

(a) Thinking that one sees that things are so, and its sensibly seeming to one that things are so, are not something one could be *conscious of* (or *fail* to be conscious of). For

I am conscious that I think I see that the lights are on.*

if it means anything, can hardly mean more than

I think I (can) see the lights.

Similarly,

I am conscious that it visually seems to me that the wall is red.*

if it means anything, means no more than

It looks to me as if the wall is red.

That is, the sentence-forming operator on sentences "I am conscious that", in such cases, is vacuous (like multiplication by 1). But, ironically, one may become and then be conscious that things visually *seem to another person* to be thus-and-so – as when our attention is caught and held by Macbeth's grasping for a dagger in thin air. There is no such thing as being conscious that it sensibly seems to me that things are thus-and-so, or as being conscious that I think I see that things are thus-and-so. (I shall elaborate below.) Rather, any mature language-user *can truthfully say* (i) that he perceives things to be thus-and-so; or (ii) that it sensibly seems to him that things are thus-and-so. Of course, the former, but not the latter, may be false for all one's truthfulness. Kant confuses the ability to *say* what we perceive or think we perceive with the fictitious ability to *apperceive* all our "representations".

(b) "It sensibly seems to me that ..." ("It seems to me as if I were seeing/hearing ...") is not (contrary to what Descartes suggested) the expression of indubitable and infallible subjective knowledge. Rather, its truthfulness guarantees its truth[57] – and that is what confused Descartes. "It sensibly seems to me that *p*" is not an assertion *of consciousness* that *p* (and hence of knowledge that *p*). Nor is it the description of something (a "representation") *of which* one is conscious, and so knows (infallibly and indubitably) to be as one apperceives it to be. On the contrary, its role is to qualify the assertion that *p* or the assertion that I see that *p*.

(c) Its sensibly seeming to me that ... (the representation that another representation is in me, as Kant put it) is *not* a possible accompaniment of all my representations. On the contrary, it is *excluded* when I correctly and confidently perceive that ... Seeming to see (I think I see) is not a common constituent of both seeing and having illusions and hallucinations.[58] Macbeth seemed to see a dagger, but he did not *seem to see* the blood on his hands – he saw it. Seeing is not successful seeing to see. But one might say that seeming to see is often unsuccessful seeing. If someone satisfies the criteria for seeing a dagger, he *thereby* fails to satisfy the criteria for seeing to see a dagger. The two "experiences" could not be more different – since one involves the visible presence of a dagger in the subject's visual field and the other requires its absence. The fact that Macbeth could not, for a moment, distinguish the two does not show that they contain a common core of *seeming to see*. What it shows (unsurprisingly) is that he was hallucinating. It is not as if, when he previously did see the real dagger in his hand dripping with Duncan's blood, his seeing the dagger was a successful seeming to see it.

---

57 Cp. PPF § 319.
58 *Pace* Grice and Strawson. "It sensibly seems to me ..." is not like "I am breathing", i. e. always true but therefore not worth saying. But this is not the place to confront the contrary claim.

In short, we must disentangle the knotted threads in the putative concept of self-consciousness that is conceived to be both accompaniment and form of experience (perceptual cognition). Let us distinguish:

(i) The object of my perception, i.e. *what* (relative WH-pronoun) I perceive, namely: a material object array.

(ii) The content of my perception, namely: *that things are thus-and-so* (including, for example, that there is such-and-such a material object array before me).

(iii) My perceiving what I perceive, i.e. my seeing what I see, my hearing what I hear, etc. "To perceive" and verbs of perception signifying species of perceiving are *factive*. However, "I perceive that things are thus-and-so" is not, according to Descartes, the expression of a *cogitatio*. For it is neither indubitable nor infallible. But it is a Kantian *cognition* (i.e. an "objective perception").[59]

(iv) Its sensibly (visually, auditorily, etc.) seeming to me that things are thus-and-so (a Cartesian *cogitatio*). But now we are faced with a dilemma. Is *my thinking* (of apperception)

(a) identical with *my being conscious of...*?

Or is it

(b) *what* I am conscious of?

It seems to have to be both; but it cannot be. Nor indeed can it be the one or the other. Let us examine both possibilities.

(a) Suppose that "It visually seems to me ..." amounts to much the same as "I am conscious that I see // a so-and-so // things to be thus-and-so//" or "I am conscious of seeing // a so-and-so// things to be thus-and-so//". Then this, far from cancelling the factivity of "I see ...", reinforces it. For if I am conscious that I see, then it follows that I see. But the whole point of the Cartesian "It seems to me" was to cancel the factivity of the verb of perception. Equally, the Kantian "I

---

59 A 320/B 376.

think that ..." does not amount to an *objective* perception – a cognition. For it is supposed to be common to both "subjective" and "objective" perception, and therefore does *not* guarantee that the representation it accompanies is an objective representation.

(b) So suppose that "It seems to me that I see ..." and "I think my representation is ..." are expressions of thoughts (*cogitationes*) or of apperception. Then they seem to be candidates for being *what I am conscious of*. According to Descartes, I cannot think without being conscious of my thinking. So when it seems to me that I see that things are thus-and-so, *I must be conscious of its so seeming to me*. According to Kant "I think" must be capable of accompanying all my representations. It is, he says, a representation of a representation. But the representation that is the object of the "I think" (that is the "content" of consciousness) must be a *seeming*. Otherwise it would be tantamount to an objective perception, i.e. a perceptual cognition. So Kant is either in the same boat as Descartes, or he is in the deep blue sea. But now: what is the difference between "it sensibly seems to me that ..." and "I am conscious that it sensibly seems to me that..."? What conceivable role can the operator "I am conscious that" fulfil when prefixed to "It seems to me that I see ..." or "It visually seems to me that ..."?

It is all too easy to suppose that its role is to declare *subjective knowledge of thoughts*. The factivity-cancelling, thought-specifying operator on statements of perception – "It seems to me that" – seems to secure the indubitability and infallibility of thoughts. For while I may doubt whether I really see a given material object array, and while I may be mistaken as to whether I actually do perceive that things are thus-and-so, I cannot, it seems, doubt or be mistaken that things sensibly seem to me to be thus-and-so. Certainly, for Descartes, it is precisely this that ensures that perceptual thoughts can function as premises in the *cogito*. But the very idea of perceptual *cogitationes* or of consciousness of representations thus conceived is a dire confusion. We confuse the grammatical fact that, in such cases, *truthfulness guarantees truth* with the idea that thoughts are indubitable and infallibly known to be as they are. But it is precisely because truthfulness guarantees truth that thoughts thus conceived are *not* objects (or contents) of subjective knowledge, and so too *not* objects (or contents) of consciousness. Why so?

One role of "I know" is to declare that grounds for doubt and error have been excluded. They may be excluded by evidence, by the satisfactory concept-laden exercise of a cognitive faculty (e.g. sight, hearing), by reliable hearsay or authority. But if truth is already guaranteed by truthfulness, then ignorance (doubt and error) are *logically* excluded anyway. It makes no sense to say: "Either it sensibly seems to me that p, or it sensibly seems to me that q, but I don't know which."

(If someone were to say, "Either it (sensibly) seems to me that there is a rose in the vase, or it (sensibly) seems to me that there is bread in the bread-bin – but I don't know which" we would not understand him.) But if ignorance of such an empirical truth is *logically* excluded, if "I don't know which" makes no sense here), then so too is knowledge – *for there is no epistemic work for it to do*. What it normally serves to exclude (viz. grounds for doubt and the possibility of error) is already precluded by logic. There is no logical space within which knowledge may be located.

So the apperception of a sensible representation can be neither a form of consciousness nor an object of consciousness. So a transcendental deduction is impossible.

4 The Way Out of the Jungle

What has gone wrong? As usual in philosophy, the fault lies in the fundamental questions asked, or even further back – in their presuppositions. The first mistake lay in Kant's master-question: How are synthetic a priori judgements possible? Or: how is knowledge of synthetic a priori propositions possible? The correct questions to ask are: What is it for a proposition to be a necessary proposition? and: What is the role of necessary propositions? These are indeed the questions that lie at the heart of Wittgenstein's treatment of the variety of propositions that we deem to be necessary truths.[60] The questions, *pace* Kant, are *not* epistemological, but logico-grammatical ones. Wittgenstein's answers were that necessary truths are either norms of representation in the misleading guise of descriptions, or internally related to such norms of representation. Their role is as inference rules. They are not descriptions of anything, but rules of description. How is it possible for us to know them? To know them is to know rules. We learn these in the course of learning our language – for they are partly constitutive of the meanings of the words we use.

The treatment of the philosophical questions about necessity is to be detached from epistemological considerations. So the treatment of the philosophical problem of the conditions of the possibility of original (underived, groundless) self-ascription of experience is to be detached altogether from the treatment of the Kantian epistemological question of the conditions of the possibility of knowledge of synthetic a priori judgements. How then is *this* problem to be char-

---

60 For detailed discussion see Baker and Hacker 2009, pp. 241–370.

acterized? – *Not* by reference to the misguided question of what experience must be like in order to constitute cognition.[61] Nor is the answer to the problem to be by reference to the imaginary "science" of transcendental psychology according to which I must be aware, or be able to be aware, of a transcendental synthesis of intuitions.[62] Rather the question is to be transposed to the linguistic plane: how is it possible for a language-user to apply present-tense perceptual verbs to himself without any grounds whatsoever? Or: not "what must *experience* be like to be groundlessly self-ascribable by a subject of experience?", but rather: "what must the logico-grammatical character of *predicates of experience* be in order for their groundless self-ascription to make sense?"

Wittgenstein's treatment of self-ascribed predicates of sensation (e. g. "to have a pain") is too well known, I hope, to need much rehearsing. Criterionless self-ascription of psychological concepts is possible only on condition of mastery of the concept self-ascribed without criteria. Mastery of the concept self-ascribed without criteria involves grasp of the criteria for its other-ascription, and mastery of the language-games in which both self- and other-ascription are embedded. In the case of *having a pain*, the primitive roots of the language-game lie in natural behavioural expressions of pain. For the child learns to say "Ow", "Hurts", "It hurts" and later "I have a pain" as extensions of natural pain-expression – first as avowals, later as averrals. In learning this, the child also learns that his own pain-expressions and pain reports are a reason for others to ascribe *having a pain* to him, and hence too that the pain-utterances and pain-behaviour of others is a reason for saying of them that they are in pain. But this form of linguistic graft onto natural behavioural stock is *not* a general pattern. Each concept must be examined in its own right, and located within its own language-games.

So, how is it possible for a language-user to apply predicates of sensible experience to himself, defeasibly – but without grounds, and to apply them to others on the basis of behavioural grounds? A full reply would be lengthy. All

---

61 Misguided, because what is self-ascribed is the *experiencing*, not the *experienced*. So the question is akin to "what must seeing be like to constitute my seeing something to be so?", or transposed to sensation "what must having a pain be like for me to be able to have a pain?" These are surely nonsensical questions, the incoherence of which is masked by the deceptive nominalisation "representation", "experience", "perception".

62 The fact that Kant has to have recourse to the idea of consciousness of the power of synthesis and its exercise (A 108; B 133) is a token of the fact that the questions he is asking are misconceived. For such consciousness could not be empirical – since it is a condition of the possibility of experience. But there is no such thing as non-empirical, atemporal, consciousness of an act or activity.

that I aim to do here is indicate what sort of reply a Wittgensteinian approach would yield. But what I here briefly sketch is, I hope, in the spirit of his thought. Mastery of the perceptual vocabulary (the use of verbs of perception and their cognates), and hence possession of concepts of perception, presuppose antecedent mastery of an observational vocabulary of perceptibilia, and, by and large, a vocabulary of perceptual qualities (both special and common sensibles). This, with us, requires competence in its use in description, interrogation and command.[63] Once a significant fragment of that is mastered, indeed, *while* it is being mastered, perceptual verbs come into play: "Can you see ...?", "Did you hear ...?", "Does that feel cold?", and so forth. In response to an assertion of how things perceptibly are, the question "How do you know?" can now arise. So the child learns to reply "I saw him in the garden", and "I can hear her outside". He learns to play "I spy with my little eye", and so on, and so forth. In short, he learns the use of verbs of perception as operators on descriptions of perceptibilia, and as indicative of validating sources of knowledge. He learns the first-person use *and* the third-person use. He learns the groundless application of verbs of vision as operators on descriptions of visibilia qualified by visual sensibles, which he has been able to report on using his sight, i.e. on looking, watching, glancing and spotting. (He would not have been able to do so with his eyes closed!) And so too, *mutatis mutandis*, he learns the first-person use of the other perceptual verbs. At the same time, the child learns the use of these verbs in respect of his parents, siblings and friends: he learns to say "Look!", to ask "Can you see?", to order "Listen!" and to query "Did you hear?", not to mention "Mummy, taste!" or "Daddy, smell!". So too, he learns to apply this battery of verbs to others on the grounds of what they do and say – of their looking, listening, tasting, smelling and feeling, and the evident upshot of their perceptual activities.

Once this expansion of vocabulary and concept-acquisition is under way, illusion and error are made explicit. Perceptual descriptions and claims are not always right. Observation conditions are sometimes sub-optimal, the sense-organs are sometimes defective (temporarily or permanently), the objects of perception are sometimes deceptive and look or sound other than they are. Parental or peer correction commonly follows error. The child himself learns to correct error – by looking again, or improving the

---

63 One can readily imagine more primitive languages with only substances names and no names of perceptual qualities, or with only orders, or only questions with yes/no answers. But that is not to the point here, since we are patently concerned with any language rich enough to admit of a systematic distinction between subjective experiences (and statements of what they are experiences of) and their objects (and the descriptions of their objects).

observation conditions (moving closer, turning on the light), and so forth. So he learns to budget for the defeat and defeasibility of observation claims and perceptual self-ascriptions. He learns the use of the operators "It seems to me as if", "I think it's a ...", "As far as I can see" and so forth. The *fundamental* role (others will come later) of these sentence-forming operators on observation-sentences and on perceptual sentences is not to report the "representation of a representation that is in me", but to *qualify* an observation-sentence or perceptual sentence. The *basic* role is to indicate that the operand is not wholly reliable, that the employment of the cognitive faculty of sense was, in one way or another, non-optimal (either by way of sense or by way of recognition), that defeating conditions cannot be ruled out. Once that basic role is in place, other roles can be assigned to the operation, e.g. characterization of the manner of perceiving (at the oculist's, for example), qualifications on thought rather than on perception, characterization of the objective appearance of the object perceived by "It looks like", "It appears", "It seems to be".

Self-consciousness, as conceived in the Cartesian/Lockean tradition culminating in Kant, was, I suggest, a grammatical red-herring. There is indeed such a thing as self-consciousness.[64] But it is not a matter of the capacity for self-ascription of experience. That a child has learnt to say "Mummy, I can see you", "Daddy, I heard a noise", or "That feels hot!" does not imply any increase in, or development of, self-consciousness. That a language-user has advanced to this stage does indeed imply that he can *think about* and *express his thoughts about* his own perceptual experiences ("Oh, it is so nice to see that garden", "I enjoyed listening to you"). Is this a mark of achieving self-consciousness? One *might* say so. It is true that language-users such as ourselves, unlike the other animals, can think about our current perceptual experiences and say what we think about them. But is that sufficient for self-consciousness? To think about something (e.g. Julius Caesar) is not in general to be conscious of what one is thinking about. Why should thinking about one's perceiving what one is currently perceiving be conceived to be a mode of self-consciousness? One might rather opt for a weightier notion. Self-consciousness, taken weightily, is *related* to the bare idea of thinking about one's experiences. It is indeed *cogitative* rather than cognitive – so it belies its etymological ancestry. But unlike mere *thinking about* one's currently perceiving something, it is a reflective, cogitative *disposi-*

---

64 I deliberately disregard here the perfectly decent, but clearly irrelevant, notion of self-consciousness associated with one's reactions to awareness of other people's eyes being upon one. I also pass by the notion of self-consciousness linked with deliberation in creativity ("Flaubert was a highly self-conscious author").

tion. Moreover, its objects are not current perceptions. To be self-conscious, in this sense, is a matter of having a disposition to *think about* one's tendencies, attitudes, character traits, actions and the reasons and motives one has or had for them – but it is *not* being *conscious of them*. For those who are, in this sense, self-conscious (introspective) personalities are also much given to self-decep-tion.[65]

65 I am much indebted to Hanjo Glock, Anthony Kenny, Adrian Moore, Hans Oberdiek, Herman Philipse, Bernhard Ritter and Daniel Robinson for their comments on earlier drafts of this paper.

João Vergílio Gallerani Cuter
Five Red Apples

Consider the pieces chosen by Wittgenstein to compose the most famous of all his language-games. Consider them against the background of his philosophical development and it will be clear that the choice has a historical as well as a conceptual significance. Numbers (like five), the immediately given (like red), and physical objects (like an apple) — these are precisely the landmarks of the transition from the *Tractatus* to his late philosophy. Is it just a coincidence? I do not think so.

As is widely known, the general form of all propositions is given in the *Tractatus* without any hint as to the special forms of the elementary ones. The latter are collectively represented in aphorism 6 by a propositional variable with a bar over it: $[\bar{p}, \bar{\xi}, N(\bar{\xi})]$. The symbol is a little bit awkward,[1] but the meaning is quite unambiguous. Before logical analysis is effectively carried out, we cannot forecast the combinatorial order according to which names give rise to elementary propositions. We can only be sure that elementary propositions must be found as the end result of analysis, and that any other proposition can be built in a finite number of steps (this is the meaning of the bracketed expression as a whole) from the elementary level on up (i. e. from $\bar{p}$ on up) with the only help of

---

1 It is awkward because it does *not* generate a formal series, as a bracketed expression usually does. We do not have here a "first member", and some members can only be reached once we are able to gather an infinite number of propositions. Imagine "aRb" is an elementary proposition. We can reach "$(\exists x)(aRx \& xRb)$" by selecting the totality of values of the propositional function "$aRx \& xRb$", and then negating the simultaneous denial of those values. A similar move will give us each member of the *formal* series mentioned in aphorism 4.1273:

   aRb

   $(\exists x)(aRx \& xRb)$

   $(\exists x, y)(aRx \& xRy \& yRb)$

   etc.

If we now consider this formal series as a whole, we will be able to negate the simultaneous denial of all its members, and obtain the (equivalent of the Fregean) proposition "*b* follows *a* in the R-series" (without the need of second-order quantifiers and R-hereditary properties).

formal mechanisms of selection[2] (this is the meaning of $\bar{\xi}$) and truth-operations (aptly represented here by the operation N) applied to those selections.

Taken as a totality, elementary propositions have two characteristic marks: (i) they must be sufficient to build any descriptive sense according to the recipe given in the general form of proposition, and (ii) they must be logically independent of one another. This independence was at the heart of the crisis announced in the lecture on logical form.

Let us carefully read aphorism 6.3751 in order to understand the exact nature of that crisis. It has three paragraphs. The first and the last ones state an apparently serious problem; the second hints at a possible solution by means of an analogy.

6.371 comes as a remark on aphorism 6.375, according to which every necessity and every impossibility must be logical in nature. If so, then we must come to terms with ascriptions of colour made at the phenomenal level. If we have reasons to think that it is *impossible* for two colours "to be at one place in the visual field", then we must hold that the logical product

a is red & a is green

(where *a* is a place in my visual field) is a hidden contradiction. The immediate consequence is that phenomenal ascriptions of colour cannot be elementary propositions. This is the conclusion we are led to by the last paragraph of the aphorism:

> It is clear that the logical product of two elementary propositions can neither be a tautology nor a contradiction. The assertion that a point in the visual field has two different colours at the same time, is a contradiction.

There are many questions we could raise about this passage, and at least one of them seems to be partially answered by the paragraph which was set aside for a moment: *Why should we consider "a is red & a is green" a hidden contradiction?* If we go to the *Notebooks*, we find a passage where this question is explicitly raised, and the physical approach is explicitly used to answer it:

---

2 Viz. those listed in aphorism 5.501.

> A point cannot be red and green at the same time: at first sight there seems no need for this to be a logical impossibility. But the very language of physics reduces it to a kinetic impossibility. We see that there is a difference of structure between red and green.
>
> And then physics arranges them in a series. And then we see how here the true structure of the objects is brought to light.
>
> The fact that a particle cannot be in two places at the same time does look more like a logical impossibility.
>
> If we ask why, for example, then straight away comes the thought: Well, we should call particles that were in two places different, and this in its turn all seems to follow from the structure of space and of particles.[3]

At first sight, we could think that we just cannot *imagine* red and green occupying at the same time the same region of our visual field. Why not blame our imagination, and take the "cannot" as expressing a merely psychological shortcoming? Were this the case, "*a is red & a is green*" would be a proposition of the same form as "*a is red & a is round*", and there would be no logical objection against the elementary character of colour ascriptions. But there seems to be more to it than the contingent limits of our imagination. The physical theories we build do not make any room for the expectation of an experience that could be described as the presence in my visual field of a patch of colour which is both red and green. Quite the contrary. Physical statements that could be linked to expectations of this kind take the form of *prima facie* contradictions, like

The velocity of this particle is both m and n.

where m and n are numbers. In the absence of any qualification, this statement should be as contradictory as

The number of persons in this room is both 5 and 3.

Moreover, it implies propositions which seem to be contradictory, like

Right now this particle is both here and there.

---

3 NB, p. 81.

Taking these physical statements as being contradictory, we close the door for the expectation of a colour which is both red and green. In doing so, we are just doing justice to our feeling that both-red-and-green is not a possible content of our visual field. In Wittgenstein's words, "we see that there is a difference of *structure* between red and green". If they were logically simple objects, they would not be incompatible with each other. This incompatibility can only be explained by a logical complexity hidden underneath surface grammar – a hidden structure that logical analysis is in charge of digging out. Can we foresee the end results of analysis at this point? In outline, we can. Once again, the physical way of dealing with colours will give us a precious clue: physics arranges colours in a *series*, and then we see "*how the true structure of the objects* is brought to light".

Physical theories deal with chromatic difference associating each colour to a certain velocity of particles, or to a certain wavelength. So instead of the apparently discrete and independent elements named as "violet", "blue", "cyan", "green", etc., we would have a sequence of indefinite descriptions (roughly) like

a radiation whose wavelength lies between 380 and 450 nm
a radiation whose wavelength lies between 451 and 475 nm
a radiation whose wavelength lies between 476 and 495 nm
etc.

Serially organized, colours acquire a definite logical structure, and physical ascriptions of colour become (or at least should become) reducible to formal series like

There is no apple in this bag.
There is exactly one apple in this bag.
There are exactly two apples in this bag.
etc.

As such, they should be expressible in the Tractarian notation which uses numbers as exponents of recursive operations: $0^{0'}p, 0^{1'}p, 0^{2'}p$, etc., and it should be clear *why* ascriptions of colour clash the way they do. Physical red is incompatible with physical green in the same sense as the existence of exactly five apples in this bag is incompatible with the existence of exactly three. Our hope is that *phenomenal* colours can be analysed along the same lines. But how?

By the time Wittgenstein was writing the *Tractatus*, his future editor Wilhelm Ostwald published a series of books[4] where he tried (among other things) to organize colours in a kind of coordinate space, where each possible variation of each spectral ("pure") colour was associated with a triad of numbers. His criteria were not purely phenomenal, as he used a physical disk to produce physical mixtures of spectral colours with different physical amounts of black and white. Even so, the Ostwald notation for colours was able to suggest a way of organizing phenomenal colours in a structure within which any chromatic element would find its place.

The idea itself was not new. After reading Alois Höfler's Psychologie, or Ebbinghaus' Grundzüge der Psychologie any student of psychology would be familiar with a theoretical device that was to appear many times in Wittgenstein's manuscripts: the colour octahedron.[5] The geometrical structure of the octahedron was thought of as a mirror of the relations borne by each colour to any other:[6]

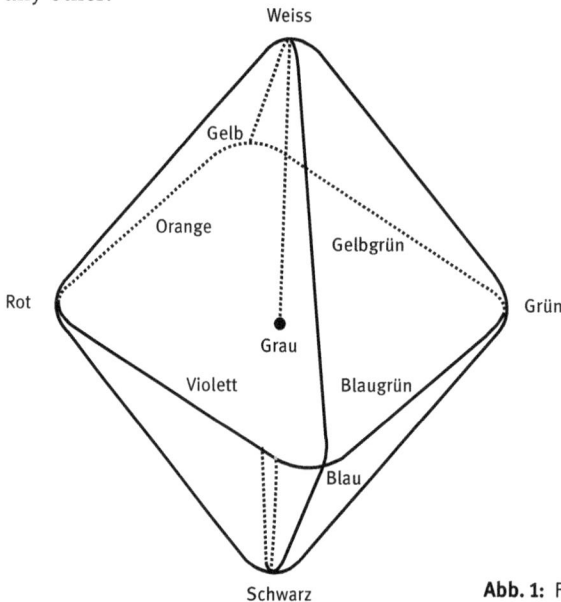

Abb. 1: Farbenoktaeder

4 *Die Farbenfibel* (1917), *Der Farbkörper und seine Anwendung zur Herstellung farbigen Harmonien* (1919), *Die Harmonie der Farben* (1919), *Farbkunde* (1923), among others. One of his aims was to create a scientific theory about the harmonization of colours for the use of professional painters. It is not difficult to imagine Wittgenstein's reaction to this kind of project. In a letter to Russell, he refers to Ostwald as an *Erzscharlatan* (a consumate charlatan). Cf. WC, p. 128.
5 Cf. Höfler 1897, pp. 108–121, and Ebbinghaus 1902, pp. 180–191.
6 Image taken from Ebbinghaus 1902, p. 184.

A first division opposes white, black and all shades of grey to spectral colours. In the octahedron this corresponds to the opposition between the vertical axis and the horizontal edges. Inside the octahedron, "lighter" and "darker" are mapped by "closer to the white pole" and "closer to black pole". Colours that can be *seen* as the phenomenal mixture of two others, like orange, are placed at some point on a horizontal edge. Pure colours, in which no other hue can be distinguished, are positioned at the four corners of the central square: red opposite to green, blue opposite to yellow, since there is no reddish green, and no yellowish blue. Ebbinghaus even makes the central square of the octahedron to bend a little bit so as to make the whole construction reflect the "fact" that yellow is nearer to the white pole than to the black one.

Different latitudes in the octahedron will be associated to differences in hue, longitudes to degrees of brightness, distances from the vertical axis to degrees of saturation. If we suppose divisions marking perceptible intermediate levels in these three chromatic dimensions, it will be possible to make reference to any colour by means of a triad of numbers. We could describe the way leading from a given colour to any other one by means of discrete transitions inside the octahedron: "2 steps to the right, 3 upwards, then 1 to the centre". Ebbinghaus recognizes that it would be difficult to do this in practice, and it would have scarcely any importance in everyday life.[7] But that is not the point. What really matters is that the octahedron gives us "insight into the inner constitution of the realm of colours".

Now my contention is that in aphorism 6.3751 Wittgenstein is suggesting this horizon of analysis. For sure, ascriptions of colour cannot be elementary propositions. But, in addition to that, the only way to make those ascriptions logically incompatible with one another (as they seem to be) is to render them logically akin to ascriptions of number. Ostwald's system could be a good example if it were not for the introduction of physical criteria to get the scales of hue, brightness and saturation. The octahedra devised by Höfler and Ebbinghaus give us a good sketch of how to carry out the numeration of colours without bringing in non-phenomenal elements. Wittgenstein's plan to analyse phenomenological statements like "There is a red circle in my visual field" was to translate it in a conjunction of the form

There is a circle in my visual field of hue *k* & brightness *m* & saturation *n*

---

7 Ebbinghaus 1902, p. 187.

where each of the conjuncts is a member of a formal series like

There is a circle in my visual field of hue 1
There is a circle in my visual field of hue 2
There is a circle in my visual field of hue 3
etc.

Each of the members of a formal series like this should be analysed in terms of quantified statements of the form "there are exactly n...", where the numeral n would be analysed away, and replaced by quantificational structures. In the *Tractatus*, as is well known, numbers were not introduced at the basis of language. They were only abbreviatory devices, marking the place of a proposition inside a formal series. Physics arranges ascriptions of colours in *series* (i.e., formal series of *propositions*) whose members are logically incompatible with one another. Phenomenal ascriptions of colour should do the same. Octahedric presentations show a possible way to carry out the idea.

I think it is not quite correct to associate the fall of the Tractarian project with the "colour exclusion problem". Colour exclusion was there since the beginning, and Wittgenstein had a definite plan to overcome it. What is more important – the plan would outlive the downfall of the original project. We find numbers clearly associated to colours in the 1929 lecture on logical form, and the octahedric presentation throughout the *Philosophical Remarks*. Colours have nothing to do with the abandonment of the *Tractatus*. Numbers, and not colours, were at the centre of the crisis.

What Wittgenstein discovers in 1929 is that Tractarian numbers could be good (at most) to count, but were useless to measure. Numbers could not be analysed away. They could not be replaced by quantificational structures. They should be introduced *as such* at the basis of language – at the very level of elementary propositions. There can be no doubt about this, since he is quite explicit:

> If now we try to get at an actual analysis, we find logical forms which have very little similarity with the norms of ordinary language. We meet with the forms of space and time with the whole manifold of spatial and temporal objects, as *colours*, sounds, etc., etc., *with their gradations, continuous transitions, and combinations in various proportions*, all of which we cannot seize by our ordinary means of expression. And here I wish to make my first definite remark on the logical analysis of actual phenomena: it is this, that *for their representation numbers (rational and irrational) must enter into the structure of the atomic propositions themselves.*[8]

---

8 "Some Remarks on Logical Form" in PO, p. 31.

Let us repeat the idea. Wittgenstein is saying that for the representation of space, time, *colours*, sounds, etc., etc. numbers must enter into the structure of *elementary propositions*. Here is the novelty. As I said, the crisis has nothing to do with "colour exclusion" – no more at least than it has to do with "sound exclusion", "temporal exclusion", or "spatial exclusion". They are all at stake, it is true, but *only* in so far as they are all special cases of *gradation, continuous transition, combination in various proportions*. They all involve (or seem to involve) some kind of *measurement*, and the results of measurement cannot be expressed by means of quantifiers.

The argument is very well known. It runs like this. If I say that there are five apples in this bag, I am saying that there is one, and another, and another, and another, and another, and no other. Now if we apply the same rule of translation to express the measurement of this table, the word "another" has to be dropped, on pain of multiplying the patterns. If there were "one" meter and "another" one, a question could be raised as to the measurement of each meter – "are they of the same length, or not?". On the other hand, if we get rid of the word "another", we are left with a single incomparable pattern. But in this case quantifiers cannot be applied to say "there are two". As there is only one meter, there cannot be more than one variable running through different meters.[9] The conclusion is that we cannot use quantifiers to analyse numbers away. Numbers must be introduced at the basis of language, inside the structure of elementary propositions themselves.

This may sound like a *non sequitur*. Why should we take patterns of measurement as being logically simple objects, hence as being the reference of certain names, and hence as being possible arguments for variables? We could suppose that statements of degree are highly complex, and that after analysis meters, pounds, degrees of brightness, etc. would simply disappear. Could we not just tell a story about the superposition of an ordinary wooden rod as a good rendering of the statement "this table is three meters long"? Why should a story like this be logically more problematic than any other as far as logical analysis is concerned?

The truth is that no such story would be able to match the logical relations involved in measurement – that is what Wittgenstein seems to have realized in 1929. If this table is 3 meters long, it cannot have any other length. As a matter of fact, if I measure it now, and measure it again, then (if nothing happens to

---

9 I am applying the Tractarian convention as to the use of variables. Without applying it, the result would be exactly the same: "$a \neq b$" would be a contradiction when a pattern of measurement was concerned, and "$(\exists x, y): \varphi x. \varphi y. x \neq y$" would be a contradiction as well.

the table) I will find the same result. But although that is the expected outcome of measurement episodes, from a logical point of view it is not necessarily so. It is possible (i.e. it makes sense) to tell a story in which I find 3 meters now, and 2 meters afterwards. It would be futile to reduce measures to *single acts of measurement* — i.e. to interpret "this table is 3 meters long" as "at time *t* and place *s* I made 3 superpositions of that particular rod". If two different tables are 3 meters long I must be able to conclude that they coincide, that is to say, that I could superpose *them*. Singularized measurement would not have this logical consequence. The sense of "same measure" would be completely subverted.

So Wittgenstein had good reasons to abandon the arithmetic of the *Tractatus*. Ascriptions of number of any kind should involve (sooner or later) quantified structures of the form

$$(\exists x_1 \dots x_k) \dots \& \sim (\exists x_1 \dots x_{k+1}) \dots$$

We would have to be able to express the results of measurement in statements with this form, and that is what Wittgenstein realizes that could not be done.[10] Numbers would have to be included in the basic toolkit of language, alongside names and truth-operations.[11] This is an idea he repeats many times (for instance, PR § 76, WVC, pp. 73, 81), and he could hardly have been more explicit than he was.

---

10 No similar problem occurs when we are using numbers to count. If I say that there are 3 people in room A, and 2 people in room B, then we can immediately conclude that there are more people in room A than in room B. To express this last statement in Tractarian terms we just have to consider the formal series

$(\exists x)Ax \, \& \, (E0x)Bx$
$[(\exists x,y)(Ax \, \& \, Ay)] \, \& \, (E1x)Bx$
$[(\exists x,y,z)(Ax \, \& \, Ay \, \& \, Az)] \, \& (E2x)Bx$
etc.

where "$(Enx)Bx$" means "there are exactly n people in room B". If we affirm that one member of this series is true (i.e, if we negate the simultaneous negation of all members of the series), we obtain the proposition we need. This proposition is now an immediate consequence of the conjunction

$(E3x)Ax \, \& (E2x)Bx$

In measurements we must have a similar logical relation, but Wittgenstein realizes that it cannot be based on the working of quantifiers.
11 Or what will be left of these two notions.

The interesting thing is that he did *not* give up the horizon of analysis of ascriptions of colour announced at aphorism 6.3751. Not completely at least. As late as January 1930 (more than six months after having written his paper on logical form) we find him talking about a metric of colours to be established with the help of a coordinate system:[12]

> Of course colours have not the multiplicity of lengths – they cannot be measured with *one* yardstick. Instead of describing the distribution of colours by means of propositions, I could also do it by means of a system of yardsticks. I take as many yardsticks as the coordinates occurring in my description, and *put the scales in a certain position*:

Wittgenstein is still considering the possibility of using numbers to give colours an adequate logical structure – to make them incompatible with one another, as they should be. The use of actual yardsticks would make it *physically* impossible to ascribe different colours to the same region of my visual field. In a coordinate language, physical impossibility gives place to the syntactical rules associated to the use of numerical parameters. In both cases we have the same result.[13]

It is easy to see the advantages of this kind of approach. Even if numbers cannot be analysed away, it would be highly desirable to have a unified explanation of logical relations between statements of degree. If a patch in my visual field has a certain degree of brightness, then it cannot have any other. If a sound has a certain pitch, then it cannot have any higher (or lower) one. If a body is here now, then it cannot be there. And if an event began 5 minutes ago, it cannot have begun at any other time. Space, time, sounds and colours would certainly have specific logical properties, but there would be a certain core that could be completely mapped by the mere use of coordinates and numerical parameters. Colour exclusion would clearly belong to this core. So it is not surprising to see Wittgenstein flirting with a metric of colours, and with coordinated languages in general.

But in spite of all its advantages, the idea of a *metric* of colours will be clearly abandoned in the final chapters of the *Remarks*. A metric presupposes the identification of distances and intensities, and that is what we cannot do within the phenomenal level:

---

12 WVC, p. 76. Almost the same ideas can be found in PR § 84.

13 "We give one coordinate to reality: one colour, one brightness, one hardness, and so on. The description must take place in such a way that it does not determine twice the same coordinate. In order to avoid this, we use a syntax. We can also do without syntax by employing a system of description which cannot give two different coordinate values to reality." (WVC, p. 76)

> We can see that a colour is redder than another or whiter, etc. But can I find a metric of
> colours? Does it have sense to say, for instance, that as far as the amount of red in it is con-
> cerned one colour is *halfway* between two others?[14]

The implicit answer is that it does not make sense to "measure" the distances between chromatic determinations at the phenomenal level. We are perfectly able to recognize a colour as being redder than another. But, given two colours, does it make sense to say that one of them is *twice as red* as a third one? And even if we decide to use this form of expression, would we be prepared to say that a distance in redness between a pair of colours is exactly the same as the distance in greenness between another pair? Which criteria should we use in case of doubt? Suppose you have three reddish colours in your visual field, two of them being very close to one another. Which criteria would you use to decide that *this* colour, and not that one, is *exactly twice* as red as the third? Ebbinghaus' octa-hedron is excellent to display logical relations among colours, but it is of little help as a yardstick. And colours are not the only problem. There is no place for yardsticks at the phenomenal level – as Wittgenstein says, "there is no measuring in the visual space".[15] The problem is very simple and straightforward. In order to measure we must have an equivalence relation of a certain kind. If we want to measure distance, for example, we must be prepared to say that this distance is the same as that one. Now sameness of distance (like sameness of hue, saturation, brightness, temperature, timbre, pitch, etc.) must be a transitive relation in order to be a kind of equivalence, and when we are inside the world of phenomena transitivity is completely lost. If we put the prefix "seems to be" before any of the aforementioned equivalences, the resultant relation will not be transitive. Let me use one of the many explanations inserted in the last pages of the *Remarks* to establish this point:

> If any pair of contiguous segments seem to be equal, I cannot infer that a pair of distant
> segments will seem to be equal as well. Numbers simply fail to depict the relations between
> magnitudes and intensities at the phenomenal level. They make us expect a transitivity that
> simply does not hold.[16]

---

14 PR, p. 273.
15 PR, p. 266.
16 Cf. PR, p. 270.

So the situation seems to be as follows. In the *Tractatus*, phenomenal ascriptions of colours could not be elementary propositions, since they are not logically independent. At that time Wittgenstein thought he could deal with those propositions using numbers. Ostwald's system suggested a rough way of doing that, and Höfler's octahedron presented a way of organizing colours according to purely phenomenological criteria. To each colour we could associate a triad of numbers, and each ascription of colour could be analysed as a conjunction of three assignments of numbers determining the hue, brightness and saturation of the colour to be ascribed. Then numbers could be analysed away, being substituted by quantificational structures, and quantificational structures could be reduced to truth-functions of elementary propositions, fitting the general mould given at aphorism 6. When Wittgenstein resumed his philosophical activities, he was led to admit that this solution would not work. In the lecture on logical form, the burden was put on the reduction of numbers to quantificational structures. Quantifiers were good to count, but useless to express the degree of a property. Numbers would have to be brought to the basis of language, inserted as such into the structure of elementary propositions. Then they would be able to measure phenomenal colours, sounds, spans of time, and so on. The bad news came in the final portion of the *Remarks*. Even that solution would not do. It is impossible to project a measuring system inside the visual space, since appearance of equality is not a transitive relation. So colours would have to be dealt with primitively, without the benefit of a metric. The octahedron can be used to give a perspicuous access to all chromatic relations, but not to build a coordinate system to which numbers could be applied.

This is obviously linked to the opposition between propositions and hypothesis during the intermediate period. Any sentence making reference to physical objects (like an apple, for instance) is called by Wittgenstein a "hypothesis". Hypotheses are not capable of being true or false, since they cannot be verified. They are not propositions, but only "rules for the construction of propositions".[17] Only descriptions of what is immediately given to me at a given moment can be properly called "propositions". When I say that there is an apple in this bag I am saying that if I look at it I will have visual impressions of a certain kind. I expect to have such and such immediate experiences, and these expectations would have a propositional character, since they can be met (or not). Expectations do have a pictorial nature – they can agree or disagree with reality. Imagine the bag is closed. I say that there is an apple inside it. This creates a "visual expectation" which is not met at the present moment. Then I open the bag, and see what I was

---

17 PR, p. 285.

expecting to see: a round red patch right in the middle of my visual field. The expectation turned out to be true.[18]

Did phenomena play any role in the *Tractatus*? Were elementary sentences to be considered descriptions of what is immediately given from a solipsistic perspective? Would Wittgenstein treat propositions about physical objects as mere "hypothesis", as he would explicitly do some years later in the *Remarks*? I think it is impossible to read aphorism 6.3751 without answering "yes and no" to these questions. He is not *committed* to the view that elementary propositions should deal with phenomena; but he is clearly *inclined* to look for elementary propositions at the phenomenal level. At least I cannot see any better way of explaining his talk about the "visual field" in that place. After all, immediate experience is the place where *anyone* would expect to find logically simple objects which would be presupposed in any description of the "world as I found it". On the other hand, the same aphorism gives us excellent reasons to realize that the immediately given has not an *immediately given structure*. Red looks like an ultimate element, but it is not. So we must be cautious. Phenomena are not the place where Tractarian elementary propositions dwell. They are at most the direction in which they should be searched for.

Be that as it may, the crisis of the *Tractatus* was clearly marked by difficulties in the actual analysis of phenomena. Wittgenstein believed that elementary propositions would be found by probing propositions like "There is a red round patch in my visual field", and then using numbers to reproduce the logical behaviour or words like "red". On the other hand, it is impossible to be sure about the logical analysis he would endorse for a word like "apple", but it is possible at least to surmise. When you take phenomena as your point of departure, physical objects are condemned to be found at a level you will have to ascend to. They can be in the mind of God, as Berkeley contended, or be logical constructions, as in Russell's external world, or finally be mere hypotheses, as Wittgenstein himself would think in the early 1930s. In any case, they will be part of a physical world opposed from the very beginning to the world of our private experiences. If you assume that reference is a private action to be performed by a lonely subject, you will have a set of specific problems when you try to give explanations for the workings of words like "red" and "apple". The philosophical agenda associated to this perspective is clearly recognizable as one of the main targets of Wittgenstein's philosophy after the *Blue Book*.

---

18 "It is essential that the expectation must be capable of being compared not only with what is considered the final answer (verification or falsification) but also with the present state of things. That is the only thing which makes the expectation to be a picture." (PR, p. 286)

Numbers were right at the centre of the crisis. When he wrote the *Tractatus*, Wittgenstein believed he had reached a very elegant and powerful version of logicism. His central idea was both simple and ingenious. Pure arithmetic has no statements. It consists entirely of equations, and equations are simply substitution rules. They deal with signs – marks of ink which are part of a vast uninterpreted game. The equation "5 + 7 = 12", if it says anything at all, says simply that the signs (or pieces) "5 + 7" and "12" are interchangeable within the game. This is not much different from saying that when the pawn reaches the eighth row it may be replaced by a queen. The only difference is that arithmetical pieces are used in ordinary language inside sentences that have a definite sense, such as

There are 5 red apples in this bag.

But in these sentences the sign "5" is what Russell would call an "incomplete symbol". It does not have any meaning in isolation, although it can take part in meaningful contexts like this. Under analysis, it is doomed to disappear, giving place to nested quantifiers and maximal clauses. The sentences we reach after analysing numbers away can be organized in formal series – series of propositional signs that can be recursively characterized. In other words, these sentences form a totality of signs which is given by the direct description of the first member and by a formal rule saying how to get a new member out of a given one. This amounts to saying that ascriptions of numbers are organized in series governed by recursive operations. What the *Tractatus* shows is that the series of natural numbers is a logical mirror of all these formal series of propositions, and that non-quantified arithmetic mirrors the logical relations holding among the members of any formal series of propositions.[19] So the arithmetical substitution rules are logically grounded. They are not wholly arbitrary, like the rules of chess. They answer to essential features which must be present in any symbolism. If I take the fifth member of a series as the first member of another one, and use in the construction of the new series the same rule that was used to construct the first, the seventh member of the second series will coincide with the twelfth member of the first. That is the logical ground for accepting the equation "5 + 7 = 12".

---

19 I showed this in my PhD thesis "A Teoria dos Tipos e a Teoria da Figuração: O Tractatus no Contexto do Projeto Logicista", written in 1993. In the next year, Frascolla published his book *Wittgenstein's Philosophy of Mathematics*, whose first chapter has an exposition of the philosophy of arithmetic we find in the *Tractatus*. In general lines, Frascolla's account coincides with mine.

In the *Tractatus* numbers are just abbreviatory devices – "exponents of operations", meaningless signs marking the place of a proposition inside a formal series. The proposition "There are five red apples in this bag" is the fifth result of recursively applying a formal operation: "There is no...","There is exactly one...","There are exactly two...", and so on, up to five. Instead of "There are five apples in this room", we could write

$$0^{5\prime}p$$

Where *p* is the proposition "There is no red apple in this bag". In its unabbreviated form, it has no numbers at all. It will just be an ordinary truth-function of elementary propositions.

This is what disappears in the early 1930s: numbers come back to the foreground, and cannot be analysed away. That is the most radical (and I would say — the most central) departure from the Tractarian doctrines that we find in the *Philosophical Remarks*.

So we see that "five red apples" is not simply a group of words chosen at random. The language game of §1 certainly has a function in the internal economy of the *Investigations*, standing in sharp contrast, for instance, with the language games introduced in the second and eighth sections. But it has also historical references that cannot be ignored. These three words summarize the crisis of the Tractarian project as Wittgenstein faced it. The inclusion of this language game right at the beginning of the *Investigations* should even invite us to recognize that the expression "Tractarian project" has to acquire a wider meaning. It should not be exclusively applied to the book published in 1921, and to the manuscripts which gave rise to it. The project goes from 1913 until at least the first months of 1930, when the typescript of the *Remarks* was finished. It is against the philosophy produced along all this rather long period that the *Investigations* will be directed. Some of his arguments even make much clearer sense if understood against the background of the *Remarks*. It is in that work, for instance, that private experience is explicitly brought to the core of the semantic discussions. In the *Tractatus*, we must recognize the presence of the concept, not directly, but by way of consequence. It is in the *Remarks* that following a rule becomes an *activity* in the full and usual sense of the word. In the *Tractatus*, the "activity" of following the logical rules of language was the atemporal job of a transcendental subject dwelling at the limits of the world. In the *Remarks*, it takes time, and is inserted into the physical time of our lives. The *Tractatus* is certainly hit by the criticism of the *Investigations*, but only at a certain distance, and after a lot of intermediate steps. In the *Remarks*, the target is right in front of you. There is no distance to be transposed. From Wittgenstein's point of view, the *Tractatus* was the *Tractatus* and its circumstances – its antecedents and also the many attempts he made to save some substantial parts of the building from a devastating fire. The Tractarian project was for him the story of a failure that begins with the first letters to Russell and will finish in the intermediate period of his philosophical career. The words "five red apples" are a kind of emblem of this failure: a schematic reminder of the dead ends to which the Augustinian picture of language can lead us.

Jesús Padilla Gálvez
Are "Sentence" and "Language" Blurring Concepts?

In Ludwig Wittgenstein's work *The Big Typescript* we find a chapter that is entirely dedicated to concepts. It is entitled "'Sentence' and 'Language'" and its subtitle reads "Blurring Concepts"[1] Referring to the English translation of the subtitle, it is noteworthy that Wittgenstein had originally used the expression "*verschwimmende Begriffe*" in his German version which literally translates into "blurring concepts". He used the present participle to indicate that once we use concepts their reference tends to disappear. However, the translators replaced the present by the past participle which produces a slight shift in meaning.[2] It seems that Wittgenstein wanted to emphasize the circumstance that in the process of using a term it tends to lose its reference.

In the chapter mentioned, Wittgenstein reflects on the meaning of proposition. Actually, in this context the subtitle appears rather strange and one may ask what the translator actually understood by "Blurring Concepts"? Are we confronted with a polysemous adjective? In German the word "blurred" means "to become indistinct or unclear" (*wird undeutlich*) or else something "becomes obliterate or faint" (*verliert seine klaren Umrisse*). But does this indicate that terms such as "sentence" or "language" are both vague and lack sharp contours? In this paper I will deal with the question of how these terms are determined in Wittgenstein's philosophy of the middle period. The aim is to give an outline of the arguments that the philosopher used in order to clarify the supposed vagueness of language in general and sentences in particular.

---

1 BT, pp. 15, 50, 60. Cf.: "Und, wenn man sich in die Erinnerung ruft, 'daß die Tabelle uns nicht zwingt', sie aufeine bestimmte Weise<,>,<–> noch, sie immer auf diegleiche Weise zu benützen, – so wird es <(>ganz<)> ᴶᵉᵈᵉᵐ klar, daß unser Gebrauch des Wortes 'Regel' & 'Spiel' ein schwankender ɪ̶s̶t̶ (nach den Rändern zuverschwimmender) ist." (MS 114: X, 74)
2 BT, pp. 15, 50e, 60.

1 The Background of the Discussion on "Concept"

Wittgenstein mentioned in *The Big Typescript* that one has to take distance from what he called "false prophets" when analysing "blurring concepts". The problem of a "blurring concept" is that it is opposed to a definite distinction of various or different concepts. We shall briefly make reference to the arguments that proponents of an unambiguous delineation of concepts give for the importance of exactness in this field.

According to G. Frege, logicians must seek to define concepts clearly and unequivocally. Frege insisted that any concept shall be defined for all arguments of the appropriate category. Moreover, each argument must be assigned exactly one object. He argued that scientific rigor can only be achieved if certain conditions are met. The most important precondition is that in logic and science an expression can never be meaningless. This implies that one shall never act with empty terms and wrongly assume that these stand for objects. His program of scientific rigor reads as follows:

> Man kann dies bildlich so ausdrücken: der Begriff muss scharf begrenzt sein. Wenn man sich Begriffe ihrem Umfange nach durch Bezirke in der Ebene versinnlicht, so ist das freilich ein Gleichnis, das nur mit Vorsicht gebraucht werden darf, hier aber gute Dienste leisten kann. Einem unscharf begrenzten Begriffe würde ein Bezirk entsprechen, der nicht überall eine scharfe Grenzlinie hätte, sondern stellenweise ganz verschwimmend in die Umgebung überginge. Das wäre eigentlich gar kein Bezirk; und so wird ein unscharf definierter Begriff mit Unrecht Begriff genannt. Solche begriffsartige Bildungen kann die Logik nicht als Begriffe anerkennen; es ist unmöglich, von ihnen genaue Gesetze aufzustellen. Das Gesetz des ausgeschlossenen Dritten ist ja eigentlich nur in anderer Form die Forderung, dass der Begriff scharf begrenzt sei.[3]

In order for concepts to be uniquely determined, it is required that they must be strictly limited. Concepts without such delineation cannot be determined unequivocally. Following Frege, the extension of a concept must be clearly determined by its "scope" (*Bezirk*). The interesting thing is that the German expression "*Bezirk*" used by Frege is in itself a polysemous expression. On the one hand "*Bezirk*" is a specific territory or region which is determined extensionally and stands for a hierarchical order. As such, the expression remains unclear since it refers to both, a horizontal and a vertical segmentation. Additionally, it implies that such order may change over time. In fact, Frege himself used several artificial conditions in order to provide criteria for a definition of the exactness of con-

---

3 Frege 1966, vol.II, p. 69.

cepts. He attempted a clarification by pointing to a contradiction which occurs in the requirement of scientific rigor. Even if a concept needs a sharp boundary as to its scope, we have not yet defined its actual content. In other words, despite defining the boundaries of a concept, we are still not sure which elements this concept refers to.

Although the reference of a term may remain extensionally or vertically unchanged, it may still vary over time. No concept is extensionally determined, vertically invariant and at the same time temporally unchangeable. The whole argument presented by Frege is based on a linguistic illusion of symbolism. What is possible is that we can use a character (*Zeichen*) such as, for instance, a singular term "a" and put it in correlation with a predicate "F" called "Fa". This correlation remains unchanged. For instance, if I say "*Laufen* is beautiful" (and "*laufen*" means "to run"), then, the word "*laufen*" refers to a castle in Switzerland and corresponds to a name "a". But I could just as well use "*laufen*" as a predicate and thereby indicate "to go fast", "to run" and call this "F".

Thus it becomes obvious that the Fregean thesis can easily be refuted. A language consisting of definite concept with a distinct extension still has its limits due to the polysemous character of language. If we do not have any tool for a distinction of "*laufen*" as a proper name and as a predicate, then we are doomed to fail. Let us first examine the extensional aspects of concepts. The question is whether each term has a clear delineation. In other words, can we ever determine the definite extension of a concept? In his letter to Husserl of May 1891, Frege summarized his view of concept-words in the following statement:

> In the conceptual term there is one more *step* before the object than in the proper name, and the last *step* may be omitted – this means that the concept can be empty – but nevertheless the concept word may still be scientifically useful.[4]

---

4 "Beim Begriffsworte ist ein Schritt mehr bis zum Gegenstande als beim Eigennamen und der letzte kann fehlen – d.h. der Begriff kann leer sein –, ohne dass dadurch das Begriffswort aufhört, wissenschaftlich verwendbar zu sein". Frege 1976, p. 96 (Letter from Frege to Husserl, 24.5.1891).

Frege criticized Husserl's simple semantic perspective and described the phenomenological position in the following quote:

Begriffswort	Concept-word
↓	↓
Sinn des Begriffswortes (Begriff)	Sense of concept-word (Concept)
↓	↓
Gegenstand, der unter den Begriff fällt.	Object that belongs to a concept.

Husserl's Scheme (Frege 1976, p. 98 (Letter from Frege to Husserl, 24.5.1891))

In his *Logische Untersuchungen* Husserl underlined that a theory of concepts should avoid blurring concepts.[5] According to Frege's scheme, a relation between word and concept is only created by its meaning. Following Frege, objects and concepts are equally objective and a concept-word has both a sense and a meaning. The extension of a concept corresponds to objects.[6] In his view, the fact that a word has a sense is a sufficient criterion for its literary use. In order to use a concept in scientific terms it must also have a meaning. He considered the meaning of a concept as primarily important. The meaning is the object (*Gegenstand*) which is subsumed under the concept. To illustrate this difference Frege presented the following scheme:

Begriffswort		Concept-word	
↓		↓	
Sinn des Begriffswortes		Sense of concept-word	
↓		↓	
Bedeutung des Begriffswortes (Begriff)	→ Gegenstand, der unter den Begriff fällt	Meaning of the concept-word (concept)	→ Object that belongs to a concept

Frege's Scheme (Frege 1976, pp. 96ff. (Frege to Husserl, 24.5.1891))

---

5 Husserl 1968, p. 54.
6 Frege 1977, § 47.

These two schemes show relevant differences. In Frege's scheme the meaning of a concept-word remains indefinite whereas for Husserl the meaning of a concept-word is the concept itself. The carrier of meaning refers to the object that is subsumed by the concept-word. The object arises from the meaning expressed by the concept-word. As such, Wittgenstein's strict attitude towards language was perhaps a reaction to Frege's radical approach. In this context Wittgenstein asked which role "sentence" and "language" actually played within a rigid concept system.

2 "Sentence" as Blurring Concept

It is interesting what importance the question of meaning had. Frege's semantic position is dominated by logic whereby the meaning of an expression is delimited by its formal structure. This formal frame is critically reflected on. If the content of a concept is determined on the basis of logic operations, concepts would not exist. The argumentation reads as follows:

> Incidentally, that this sentence follows from that, although not yet thought of it //if you are surprised that one proposition follows from another even though you don't think of the latter when you think of the former//, then just consider that p v q follows from p, and I certainly don't think all propositions of the form p v ξ when I'm thinking p.[7]

The point goes back to Wittgenstein's observation in which the determiner of the content of a concept, p → (p v q) induces us to say that the sense of a sentence S implies the sense of a sentence S or S', whereby S' stands for any sentence whatever. Thus, Frege's account of the content of concepts produces a semantic collapse in which the sense of each sentence of language is the disjunction of the senses of every sentence of that language. The sense of each sentence of a language includes and is included in the sense of every sentence. For instance, the meaning of "man" refers to the whole range of meanings such as "gentleman", "guy", "male", "fellow", "chap", and so on. Hence, the content of every sentence is the same as that of every other sentence; in other words, all sentences are synonymous. Therefore, the problem of meaning must be approached from the perspective of natural language.

---

7 BT, pp. 234, 301.

Wittgenstein assumed that once a concept is applied its meaning becomes blurred because of its polysemous nature. He explains his assumptions in the following quote:[8]

> When Frege says that logic doesn't know what to do with vague concepts, this is true //is a the truth// in so far as it is precisely the sharpness of concepts that belongs to the method of logic. That is what the expression "Logic is normative" can refer to.[9]

In this quote he deals with the correlation between clear concepts and logic. He underlines that the method used in logic has to do with the quality of definiteness. Wittgenstein goes one step further than Frege and demonstrates that normativity in logic can only be based on the accuracy of terms. According to his view, normativity refers to how language *should be* and how it should be assessed, whether it is applied correctly or incorrectly and which structures are essential. However, this approach has nothing to do with the descriptive point of view because descriptive statements are made about reality and can be proved and also be refuted.

Wittgenstein used the term "normative" in connection with logic to show the difference between exact and indefinite concepts. Normative sciences are not aimed at justifying a predetermined standard or target. Rather they assume a norm as hypothetically given, without giving reasons why it should be followed. However, normative theories name the necessary conditions or standards that must be accomplished in order to comply with a specific norm. As such, normative theories are descriptive in a way.

However, Wittgenstein did not adopt such a radical standpoint nor did he reject logic as a whole. He said this:

> It is essential to logic to draw boundaries, but no such boundaries are drawn in the language we speak. But this doesn't mean that logic represents language incorrectly, or that it represents an ideal language. Its task is to portray a colourful, blurred reality as a pen-and-ink drawing.[10]

According to his view, logic is characterized by metaphor and thereby portrays the blurredness of language.

---

8 BT, pp. 50ff.
9 BT, pp. 55, 68v.
10 BT, pp. 56, 68v.

3 What Does "Sentence" Mean?

Wittgenstein analysed two solutions in order to clarify the content of a concept, all of which shall be presented in the following section:

(1) "A proposition is everything with which I mean something"[11]
(2) "The concept: to communicate something to each other"[12]
(3) "Socrates always rejects talking about particular instances of knowing, in favour of talking about knowledge"[13]

The first alternative is discussed in more detail. Quote (1) says that generalization itself is something specific. In that case, a concept can be interpreted as a sign, within which the grammatical rules are pre-determined. If the general is unclear, then logical indeterminacy is ruled out. If we use the metaphor mentioned above we could say: if someone draws a pen-and-ink-drawing and uses colour, then the soft focus never affects the pen-and-ink-drawing but rather the colour, which is an aggregate. Therefore, the question on the general form of a "proposition" can to be reformulated to: do we have a general concept of "proposition" that can be exactly understood?

Proposal (2) could be described as a communicative approach. Although a detailed description of this viewpoint would go beyond the scope of this essay, I shall still exemplify some aspects. Concepts are not normally discovered but they are rather entities that we tend to utilize. We learn to use concepts correctly. What it means to know a concept is nothing more than to know the techniques of how to apply them in a certain language. By applying a concept correctly, we indicate what it means in a certain context. Consequently, the technique of language use is rule-governed. It is probably this view that took Wittgenstein to criticize the platonic perspective. Quote (3) deals with the Platonic view in which basic structures are developed. We shall deal with this approach in more detail.

---

11 BT, pp. 50, 61.
12 BT, pp. 53, 66.
13 BT, pp. 54, 66.

4 The Meaning of Concepts

In quote (1) a theory of the meaning of terms is reduced to mere opinion. The concept of "sentence" is reduced to a speaker's opinion. In this context Wittgenstein asks: "What does, '*to mean "something"*', mean?". This question can be answered by giving examples. However, such examples would only reveal the scope of a meaning. The generalization of concepts is characterized as a sign with pre-determined grammatical rules. To the question: what exactly does the concept "proposition" mean, the answer might be: "... a proposition is any sign by which we mean something". But this is an inappropriate response because one has to define what is meant by "proposition".

The problem arises because of a false assumption. To explain this let us assume that a new sentence is included in a language. Which criterion do we have to determine whether this new combination is actually a sentence? How does the hearer know what the speaker wants to express by a sentence? Do we have to describe it in the same way as if we had made a new experience? How and why do we use concepts such as "sentence" or "experience"? How can we recognize a newly introduced "sentence" or "experience" compared to old "sentences" or "experiences"? This thought is described as follows:

> Have I to a certain extent already characterized what has happened in saying that it's an experience? Obviously, *not at all*. But still it looks as if I had already done that, as if I had already stated something about it: "that it is an experience". Our entire problem lies in this false appearance. For what holds true of the predicate "experience" also holds for the predicate "proposition".[14]

Wittgenstein criticized Frege and Husserl for not taking the fact into account that concepts do already have a particular grammar of their own. And what is more, this grammar does not depend on future events but rather must be established in advance.[15] The meaning of such concepts as "sentence" and "experience" "is [...] laid down in grammar".[16] Therefore, the problem is this: How does the grammar of a concept relate to the grammar of the concept once it is used? Or more precisely:

> How does the grammar of the word "proposition" relate to the grammar of propositions?[17]

---

14 BT, pp. 51, 62.
15 Ibid.
16 BT, pp. 51, 63.
17 Ibid.

The term "proposition" is understood as the "heading for the grammar of propositions".[18] "Heading" refers here to a short and precise description of a concept. If the term is defined as a heading, it is revealed as the concept of the grammar of sentences.

The next issue in need of clarification is that terms have a restricted extension. By systematically comparing terms, Wittgenstein noticed that he could form new sentences. Does this mean that a concept changes once it is applied to a new context? According to Wittgenstein, this is not the case because the grammar of terms remains constant, or as he says: "[...] that surprises do occur in the world, but not in grammar".[19]

Another aspect of criticism referring to the meaning of terms goes back to a mythological conception. If one is asked which "proposition" is pronounced by a specific term, the first reaction is that one is first captivated. Wittgenstein argued against this magic effect of terms by rephrasing the whole question by saying that what we are actually asked for is the mode of expression. Expressions determine the meaning of a concept and we cannot find any magic aspect in these expressions.

We might expand the meaning of terms by adding new concepts in propositional structures. Thus, the notion of "construction" as the most relevant part of the term itself, the method of "design" itself is a concept of "language". We cannot understand grammar as general discourse about language.[20]

5 Rules, Over-rules, and Other Considerations

Let us suppose a concept has several meanings, such as in the case of polysemous words. But how do we determine which rule is used to define the meaning of a concept? Wittgenstein rejected any visual explanation, because he did not consider this a rule and therefore it does not tabulate.[21] This is mainly because a visual explanation does not show the application of a term. Therefore, images are no adequate means to provide a definition of polysemous concepts.

The concept of "calculus" seems useful to define boundaries. If philosophy had to deal with the concept of "calculus" and especially with calculations,

---

18 BT, pp. 51, 62

19 BT, pp. 52, 63

20 BT, pp. 54, 66.

21 BT, pp. 54, 67.

we would be confronted with some sort of meta-philosophy.[22] Yet Wittgenstein rejected any such meta-philosophy. First, we calculate and apply certain calculations and only then can we define the concept of calculus. We proceed as follows: If I tell a child that 2 + 2 equals 4, then I do not need the concept of "calculus". I explain the meaning of "2", "+" (*plus*), "=" (*equals*) and "4" whereby I introduce the explanation of "2" and "4" by the ranking of the numbers, "1, 2, 3, 4, 5, 6, etc."

The relevant question is: How do we use the concept of the rule, for instance in a game?[23] A player has the following options:

a. The speaker may say "This follows from that rule". But then we could cite the rule itself and thus get rid of the word "rule".[24]

b. The speaker mentions of "all the rules of the game" and then he has to enumerate all the rules.

c. The speaker refers to the concept of "rule" as a group that is generated in a certain way from certain basic rules (*Grundregeln*). The term "rule" stands for the expression of these basic rules and operations.

d. The speaker determines what is considered a rule and what falls beyond it. This distinction is an agreement.

Wittgenstein shows that for a definition of a concept of meaning we rarely define the boundaries.[25] The use of concept-words in language is characterized by their blurredness. In contrast to Husserl, Wittgenstein shows that this blurredness can be useful.[26] This brings him to the following conclusion:

> If I want to draw sharp boundaries in the area of (such) blurred language use in order to clear things up and to avoid misunderstandings, then the sharply demarcated areas will

---

22 Ibid.
23 Cf.: "Man sieht dann vor allem, wie der Begriff des Spiels und damit der Spielregel ein an den Rändern verschwimmender ist". TS 212, 578; BT, TS 213, 239; and: "Und, wenn man sich in die Erinnerung ruft ^daran erinnert, 'daß die Tabelle uns nicht zwingt', sie so & so zu benützen, noch, sie immer auf die gleiche Weise zu benützen, so wird es ganz ^jedem klar, daß unser Gebrauch des Wortes ~~'Siel'~~ 'Regel' & des Wortes 'Spiel' ein schwankender ist. (Nach den Rändern zu verschwimmt.)". (BT, TS 213, 42)
24 BT, pp. 55, 68.
25 BT, pp. 55, 69.
26 BT, pp. 56, 70.

relate to real language use like the contours of a pen-and-ink drawing to the gradual transitions of colour patches in the reality that has been sketched.[27]

Consequently, Wittgenstein rejects the Husserl-Frege position against blurring concepts. Moreover, he points to another relevant aspect of language. In the next section we shall examine the Platonic position against blurred concepts in more detail.

6 Against Platonism

The third proposal is a critique of the Platonic idea of concept. But before analysing this view we need to clarify whether the concept of meaning originates in a primitive philosophical view of language. Let us start at the beginning.[28] Wittgenstein says:

> Augustinus, wenn er vom Lernen der Sprache redet, redet ausschließlich davon, wie wir den Dingen Namen beilegen, oder die Namen der Dinge verstehen. Hier scheint also das Benennen Fundament und Um und Auf der Sprache zu sein.
> Diese Auffassung des Fundaments der Sprache //Diese Betrachtungsweise der Sprache ist offenbar äquivalent mit der, die// ist wohl die, welche die Erklärungsform "das ist ..." als fundamental auffaßt. – Von einem Unterschied der Worte redet Augustinus nicht, meint also mit "Namen?" offenbar Wörter, wie "Baum", "Tisch", "Brot", und gewiß die Eigennamen der Personen; dann aber wohl auch "essen", "gehen", "hier", "dort"; kurz, alle Wörter. Gewiß aber denkt er zunächst an *Hauptwörter* und an die übrigen als etwas, was sich finden wird. (Und Plato sagt, daß der Satz aus Haupt- und Zeitwörtern besteht.)
> Sie beschreiben eben das Spiel einfacher, als es ist.
> Dieses Spiel kommt aber wohl in der Wirklichkeit vor. – Nehmen wir etwa an, ich wollte aus Bausteinen, die mir ein Andrer zureichen soll, ein Haus aufführen, so könnten wir erst ein Übereinkommen dadurch treffen, daß ich auf einen Stein zeigend sagte "das ist eine Säule", auf einen andern zeigend "das heißt Würfel", – "das heißt Platte" u.s.w.. Und nun bestünde die Anwendung im Ausrufen jener Wörter "Säule", "Platte", etc. in der Ordnung, wie ich die Bausteine brauche. Und ganz ähnlich ist ja das Übereinkommen
>
> a | ↓
> b | ↑
> c | →
> d | ←
>
> und etwa eines, das mit Farben arbeiten würde.

---

27 BT, pp. 56, 70.
28 BT, pp. 25ff., 23ff.

Augustinus beschreibt wirklich einen Kalkül; nur ist nicht alles, was wir Sprache nennen, dieser Kalkül.
(Und das muß man in einer großen Anzahl von Fällen sagen, wo es sich fragt: ist diese Darstellung brauchbar oder unbrauchbar. Die Antwort ist dann: "ja, brauchbar; aber nur *dafür*, nicht für das ganze Gebiet, das Du darzustellen vorgabst".)[29]

In this long quote the Augustinian model of language is compared to the Platonic model. Wittgenstein criticized the Platonic view of language as consisting of a simple grammar focused on subject and predicate. However, the meaning of language cannot be described by such a simple model. Explanations are reduced to the basic structure of: "this is ...". Here the strategy is to reduce the abstract concept to a simple structure of names.
Additionally, Wittgenstein pointed to another problem. Plato neither answered the question of what knowledge actually is nor did he indicate how the term "knowledge" would have to be used. In general, he failed to explain how a theory of meaning would function.

In Plato when a question likes "What is knowledge?" gets asked, I don't find as a provisional answer: "Let's look and see how this work is used". Socrates always rejects talking about particular instances of knowing, in favour of talking about knowledge.[30]

Wittgenstein concluded that a general concept of language "dissolves"[31] and he added that the task was "[...] to remove certain misunderstandings from our language".[32] Later he referred again to the difficulty by saying:

(Socrates asks the question what knowledge is and he isn't content with an enumeration of instances of knowledge. But we don't pay much attention to that general concept, and are happy if we understand shoe-making, geometry, etc.)[33]

The Platonic model of language is therefore deficient and inadequate as it does not provide any explanation on how concepts function.

29 BT, pp. 25, 23.
30 BT, pp. 53ff., 66.
31 BT, pp. 54, 67.
32 BT, pp. 54, 66v.
33 BT, pp. 56, 69.

7 Conclusion

Wittgenstein's position on "concept" is a criticism of Frege's proposal. Frege insisted that any concept shall be defined for all arguments of an appropriate category. Each argument must be assigned exactly one object. He claimed that scientific rigor could only be achieved by taking certain precautions. The most important precaution is that a logic or scientific expression can never be meaningless. Each term must be sharply limited and each concept must be clearly defined. In contrast to this view, Wittgenstein described concepts as undergoing a process of merging with their surroundings in a blurring way once they are applied. Therefore, concepts are never clear. This assumption is based on the polysemous character of concept use. In order to clarify the blurring meaning of concepts Wittgenstein studied their grammar. The question to be answered is the following: how does the grammar of a concept coincide with the grammar of the term in a certain context? The concept of "sentence" is regarded as the "heading for the grammar of propositions".

He noticed that the grammar of concepts remains constant, but not their meaning. In fact, we can expand the meaning of concepts. As such, we can include concepts in new propositional structures. Finally, Wittgenstein criticized the Platonic theory of grammar and considered it as inadequate as Platonism "dissolves" into a general concept of language.

Nikolay Milkov
Wittgenstein's Method: The Third Phase of Its Development (1933–36)

Introduction

Wittgenstein's interpreters are practically undivided that method plays a central role in his philosophy. This comes as no surprise if we bear in mind the Tractarian dictum: "philosophy is not a body of doctrine but an activity".[1]

After 1929, Wittgenstein's method evolved further. In its final form, articulated in *Philosophical Investigations*, it was formulated as different kinds of therapies of specific philosophical problems that torment our life.[2] But how did Wittgenstein reach that conception?

In order to answer this question, we shall follow the changes in Wittgenstein's thinking in four subsequent phases and in three dimensions: (i) in logic and ontology; (ii) in method proper; (iii) in style.

1 First Phase – the *Tractatus*

1.1 Criticism of the Diamond-Conant Thesis

Some twenty years ago, a group of American philosophers, Cora Diamond and James Conant among them, suggested a "resolute" reading of Wittgenstein's *Tractatus*: the propositions of the *Tractatus* are plain nonsense and nothing beyond that. They are gibberish, with phrases like "piggly wiggle tiggle".[3] The main idea of the book is expressed in 6.54 which reads:

---

1 TLP 4.112.
2 PI §§ 133, 255, 593.
3 Diamond 2000, p. 151.

> My propositions are elucidatory in this way: he who understands me finally recognizes them as senseless, when he has climbed out through them, on them, over them. (He must so to speak throw away the ladder, after he has climbed up on it.)[4]

This was the real message of the *Tractatus*.

By way of criticism of the Diamond-Conant thesis, we would like to note that, in fact, the initial task of the *Tractatus* is quite clear: to advance a new logical symbolism or new "Conceptual Notation" (a term of Frege's that Wittgenstein widely used in the *Tractatus*). Of course, the program for a new Conceptual Notation that correctly expresses the logical operations of our thinking and language was first set out by Frege. The latter insisted that we can "compare it[s role] to that which the microscope has to the eye".[5] In Frege's hands, however, it was not so radically evolved as in the hands of Wittgenstein.

The leitmotif of the Tractarian Conceptual Notation was that

> we can recognize in an adequate notation the formal properties of the propositions by mere inspection [of propositions themselves].[6]

It is already clear at this point that, according to the *Tractatus*, the task of philosophy is radically different from the task of philosophy as understood by Christian Wolff or Hegel. Philosophy has no autonomous message, no story to tell, and thus has no meaning in itself. It is just like an optical instrument, a means for better seeing (better understanding) the world.

1.2 What are the Tractarian Elucidations?

In order to answer this question, we will review the ways in which we speak about elucidations in life and in ordinary language.

We typically need elucidations when we are confronted with a new appliance (a new gadget). The elucidations tell us how it functions. When we have already learned how the gadget (the logical symbolism, in this case) works, we can throw away the instructions of how to use it. In contrast, science suggests explanations.

---

4 TLP 6.54.
5 Frege 1879, p. xi.
6 TLP 6.122.

Special cases of elucidation are the textbooks that teach us how to speak a foreign language. If we want to learn Portuguese, for example, we will buy ourselves a textbook of instructions that will teach us to speak that language which already exists in the literature and on the streets of Luanda, Lisbon and Rio. If, in some point of time, we have already learned to speak that language, we can throw our "book of elucidations" away.

In short, our thesis is that in a similar way Wittgenstein's *Tractatus* teaches – *trains* – its reader to better see how the propositions of science logically relate one to another, how the logic of our everyday language functions, and how logic itself functions. In this way, it serves as a "logical clarification of *thoughts*"[7] and develops our skill of thinking. Tractarian propositions, however, have no proper content – "no existential import". Indeed, similar to the learning Portuguese example, human thinking is already there. The thinking-training must not invent it; it just teaches us how to make better use of it.

This interpretation of the Tractarian elucidations fits perfectly well into the description of its propositions as a ladder. To be sure:

(1) We typically throw away the instrument of training after we have reached a new level of command of a certain skill – we have no interest in the instrument which brought us up to that level.

(2) What is important with such instruments is not their content but their form. Perhaps another person might construct a different type of instrument, with the help of which we will be trained in the same skill. In this sense, the propositions of the *Tractatus* do not express something necessary; they are contingent. Diamond is especially insistent on this point. Unfortunately, she drew from it false conclusions: the propositions of the *Tractatus* are gibberish.

Furthermore, we discern three types of Tractarian elucidations:

(i) First of all, Wittgenstein's New Symbolism elucidates all problems of the old logic, including Frege's and Russell's. When we construct graphically (geometrically) correct symbols, all problems of logic are *eo ipso* resolved. Hence, "we cannot make mistakes in logic".[8] Moreover, all superfluous entities in logic and philosophy such as logical constants and logical objects will

---

7 TLP 4.112; my italics.
8 TLP 5.473.

be put in brackets. A consequence of the latter position was Wittgenstein's belief that there are no propositions of logic and also no logical truths. Logical propositions are tautologies – a position that can be called a "redundancy theory of logic".

(ii) More importantly, the New Logical Symbolism elucidates being a means (an instrument) for recognizing (clarifying) the logical properties of all available propositions of science and everyday life.

(iii) Besides propositions that set out the New Symbolism, there are also Tractarian propositions that are elucidations of this Symbolism. Moreover, these propositions form the bulk of the book.

1.3 Tractarian Ontology as Logic

The leading motive behind the conception of Diamond and Conant is the denial that the *Tractatus* advances metaphysical truths. But our interpretation of the Tractarian method also eschews any metaphysical assumption. In fact, there is no "Tractarian metaphysics". But what about the numerous "ontological propositions" of the *Tractatus*, for example, TLP 1–2.063?

In order to answer this question, we will turn back to David Pears who has noted that the logic of the *Tractatus* is "approximately Aristotelian. [...] The forms revealed by logic are embedded in one and only one world of facts".[9] In other words, Tractarian logic and ontology are identical, an identity best shown in the fact that the general logical form (or the "general form of truth-function")[10] is identical with the general form of compositionality: "such and such is the case".[11]

The identity between logic and ontology finds expression in two ways:

(i) Objects, states of affairs and facts have formal properties and relations that are *identical* with the formal concepts signified by propositional variables and have objects as their value.[12]

---

9 Pears 1987, vol. I, p. 23. Not only the facts, however. Tractarian objects too have a "logical form" that is embedded in them.
10 TLP 6.
11 TLP 4.5.
12 Cf. TLP 4.126.

(ii) "In the picture and the pictured there must be something *identical* in order that the one can be a picture of the other at all".[13]

Apparently, Tractarian ontology is a part of Wittgenstein's new Conceptual Notation. Moreover, Tractarian logic can be seen as built up with the help of ontological elements: objects, facts, indefinables – points that the plain man knows quite well.[14] In this way, the elucidation of our thinking is also connected with a lucid and extremely simple picture of the world: something that Diamond and Conant resolutely deny.

Technically, the principle of identity between logic and ontology can be illustrated with the help of the concept of "logical scaffolding".[15] Logical scaffoldings surround and support every newly constructed picture, or proposition; they, however, have no ontological import. They *can* help to bring the objects of a state of affairs – in propositions – together. Without it, the construction *may* be scattered, so that we cannot grasp them in the formation they now build. The point is that (i) language (and thinking) is a construction – an experimental arrangement of possible forms of objects.[16] But (ii) the objects of a state of affairs stick together thanks to their topology alone, not thanks to the logical scaffoldings. This means that there is *no mortar* between objects that connects them[17] – in the same way in which there are no logical constants between elementary propositions. The logical scaffoldings only support the objects in the state of affairs/proposition from outside and can be "thrown away" any time after the "experiment" of building up a new proposition is over.

2 Second Phase (1929–1932)

(a) Wittgenstein's Logic and Ontology

After 1929, Wittgenstein's logic-ontology developed further, without losing its character as an exercise tool or ladder that brings our ability to think up to a higher level of development. Above all, his attitude to mathematics experienced

---

13 TLP 2.161; my italics.
14 Cf. § 3 (b), below.
15 Cf. Milkov 2001.
16 "In the proposition a state of affairs is, as it were, put together for the sake of experiment." (TLP 4.031)
17 Cf. Waismann 1967, p. 252.

a major change.[18] While in the *Tractatus* Wittgenstein accepted that logic has primacy over mathematics ("[m]athematics is a method of logic"),[19] in 1929 he came to believe (arguably, under Brouwer's influence) that mathematics has a primacy over logic.

In consequence, arithmetical calculus replaced the truth-functions as mediator between elementary and complex propositions. This step was supported by the discovery that from an elementary proposition we can infer other elementary propositions. For example, from "a is now red" there follows "a is now not green". In contrast, in the *Tractatus* Wittgenstein claimed that all complex propositions (both general and molecular) are truth-functions of elementary propositions.

Furthermore, in 1929 Wittgenstein embraced the view that the inventing of new calculi is synthetic a priori. From this point on, problems of creativity gained prominence in Wittgenstein's writings. Connected with Wittgenstein's increased interest in creativity was the change of his attention from propositions stating facts to propositions exercising force; or from indicative to imperative propositions.[20]

The most significant part of this transformation was that human actions were put at the centre of philosophy of language – a step further stimulated by Piero Sraffa's insistence that Wittgenstein's logic must also explain such means of communication as gestures. Now Wittgenstein elaborated a logic–ontology that not only starts from making pictures of states of affairs; it also starts from learning model-actions and language expressions. In short, he did not merely explore the problem of how we form sentences but also how we form actions.

(b) Method

In 1929–32 Wittgenstein's method developed in the direction of extensive use of analogies, comparisons, descriptions, etc., and of striving for a clear, or perspicuous, representation of all cases under examination. In these years, he also stopped exploring ideal languages and showed more interest in ordinary language: the latter is in order as it is and is not to be improved. Wittgenstein also changed his attitude to science. Whereas in the *Tractatus* he claimed that what can be said are only the propositions of science, in *Philosophical Remarks* (see its motto!) he openly criticized the method of science and opposed to it the methods of conceptual analysis.

---

18 Cf. Hintikka 1993.
19 TLP 6.234.
20 Cf. Kenny 1973, p. 121.

(c) Style

A characteristic of the second phase of Wittgenstein's philosophical development was that now he showed an inclination to abandon the linear way of expression and gradually adopted the dialogue form, above all, a dialogue with himself.

All these changes, however, failed to satisfy Wittgenstein. Another phase of his philosophical development was to come.

3 Third Phase (1933–1936)

Today it is widely accepted that "the *Philosophische Bemerkungen* [...] displays many signs of Wittgenstein's contact with the Positivists and their influence upon him".[21] Apparently, under this influence, Wittgenstein partly forgot that his philosophy is only a method of training our thinking. Among other things, this explains the claim he repeatedly made in this period that to understand a proposition means to understand the method of its verification.

This point speaks against Jaakko and Merrill Hintikka's assertion that 1929 – the year he changed his view about mathematics and logic – was Wittgenstein's *annus mirabilis:*[22] the year in which he elaborated the ideas that were later to become his leading ideas in the *Philosophical Investigations*. Alternatively, Wolfgang Kienzler states that the major turn in Wittgenstein's philosophy occurred in 1931: in that year Sraffa directed Wittgenstein's attention to the fact that the logical form of gestures is much more complicated that the *Tractatus* assumed.[23]

In this essay we defend the view that Wittgenstein's *annus mirabilis* was 1933, not 1929 or 1931. The decisive turn in Wittgenstein's philosophy is clearly discernible in *The Big Typescript* and especially in *Philosophical Grammar*, written in 1932/33 and drastically revised at the end of 1933 and the first weeks of 1934.

Here is our story in more detail.

---

21 Grayling 1988, p. 64.
22 Cf. Hintikka 1986.
23 Cf. Kienzler 1997, pp. 26ff.

(a) Theory-Method

According to the Principle of Representing that lies at the centre of Wittgenstein's logic and ontology of 1921,[24] propositions and thoughts are facts. A state of affairs can be articulated (delivered), without loss of information, by any fact of the same multiplicity. Apparently, multiplicity is the hinge element that connects mind (language) and reality. It secures their identity.

As noted above, after 1929 Wittgenstein added actions into his ontology and logic. We learn both language and actions in a drill. Enriching his logic-ontology in this way, the character of the hinge elements that connect logic and ontology widened considerably. The model-action and the following action have not only the same multiplicity but they also have the same *method*, and follow the same *rule*.[25] It was precisely this enrichment that caused the first substantial change in Wittgenstein's philosophy.

In short, in 1933 Wittgenstein adopted the view that philosophy is a kind of criticism of the conventional conception of thinking and intention. Words like "understanding", "meaning", "interpreting", "thinking"[26] are not inner processes; they are not *processes* at all.[27] In particular, they are not to be seen as a "hypothesized reservoir out of which the visible water flows".[28] We learn to use these words (concepts) in a drill. Understanding an action, or a sentence (or a word), is best demonstrated in its actual use by the person who follows the action (or learns the sentence, the word). In this sense the phrase "meaning is use" became Wittgenstein's leading mantra.[29]

The point is that assuming specific processes of "understanding", or "knowing", would be of no help. Indeed, if we accept that they explain our learning actions, or sentences (or words), then another jump will be needed: from "knowing" to doing. This is a typical *tertium quid* argument later used in Wittgenstein's paradox of rule-following:[30] we cannot articulate the unique way in which the rule is to be followed – in order to do that, we would need another rule which would show how to follow the first rule.

Ultimately, in 1933 Wittgenstein elaborated a philosophy that functions as a *method of examining* philosophical, or philosophically pregnant, statements with the objective to eliminate any form of essentialism or duplicationism in

---

24 Cf. Milkov 2003a, pp. 96ff.
25 The evolution of this enrichment is clearly seen in Waismann 1967.
26 Other examples are "wishing", "expecting", "believing", etc.
27 Cf. BBB, p. 3.
28 PG §10.
29 Similar claims were already made in PR, p. 59.
30 In fact, Wittgenstein had used the tertium quid argument already in LWL, pp. 67–68.

them.[31] By way of elucidation, we would like to note that while essentialism (reductionism is one of its forms) claims that one entity determines all variants of the object under analysis, duplicationism accepts that these variants are autonomous entities. The task of the philosopher is similar to that of a judge: he judges between two parties in litigation over philosophical puzzles:

> Our only task is to be just. That is, we must only point out and resolve the injustices of philosophy.[32]

More often than not, the litigation is between essentialists and duplicationists.

Our last remark will be that the new method of examining our language was a direct continuation of the Tractarian program for philosophical activity that eliminates superfluous metaphysical and logical entities and improves our ability to think and judge.

(b) Method

The second, even more substantial change in Wittgenstein's method was inaugurated at the beginning of the "Philosophy" Chapter of the *Big Typescript*. It can be described as follows.

In the *Tractatus* Wittgenstein echoed Leo Tolstoy's claim that the intellectual (the man of letters) has no more knowledge than the plain man[33] – the plain man knows how things work quite well. The intellectual can simply better articulate that knowledge. That is his task and also his mission. Similarly, Wittgenstein's philosopher has two objectives: (i) to explicate this common knowledge;[34] (ii) to attend by this explication not to violate the common-sense understanding of how things work. In other words, he would not use concepts and conceptions that make sad work of the authentic intuitions of ordinary man.

Wittgenstein subscribed to these two principles in all periods of his philosophical development. His new insight in 1933 was that philosophy is not only a matter of knowledge but also of will. The point is that

---

31 Cf. Milkov 2003a, p. 86.

32 BT, p. 420.

33 Cf. for example: "Men have always thought that there must be a sphere of questions whose answers – a priori – are symmetrical and united into a closed regular structure." (TLP 5.4541) Good philosophy must make this thought explicit, preserving its authenticity.

34 We already referred to this point in the penultimate paragraph of § 1.3, above.

> The very things that are most obvious can become the most difficult to understand. What has to be overcome is not a difficulty of the intellect, but of the will.[35]

In fact, this insight was the ultimate turning point from what is sometimes being called the "early" Wittgenstein to the "later" Wittgenstein. It was the decisive step towards the *Philosophical Investigations*.

An important consequence of this change in method was that it prepared Wittgenstein's transition from seeing the role of the philosopher as an "elucidator" to seeing him as a "therapist". Indeed, in *The Big Typescript* and *The Blue Book* Wittgenstein still spoke about one method and did not mention the word "therapy". But he started to persistently claim that philosophy brings "peace of mind [*Beruhigung*]";[36] that we are often caught up in philosophical "traps", or that we feel philosophical "spasms" and are to be set free from them. He also spoke about "the bumps that the understanding has got by running its head up against the limits of language".[37]

(c) Style

In contrast, in 1933–36 Wittgenstein's style of expression changed little: he widely used the dialogue form but still preserved some systematic and linear elements. Moreover, in some sections of *The Blue and Brown Books* Wittgenstein showed a tendency to build theory. For example, he introduced the concepts "craving for generality", "family likeness" and "language-games" on one and the same page of *The Blue Book*.[38] *The Brown Book*, in its turn, advanced a consistent list of language-games, together with their elucidations and comments.[39] Another point that confirms Wittgenstein's respect for linear order in style until 1936 is that he did not stop Waismann from further work on a systematic presentation of his (Wittgenstein's) philosophy.[40]

All that changed in 1936, a development we shall discuss in § 4.

---

35 BT, p. 407.
36 Ibid., pp. 416, 421.
37 Ibid., p. 425.
38 BBB, p. 17.
39 However, Wittgenstein did not try to build up the whole ordinary language through adding ever new elementary language-games. Rather, particular language-games are similes that help us to clarify our conception of language. Cf. Schulte 2005, pp. 85f.
40 Cf. VW, pp. xxvi–xxx.

3.1 The Character of the 1933 Turn

It is noteworthy that it is difficult to speak about "turns" in Wittgenstein's philosophy. In fact, his philosophical development was more evolutionary than revolutionary. Wittgenstein often employed ideas he introduced in earlier periods of his development in texts compiled after his alleged "turn". We already met this point of style in notes 25 and 26: the slogan "meaning is use" as well as the application of the tertium quid argument, which became central in Wittgenstein's method only in 1933, were already elaborated in 1930–33.[41] Already in 1932 Wittgenstein noted: "Our method resembles psychoanalysis in a certain sense".

Our main claim here is that the revolutionary turn in Wittgenstein's thinking of 1933 was not a matter of a discovery but rather a waking up from the "dogmatic slumber" that he had fallen into while collaborating with the logical positivists of the Vienna Circle. Indeed, Wittgenstein started to speak about "calming [*beruhigen*]" our feelings when doing philosophy as early as 1930.[42] Even his correction of Tolstoy on the place of the will in philosophy was first made in 1931.[43] These "discoveries", however, were first ordered in a consistent method in 1933.

But what did make Wittgenstein wake up?

3.2 History of the 1933 Turn

That Wittgenstein's turn of 1933 had the character of a change in perspective is supported by its putative history which will be the subject-matter of the present sub-section.

Despite the fact that Wittgenstein acknowledged influences on himself from twelve writers, today many interpreters believe that, especially after 1921, he was hardly susceptible to outside impacts, with Spengler and Sraffa being the only exceptions in this respect. Our point here is that, at least to some extent, Wittgenstein's turn of 1933 was occasioned – if not caused – by Susan Stebbings' paper "Logical Positivism and Analysis", read to the British Academy as a Henriette Hertz lecture on 22 March 1933 and shortly afterwards published as a brochure.

---

41 Ibid., p. 69.
42 Cf. WA, vol. 2, p. 3.
43 CV, p. 17.

Stebbing's paper, in turn, made considerable use of Richard Braithwaite's piece "Philosophy [in Cambridge in 1933]",[44] which she read when still unpublished. She, however, was much more disapproving than Braithwaite was[45] and it can be comfortably seen as nothing but a list of Wittgenstein's muddles. In short, it confronted the "good philosophy" of Moore and Russell with the "bad philosophy" of Wittgenstein and the Vienna Circle. Stebbing identified the latter to such an extent that she spoke about Wittgenstein in 1932 following the latest publications of the Vienna Circle.

Her main argument against Wittgenstein was the danger of solipsism in his "insisting that the verification of a proposition which I assert must be in my own experience".[46] Indeed, in *Philosophical Remarks* Wittgenstein intensively discussed the verification principle that regulates the relation between facts and propositions.[47]

To be sure, there is no evidence that Wittgenstein read Stebbing's paper. It is reasonable to assume, however, that part of its contents were leaked to him through his friends and students. The immediate reaction was his notorious letter to the editor of *Mind*, written on 27 May 1933, in which he "disclaim[ed] all responsibility for the views and thoughts which Mr. Braithwaite [and so also Miss Stebbing] attributes to [him]".[48]

In this connection it is to be noted that at the time Wittgenstein was facing considerable resistance and also solitude in Cambridge. In January 1929 he returned to Cambridge only to find that Charles Broad did not accept his philosophy, nor did Frank Ramsey who considered it "scholastic". And while G. E. Moore attended his lectures, he was everything but Wittgenstein's disciple. In fact, in 1929–32 nobody in Cambridge was ready to work along Wittgenstein's lines. In these years Wittgenstein found devoted followers only in his native Vienna, in particular, in the person of Moritz Schlick and Friedrich Waismann.

Our hunch is that it was precisely Susan Stebbing's criticism that gave Wittgenstein the impulse needed to distance himself from the discussions with his Vienna friends and to start his project anew. It woke him up from his dogmatic slumber. This conjecture is supported by the fact that after March 1933, that is, immediately after Braithwaite and Stebbing's criticism, Wittgenstein made a

---

44 Braithwaite 1933.
45 Cf. Milkov 2003b.
46 Braithwaite 1933, p. 27.
47 Cf. § 2, above, first paragraph.
48 WC, p. 210.

change in his philosophy that seemed as if it had been specifically designed to face the criticism of Stebbing and Braithwaite. This change led to the transformation of his philosophy that we have already discussed in §3(a) and can be easily traced in *Wittgenstein's Lectures: Cambridge, 1932–1935*. After lecture 26, he practically stopped speaking of "verification", "visual field", and "private language".[49] Instead, Wittgenstein devoted a great deal of space to the rejection of the private language argument and increased criticism of essentialist and reductionist conceptions in psychology and mathematics.

In the summer of 1933 Wittgenstein initiated a revision of *The Big Typescript* on which parts of *Philosophical Grammar* and the *Blue Book* were also based. As already seen, in these works he began to prepare his "new book", *Philosophical Investigations*, more especially its *Urfassung* (MS 142).

This turn also paid back on a didactic and social level. Soon after his conversion, Wittgenstein found devoted followers in the person of his students Rush Rhees and Francis Skinner and also of John Wisdom. Wisdom's paper "Philosophical Perplexity" (1936),[50] in particular, was the first public evidence that Wittgenstein's turn had followers in Cambridge.

4 Fourth Phase

The fourth phase of the development of Wittgenstein's method was copiously prepared by him in 1936 in a long period of meditation in which he wrote his *Confessions*. In general, Wittgenstein was convinced that only a preliminary exercise in confessing his sins could make him hope to reach the level of sincerity needed to write good philosophy. However, Wittgenstein never applied this principle so consequentially as in the summer of 1936.

(a) Style
Unfortunately, these preparations produced more changes in style than in content. Indeed, the 1936 radical transformation affected above all Wittgenstein's form of exposition. The transformation is clearly discernible in *Eine philosophische Betrachtung* (the German translation and revision of the *Brown*

---

49 Cf. AWL, p. 31.
50 Cf. Wisdom 1953.

Book) in which Wittgenstein's style turned polyphonic.[51] Typically, three voices take part in a dialogue on a specific philosophical problem: that of a scientist, of common sense, and of the mediator. The task of the mediator is to show the two parties that they have lost the point of the opposite side. Embracing this style of expression, Wittgenstein completely abandoned the project to present his ideas in a linear book form. Instead, he produced an "album" of such dialogues.[52]

(b) Method

In parallel, Wittgenstein stopped speaking about "method". Instead, he was now convinced that he had "methods", or more precisely, "therapies". It is worth noticing, however, that this was an even later idea. Indeed, §133d was added later to the *Urfassung* of *Philosophical Investigations* in autumn 1937.[53] §§255 and 593, in which Wittgenstein spoke about "philosophical disease", were written down much later.

(c) Logic and Ontology

In respect of theory, Wittgenstein's turn brought only a few new elements. Very roughly, his anti-essentialism and anti-duplicationism radicalized further, thus transforming Wittgenstein into perhaps the most slippery of all "fishes" called *philosophers*.

Unfortunately – as we read in the "Preface" to *Philosophical Investigations* – the exposition of Wittgenstein's method still remained unsatisfactory after his turn of 1933.

Epilogue

Our concluding remark is that Wittgenstein's ceaseless efforts to elaborate a new method in philosophy was part of the project for a *new, "analytic", philosophy*, started by him and by Russell in 1912.[54] (Note that this project bears only a remote family likeness to what we today understand by "analytic philosophy").

---

51 A related style of exposition was already employed in belles-lettres, for example by F. M. Dostoyevsky. Cf. Bakhtin 1984.

52 Cf. Pichler 2004.

53 MS 116, p. 186.

54 Cf. Milkov 2002, pp. 60–62.

Very roughly, Wittgenstein's ultimate objective was to help his readers to develop a better ability to judge. Hence, it is intrinsically misleading to connect it only with therapy, as Diamond and Conant do. Wittgenstein started to speak (and think) about philosophy as a kind of worry first in the early 1930s, developed the theoretical grounds of his new conception of philosophy as therapy in 1933, but introduced the term "therapy" only in 1937.[55]

55 Ideas expressed in § 1 were delivered at the Open Sections of the Mind Association and the Aristotelian Society 2011 Joint Session in Brighton (Sussex). Thanks for stimulating remarks are due to Guy Stock, Chon Tejedor and Carolyn Wilde.

Rui Sampaio da Silva
Meaning and Rules in Wittgenstein's Philosophy

1

The problem of rule-following plays a crucial role in Wittgenstein's philosophy, not only in the *Philosophical Investigations*, but also in previous works. The present paper has two main goals: to analyse the evolution of Wittgenstein's views on the nature of rules (from the 1930s until the *Philosophical Investigations*) and to defend an interpretation of Wittgenstein's reflections on rule-following that will be largely inspired by McDowell.

Wittgenstein is usually considered a prominent advocate of the normativity of meaning and, more generally, intentionality. According to this perspective, the meaning of a linguistic expression presupposes a distinction between correct and incorrect uses, and the content of intentional states is equally dependent on a distinction between correct and incorrect ways to act or think. Many philosophers influenced by Wittgenstein take the normativity of meaning as a kind of platitude:

If there cease to be right and wrong uses of a word, the word loses its meaning.[1]

The relation of meaning and intention to future action is normative, not descriptive.[2]

The starting point of his [Wittgenstein's] investigations is the insight that our ordinary understanding of states and acts of meaning, understanding, intending, or believing something is an understanding of them as states and acts that *commit* or *oblige* us to act and think in various ways. To perform its traditional role, the meaning of a linguistic expression must determine how it would be *correct* to use it in various contexts. To understand or grasp such a meaning is to be able to distinguish correct from incorrect uses. The view is not

---

1 Dummett 1991, p. 85.
2 Kripke 1982, p. 37. Kripke is usually considered an advocate of semantic normativity. However, some commentators disagree with this standard interpretation of Kripke; Kush (2006) is a case in point.

restricted to meaning and understanding but extends as well to such intentionally content-ful states as believing and intending.[3]

In his later work, Wittgenstein struggled to explain the normativity of meaning and intentionality, and, particularly, to clarify the nature of rule-following. However, the problem of rule-following was already present in works from the middle period, although his treatment of the problem left him unsatisfied. In order to analyse the evolution of Wittgenstein's reflections on rule-following, it will be convenient to bear in mind a terminological distinction proposed by Brandom between regulism and regularism. Regulism is the view that "what makes a performance correct or not is its relation to some explicit rule".[4] One thereby erases the distinction between rules and norms: "Rules are the form of the norm as such".[5] Brandom attributes this "intellectualist and Platonist conception of norms" to Kant and Frege, and praises Wittgenstein for showing that "norms that are *explicit* in the form of rules presuppose norms *implicit* in practices".[6] The main objection against regulism is Wittgenstein's regress argument, which concludes that to reduce norms to rules entails an infinite regress. In fact, if regulism is right, then any performance according to a norm presupposes a rule, but the application of rules is also a performance that must be subject to a rule; there must be, therefore, rules for applying rules (or what Wittgenstein calls an interpretation, *Deutung*, which he describes as a substitution of one expression of the rule for another). If any application of a rule presupposes another rule, we embark on a frustrating infinite regress that does not clarify the process of rule-following. The upshot of Wittgenstein's regress argument is the idea that, at a fundamental level, correct or incorrect performances must be discernible in practices, independently of any appeal to explicit rules. In Brandom's words: "rulish proprieties depend on some more primitive sort of practical propriety".[7] It is in this sense that Brandom interprets the following well-known passages from the *Philosophical Investigations*:

> Every interpretation hangs in the air together with what it interprets, and cannot give it any support. Interpretations by themselves do not determine meaning.[8]

---

3 Brandom 1994, p. 13.
4 Ibid., pp. 18–19.
5 Ibid., pp. 19–20.
6 Ibid., p. 20.
7 Ibid.
8 PIr § 198.

> There is a way of grasping a rule which is *not* an interpretation, but which, from case to case of application, is exhibited in what we call "obeying the rule" and "going against it".[9]

According to Brandom's interpretation, Wittgenstein's regress argument leads us to the idea that rules presuppose a more fundamental kind of normative force that is implicit in our practices. But now we face a bifurcation, because there are two quite different ways to conceive of practices, depending on whether we choose to describe them using a normative or a purely descriptive vocabulary.

The latter option is what Brandom calls regularism, the view that rules boil down to behavioural regularities (in opposition to rules). Regularism has an important advantage over regulism because it avoids the regress argument, but in fact regularism fares no better than regulism because it generates its own problems. Regularism is the "view that to talk about implicit norms is just to talk about regularities of behaviour – that practices should be understood just as regularities of behaviour".[10] According to regularism, norms are neither rules nor interpretations, but behavioural patterns, which could be characterized by a descriptive vocabulary that does not appeal to normative notions.[11] The main problem of regularism is the fact that it conflates the correct/incorrect distinction with the regular/irregular distinction. However, regularities of use are empirical facts and as such they lack normative force. This point motivates the main Wittgensteinian argument against regularism: what Brandom calls the gerrymandering objection. On the basis of this objection lies the claim that "there simply is no such thing as *the* pattern or regularity exhibited by a stretch of past behaviour which can be appealed to in judging some candidate bit of future as regular or irregular".[12] Kripke's example of the *quus* function constitutes a good illustration of this point. In fact, the same regularity can be subsumed under different rules; the same arithmetic series can be generated by different functions, the same sample of linguistic acts may be accommodated by different linguistic rules ... We could say that regularism is wrong because rules are underdetermined by regularities.

To sum up, regulism fails because it conceives of norms as something that transcends practices and regularism fails because it misconceives practices by characterizing them in purely descriptive terms. What is required is an account of normativity that goes beyond rules and regularities. The dilemma of regu-

---

9 PIr § 201.
10 Brandom 1994, p. 27.
11 The naturalization projects for semantics that have been developed in various forms in analytic philosophy can be considered a form of regularism.
12 Brandom 1994, p. 28.

lism and regularism corresponds, still according to Brandom, to a well-known passage where McDowell tries to explain the fundamental dilemma against which Wittgenstein struggles:

> Wittgenstein's problem is to steer a course between a Scylla and a Charybdis. Scylla is the idea that understanding is always interpretation. We can avoid Scylla by stressing that, say, calling something 'green' can be like crying "Help" when one is drowning – simply how one has learned to react to this situation. But then we risk steering on to Charybdis – the picture of a level at which there are no norms.[13]

Brandom claims that Scylla stands here for regulism and Charybdis for regularism. One must emphasize, however, that in an article published in 2002 with the suggestive title "How Not to Read *Philosophical Investigations*: Brandom's Wittgenstein",[14] McDowell criticized Brandom's interpretation of the rule-following considerations as presented in the *Philosophical Investigations*. In the last section of the present paper, I will analyse McDowell's critique of Brandom, in order to shed light on the Wittgensteinian reflections on rule-following in the context of his later work. Meanwhile, I will use the regularism/regulism distinction as a tool to interpret the evolution of Wittgenstein's thought on this subject.

2

We may say that Wittgenstein always tried to avoid both regulism and regularism; the idea that norms are explicit rules and the idea that norms consist of behavioural regularities. Both positions have unpalatable consequences. In his first reflections, Wittgenstein struggled mainly against regulism, and later on, when he moved towards a practice-based account of language, his major concern was to avoid regularism.[15]

Wittgenstein's interest in the problem of rules arose in the context of his conception of language as a calculus, a notion that presupposes rules. And when, in the *Philosophical Grammar*, he introduces the model of games to understand language, he does not distinguish yet the notions of calculus and game; in this period both concepts express the idea that language is a rule-governed activity. Later on, Wittgenstein preferred to speak of games rather than of calculi; one

---

13 McDowell 1984, p. 242.
14 McDowell 2002.
15 In this section, I am indebted to the excellent study of José Medina (Medina 2002).

reason for this terminological preference is the fact that the notion of calculus has strong connotations with formal languages or formal rules, and in this sense it does not provide an adequate model for understanding natural language. Another reason lies in his rejection of the idea that language is a unified system.[16]

The importance of rules is well expressed in the close connection that Wittgenstein establishes in his middle period between meaning and rules. In the *Philosophical Grammar*, Wittgenstein rejects clearly any attempt to subordinate rules to previously given meanings; on the contrary, the primacy belongs to rules: "It is grammatical rules that determine meaning (constitute it)".[17] In a Cambridge lecture from 1932/33 he stresses the same point: "Are the rules, for example, ~ ~p = p for negation, responsible to the meaning of a word? No, the rules constitute the meaning, and are not responsible to it".[18]

As a result, meanings, far from being entities (physical, mental or abstract entities), are roles established ultimately by rules. It is in this sense that he claims, in the *Philosophical Grammar*, that "the meaning of a word is its role in the calculus of language"[19] and that "the role of a sentence in the calculus is its sense".[20] These passages evoke similar passages from the later works. However, one should bear in mind that the notions of role and use do not have the same meaning in this period and in his later work. In the early 1930s, "use" means the domain of possible applications of a rule, and not properly the actual linguistic practices. In the *Cambridge Lectures* from 1930–32, Wittgenstein claims that the place of a word in a language is fixed by rules (or explanations), which are prior to use.[21] And he adds: "The rules prepare for the game which may afterwards be used as language. Only when the rules are fixed can I use the game as a language".[22]

In the early 1930s, Wittgenstein argues for the primacy of rules over use, whereas in the later work he gives priority to the actual use of language. This difference can be explained by the calculus view of language, which stresses the

---

16 Cf. PG § 72, where he claims that there is not a calculus of all calculi.
17 PG § 133.
18 AWL, p. 4.
19 PG § 31.
20 PG § 84.
21 LWL, p. 49.
22 Ibid., p. 57.

notion of rule and neglects the dimension of practices and natural facts.[23] The primacy of rules shows that Wittgenstein was, in his first reflections on rules, too close to what Brandom calls regulism. He claims to be "interested in language as a procedure according to explicit rules"[24] and contrasts the fluctuating character of use with fixed rules:

> If we look at the actual use of a word, what we see is something constantly fluctuating. In our investigations we set over against this fluctuation something more fixed [...]. When we study language we envisage it as a game with fixed rules.[25]

In other terms, rules constitute an autonomous domain, which is in a certain sense independent from real practices. However, while defending that rules constitute an autonomous domain (a regulist insight), Wittgenstein also stresses that the relation between a rule and its application is an internal relation (an anti-regulist insight). In other words, rules should not be conceived as abstract formulations that can be considered independently of their application. Normativity cannot be explained by mere rule formulations; rules involve what Wittgenstein calls a "method of projection" or a "method of application".

> The rule of projection is expressed in projecting, the intention in intending. The internal relation is only there if both things related are there. You cannot anticipate the result which you project.[26]

> The rule which has been taught and is subsequently applied interests us only so far as it is involved in the application. A rule, so far as it interests us, doesn't act at a distance.[27]

The relation between a rule and its application is an "internal relation", in the sense that the *relata* cannot be considered in isolation and that there are no intermediaries. The latter point is particularly important because it anticipates a key argument of the *Philosophical Investigations*, the already mentioned regress argument.

---

23 Cf. Medina 2002, p. 62: "The priority of rules over actual applications and their independence from facts of natural history will be questioned in the mid and late 1930s when Wittgenstein abandons the calculus view and starts to regard language as an actual practice of use."
24 PG § 32.
25 PG § 36.
26 LWL, p. 32.
27 BBB, p. 14.

> In all language there is a bridge between the sign and its application. No one can make this
> for us; we have to bridge the gap ourselves. No explanation ever saves the jump, because
> any further explanation will itself need a jump.[28]

In the absence of an internal relation, or in the presence of intermediaries, there would be an "unbridgeable gulf" between rule and application.[29] The phrase "unbridgeable gulf" anticipates a target of many remarks from the *Philosophical Investigations* where Wittgenstein rejects the transcendence of rules with regard to practices, arguing precisely that any form of transcendence would create an unbridgeable gap. At any rate, one should notice that the gap is not conceived in the same terms in the middle period and in the later work. In both periods Wittgenstein refuses to treat rule-following as a mere obedience to rule-formulations and claims that there is a constitutive relation between the rule and its application, but rules in the early 1930s are conceived of as infinite rails (to use Wittgenstein's famous metaphor from § 218 of the *Philosophical Investigations*), which are independent from the "natural history of the use of a word";[30] on the contrary, the later Wittgenstein dismisses the idea of infinite rails as a Platonist misunderstanding of the nature of rules that neglects the fundamental role of actual practices. This difference shows again how close he was to regulism in his first reflections on rules.

Wittgenstein faced serious difficulties in explaining the nature of internal relations, and these difficulties are reflected in another problem that called Wittgenstein's attention in the 1930s: the distinction between following a rule and acting in accordance with a rule. In the *Blue Book*, for instance, Wittgenstein anticipates famous passages from the *Philosophical Investigations* that emphasize this problem: "We must distinguish between what one might call 'a process being *in accordance with* a rule', and 'a process involving a rule'." As an example, he offers the following arithmetic series: 1, 4, 9, 16, and remarks that this row of numbers "is in accordance with the general rule of squaring; but it obviously is also in accordance with any number of other rules".[31] So there is more to following a rule than simply acting in accordance with a rule. But what, precisely? Wittgenstein offered in the 1930s three main answers to this question.[32] Firstly, he suggested that what distinguishes rule-following from a mere behavioural con-

---

28 LWL, p. 67.
29 PR § 164.
30 PR § 15.
31 BBB, p. 13.
32 Cf. Medina 2002, pp. 118–125.

formity to a rule is an "act of insight". He claimed, for instance, that following a rule requires understanding the internal relation between rule and application:

> An internal relation holds by virtue of the terms being what they are. Inference is justified by an internal relation which we see; the only justification of the transition is our looking at the two terms and seeing the internal relation.[33]

> I must recognize each time afresh that this rule may be applied here. No act of foresight can absolve me from this act of *insight*.[34]

It is important to note that the last passage was later corrected by Wittgenstein in a marginal annotation where one can read: "Act of *decision*, not of *insight*". It is easy to explain Wittgenstein's dissatisfaction with appeals to insights. Mental acts or states are not an adequate ground for the process of rule-following, because they are not publicly testable and do not allow us to establish the important distinction between thinking that one is following a rule and following effectively a rule. For this reason, he appeals to acts of decision. However, the subjectivism of acts of insight is also present in acts of decision: a shift from intuitionism to decisionism is not an improvement. As a result, there are passages in the early 1930s (especially in the *Philosophical Grammar* and *Blue Book*) where Wittgenstein tries to explain the nature of rule-following with an appeal to rule formulations: "We shall say that the rule is involved in the understanding, obeying, etc., if, as I should like to express it, the symbol of the rule forms part of the calculation".[35] However, this move was incompatible with his rejection of regulism and, accordingly, does not offer a solution to the problem.

3

An adequate account of rule-following only became possible when Wittgenstein embraced a practice-based conception of language. The following passage from his *Lectures on the Foundations of Mathematics* (1939) illustrates clearly this important shift in Wittgenstein's thought:

---

33 LWL, p. 57.
34 PR § 149.
35 BBB, p. 13.

> We might as well say that we need, not an intuition at each step, but a *decision*. – Actually there is neither. You don't make a decision: you simply do a certain thing. It is a question of a certain practice.[36]

This passage signals an important point. In the early 1930s, there are many texts where Wittgenstein devaluates the role of use, learning processes and actual practices, but the difficulties that he faced in explaining the nature of rule-following forced him to correct his stance. The reason why he took so long to recognize the crucial role of practices lies in a distorted view of them and of the nature of learning processes. He often claimed that actual practices are mere empirical processes, devoid of normative significance, and that learning processes are mere causal processes (devoid, again, of normative significance): "The process of learning does not matter; it is history and history does not matter here".[37] As we see, the devaluation of learning processes is based on an account of these processes as mere causal processes. Only in later works, like the *Remarks on the Foundations of Mathematics* and the *Philosophical Investigations*, did it become clear to Wittgenstein that normativity has an essential connection with practices and that learning processes are an initiation into normatively articulated practices. This recognition is not a capitulation to regularism, because practices and learning processes do not consist only of behavioural patterns, but also of normative attitudes. This is the fundamental insight that led to the rule-following reflections in his later work.

However, his previous reflections on practices and learning processes were based on an important insight that Wittgenstein always preserved: the view that we cannot explain normativity in a framework of natural causes. This view is at the centre of Wittgenstein's rejection of dispositionalism. Kripke emphasized this point in his reading of the *Philosophical Investigations*.[38] Dispositionalism is the general tendency of naturalistic theories of meaning (including the influential information-theoretic accounts of meaning), but, as Wittgenstein and Kripke stressed, dispositions do not have normative significance because there is a key distinction between what we are disposed to do and what we *ought* to do. According to Wittgenstein, meaning and intentionality cannot be reduced

---

36 LFM, p. 237.
37 LWL, p. 54. Cf. PR § 39: "The way in which language was learnt is not contained in its use. (Any more than the cause is contained in the effect.)"; and LWL, p. 116: "When we learn the meaning of a symbol the way in which we learn it is irrelevant to our future use and understanding of it. [...] It is a matter of purely historical interest."
38 Kripke 1982.

to naturalistic, causal terms, and this is a crucial thesis that sets him apart from many fashionable, contemporary theories of meaning.

Another important change in Wittgenstein's account of rule-following is related to the connection between rules and use. In the mid 1930s, Wittgenstein started to realize that this connection is much stronger than he initially thought. As Medina put it: "This link will grow so strong that the priority that he initially attributed to possible applications over actual uses will be reversed, and what can be done according to rules will come to be seen as the product of our actual and changing practices of application".[39] The notion of application was initially emphasized because it is relatively abstract and fits the calculus view of language; but when Wittgenstein moved towards a practice-based view of language, the notion of use (with all its fluctuations and indeterminacies) will occupy the centre-stage. In the *Blue Book*, for instance, there are already indications that actual practices are crucial to determine meanings. In his later work, Wittgenstein will even claim that concepts have their roots in our practices: "an education quite different from ours might also be the foundation for quite different concepts".[40]

4

Wittgenstein's reflections on rule-following culminate in the *Philosophical Investigations*. We may sum up briefly his main conclusions in five points. First, dispositions, as we have seen, cannot explain the nature of rule-following. Second, it is impossible to explain the connection between a rule and its application by invoking rule interpretations, because each interpretation would require a further interpretation, generating an infinite regress. Third, to follow a rule is not a mental process. An important objection against mentalistic accounts of rules is based on the fact that mental representations do not determine by themselves their application, because they are in fact signs that demand interpretation. Fourth, a Platonist account of rules as abstract entities amounts to explaining the *obscurum* (normative force) *per obscurius* (mysterious entities). Fifth, and in a more positive tone, Wittgenstein claims that following a rule is a practice, a custom and an institution.[41] Departing from a previous and impov-

---

39 Medina 2002, p. 133.
40 Z § 387.
41 Cf. PIr §§ 199, 202.

erished account of practice as a domain of causal processes deprived of normative significance, Wittgenstein came to realize that the notion of practice is the key for the problem of rule-following. This notion provides Wittgenstein with an alternative to mentalistic and Platonist accounts of the normativity of meaning; the roots of normativity are to be found neither in the mental life of an individual nor in an ideal sphere, but in the practices themselves. It is the notion of practice that, correctly understood, allows us to avoid the disastrous idea that following a rule requires an interpretation.

But in what sense are practices the source of the normativity? Practices involve, on the one hand, a crude training process, whereby the novice learns to react in a certain way to certain situations or stimuli (what Wittgenstein calls *Abrichtung* or drilling). The importance of this process lies in the fact that it enables the novice or pupil to grasp regularities and uniformities.[42] On the other hand, and this is a point that Wittgenstein missed in previous works, the learning processes that are at the origin of practices also involve an inculcation and development of normative attitudes. The novice is not subjected to a pure behaviouristic process; thanks to her interactions with a teacher or instructor, for instance, she masters gradually the distinction between correct and incorrect performances. This interaction should not be understood in intellectualist terms as a process based on explicit rule formulations and interpretations. The following passage is quite significant in this context:

> But if a person has not yet got the *concepts*, I'll teach him to use the words by means of *examples* and by *exercises*. – And when I do this, I do not communicate less to him than I know myself.[43]

We manifest our understanding of rules through actions, and it is also through actions that we learn rules.

The final result of these learning processes based on the interplay between natural reactions and acquired reactions is the inculcation of normative attitudes and the formation of concepts. Within this basic framework, the normativity of practices can be explained without appealing to external factors. It is in this sense that Wittgenstein claims that there must be a way of grasping rules which is not an interpretation but is exhibited in actual performances.[44] This passage

---

42 This point is made, for instance, in the *Remarks on the Foundations of Mathematics* (cf. e.g. RFM, pp. 303, 320).
43 PIr § 208.
44 PIr § 201.

and similar ones imply that practices and linguistic uses are intrinsically normative; rules are immanent to practices and standards of linguistic use are immanent to use. The gist of Wittgenstein's reflections on rule-following seems to be
the idea that the normativity of meaning is a primitive phenomenon that cannot
be explained in more fundamental, norm-free terms.

In sum, the development of Wittgenstein's account of rules is marked by two
major breakthroughs. First, he always recognized that rules presuppose a background, but this background was initially conceived of in theoretical terms as a
system of conventions and later as a background of practices. Second, learning
processes were at a first stage devaluated for having a merely causal character, but Wittgenstein eventually realized that learning processes already involve
normative attitudes (acceptance, rejection, expectations ...), which are crucial to
understand rule-following.

5

Before concluding, I would like to return to Brandom's distinction between
regulism and regularism, and to contrast his approach to the problem of rule-
following with McDowell's analysis, which I consider to be not only the most
plausible position, but also the most faithful reading of the Wittgensteinian text.
In *Making It Explicit*, Brandom proposes a reductive explanation of linguistic
practices, according to which we have to explain practices in a normative vocabulary that makes no use of intentional and semantic terms. He claims that the
intentional vocabulary can be reduced to a normative vocabulary, but not to the
language of natural science (as naturalists would recommend). To understand
intentional notions, we should appeal to deontic notions like commitments,
entitlements and obligations, as well as to the corresponding social interactions.
Intentionality can be reduced to normativity, but normativity is irreducible: it is
"norms all the way down". Brandom recognizes that his project of elaborating a
theory of practices does not fit Wittgenstein's quietism, but he claims at the same
time that his theoretical project satisfies "the criteria of adequacy Wittgenstein's
arguments have established".[45]

McDowell criticized both the application of the regulism/regularism distinction to the *Philosophical Investigations* and Brandom's project to develop a

---

45 Brandom 1994, p. 30.

theory of normativity[46]. We can identify three main points in McDowell's critique of Brandom. In the first place, McDowell rejects Brandom's thesis that there are two levels of normativity: a first level of norms that are expressed and a more fundamental level of implicit norms that should be reconstructed through a philosophical theory with the help of deontic notions. In fact, McDowell claims that:

> The thrust of his [Wittgenstein's] regress argument is not that what is fundamental is norms implicit in practice, but that what is fundamental is the ability to act immediately on an understanding – to act in a way that is not mediated by an interpretation of what is understood. [...] When Wittgenstein's regress is applied in the case of norms that are discursively explicit, its moral is not that that normativity presupposes normativity implicit in practice, but that there must be such a thing as a capacity to act immediately on an understanding of that normativity.[47]

The rejection of Brandom's distinction between two layers of normativity is closely connected with a second disagreement between McDowell and Brandom on the meaning of Wittgenstein's quietism. Brandom claims that Wittgenstein was simply not interested in elaborating a philosophical theory of implicit norms. For McDowell, if this was Wittgenstein's position, it would not be quietism, but laziness.[48] The real motivation of Wittgenstein's quietism lies in the fact that there is not a more fundamental level of normativity, as we have just seen.

Finally, McDowell claims that the regulism/regularism distinction is inadequate to understand Wittgenstein's position in the *Philosophical Investigations*. He concedes that Wittgenstein has no sympathy for both regulism and regularism, but he also claims that the label of regulism does not capture the real meaning of Wittgenstein's regress argument, as it is presented in the *Philosophical Investigations*. Brandom associates this argument with explicit rules, but in fact Wittgenstein also appeals to the regress argument in the case of sign-posts; the argument applies to both discursive and non-discursive norms, and in this sense it is independent of Brandom's notion of regulism.

This critique of Brandom is in line with the semantic primitivism that McDowell defended in his influential 1984 article "Wittgenstein on Following a Rule". The cornerstone of McDowell's and Wittgenstein's account of rule-following is based on the idea that meaning and norms cannot be reduced to a

---

46 McDowell 2002.
47 McDowell 2002, p. 103.
48 Cf. Ibid., p. 98.

meaning-free or norm-free dimension. In order to illustrate this point, McDowell emphasizes the following passages:[49]

Following according to the rule is FUNDAMENTAL to our language-game.[50]

The difficult thing here is not, to dig down to the ground; no, it is to recognize the ground that lies before us as the ground.[51]

Practices are the "bedrock", the ultimate level of normativity, so to speak. The normativity of practices can be described, but cannot be grounded or explained in more fundamental terms. McDowell explains the origin of normativity in light of Wittgenstein's work, with some influence from Aristotle and Sellars. From Aristotle, he develops the idea that the ethical upbringing is a particular instance of a general human capacity of developing conceptual capacities that open up a specific domain of action or experience. Borrowing a phrase from Sellars, he calls such a domain "a space of reasons". The Aristotelian process of acquisition of a second nature is a process whereby we initiate ourselves into a space of reasons by developing our conceptual capacities along the lines sketched by Wittgenstein, that is, by mastering practices. The sphere of human action and experience is *ab initio* meaningful and normatively structured.[52] Any attempt to explain or reduce intentionality or normativity is therefore misconceived. The idea that "it is norms all the way down" is closely related to another important thesis of McDowell's philosophy, the thesis of the "unboundedness of the conceptual". McDowell rejects "the idea that the conceptual realm has an outer boundary", claiming that "the conceptual is unbounded; there is nothing outside it".[53] He thereby solves the problem that haunts modern epistemology: experience can justify our beliefs because it is conceptually articulated.

In the light of the foregoing considerations, it also becomes clear why McDowell disagrees with Kripke's thesis that Wittgenstein formulated a sceptical paradox regarding meaning and also a sceptical solution. According to the sceptical paradox, there is no (mental or behavioural) fact that allows us to determine a rule and, therefore, meaning. The sceptical solution is based on an appeal to communal practices. McDowell considers the putative sceptical

---

49 McDowell 1984.

50 RFM, p. 330.

51 RFM, p. 333.

52 Cf. McDowell 1993, p. 277: "human life is itself already shaped by meaning and understanding".

53 McDowell 1996, p. 44.

paradox a "falsification".[54] It is true that Wittgenstein rejects traditional or commonsensical accounts of rule-following, but he also stresses that one can grasp rules in practice, without the help of interpretations. One should not, therefore, attribute to Wittgenstein a non-factualism about meaning. On the other hand, both McDowell and Kripke appeal to communal practices, but in different senses. Kripke considers the community as "a collection of individuals presenting to one another exteriors that match in certain respects".[55] But if meaning is indeterminate at the individual level, how could a collection of individuals solve the problem? McDowell avoids this objection by claiming that the normativity of communal practices is not constructed from a more fundamental level: it is a primitive fact.

---

54 McDowell 1984, p. 228.
55 Ibid., p. 252.

Nathan Hauthaler

Wittgenstein on Actions, Reasons and Causes

In this essay I examine one of Wittgenstein's seminal contributions to the philosophy of action: his discussion of the distinction between the grammars of reasons and causes of action. This discussion seems to have lost currency in the context of the received Davidsonian view as to which, *pace* Wittgenstein, the (primary) reason of an action is its cause. In the present contribution I identify the locus of disagreement between Wittgensteinian and Davidsonian views on this matter and outline ways in which, according to Wittgenstein, grammars of reasons and of causality may nonetheless be related. I argue, furthermore, for the viability of a Wittgensteinian conception of reasons, including motivating reasons, despite their apparent connection with a causalist conception. Lastly, I outline avenues for Wittgensteinian advances in current philosophy of action, which may be viewed as responses to misguided Davidsonian attempts at sublimating the grammar of reasons.

Introductory Remarks[1]

There are several important contributions from Wittgenstein in the philosophy of action. These include: his early and later discussions of the concept of the will,[2] his discussion of action as opposed to mere bodily movement,[3] and his discussions of other pivotal concepts such as *intention* and *trying*.[4] The present chapter will consider a related discussion of Wittgenstein's: of the grammars of

---

1 Thanks for discussion of this material to Lisbon and London audiences and, in particular, to Alberto Arruda, Lucy Campbell and Jennifer Hornsby.
2 See Scott 1996 and 1998 for discussions of Wittgenstein's criticism of other theories of will and volition, notably Wundt's and James's; see Hyman 2011 for similar results.
3 See the discussion surrounding his famous question in PIr § 621 ("what is left over if I subtract the fact that my arm rises from the fact that I raise my arm?").Though arguably considered misconceived by Wittgenstein himself, this has been taken as a suitable starting point for many philosophical inquiries into the nature of action.
4 See PIr §§ 591–5 on the former; PIr §§ 616–24 on the latter.

reasons and of causes of action. The reason/cause distinction used to be prominent until the work of Donald Davidson turned the tide on the matter. The basic Davidsonian causalist framework has since remained the received view on the nature of reasons and reason-explanation. Nevertheless, in current debates in the philosophy of action, ever more philosophers seem to be willing to depart from this framework and to look for a different understanding of reasons. In this context it might be useful to provide grounds as to why the Wittgensteinian approach should not be considered obsolete in light of the Davidsonian one, and to show in which sense many of Wittgenstein's views on the matter remain pertinent for current advances in the area.

Section 1 will provide an outline of the basic opposition between the Wittgensteinian and the Davidsonian views concerning the relation of reasons and causes of action. Section 2 discusses ways in which, despite the general view entertained in section 1, Wittgenstein recognizes connections between grammars of reasons and causes of action. Section 3 outlines differences between Davidson and Wittgenstein concerning different "kinds" of reasons, Wittgenstein's ability to accommodate all kinds of reasons as well as problems encompassing Davidson's approach. Section 4 sketches basic avenues for current Wittgensteinian conceptions of reasons. Section 5 concludes by briefly recapitulating the results from sections 1–4.

1 Wittgensteinianism and Davidsonianism

Davidson, in an essay on Hempel's 1961 account of rational action,[5] mentions that at the time of Hempel's 1961 and his own 1963 "Actions, Reasons and Causes", he was "swimming against a very strong neo-Wittgensteinian current of small red books".[6] Davidson elaborates on this current mentioning a view due to the Wittgenstein of *The Blue and Brown Books*, according to which "causal relations are essentially nomological and based on induction while our knowledge that an agent has acted on certain reasons is not usually dependent on induction or knowledge of serious laws".[7] Likewise, according to such views, conceptions of reasons and causes of action, respectively, ought generally to be kept distinct. In

---

5 See Hempel 1961.
6 Davidson 1976, p. 261.
7 Davidson 2001, p. xi. The books alluded to are titles in the Routledge & Kegan Paul series on the Philosophy of Psychology (Studies in Philosophical Psychology), which includes works such as Geach 1957, Melden 1961, and Kenny 1963; see also Davidson 1963, n. 1.

his 1963 and related essays, Davidson does his best to erode such a conceptual separation.

In order to come to terms with the distinction between grammars of reasons and causes of action, it will thus be helpful to consider Wittgenstein's *Blue and Brown Books*. In them, Wittgenstein famously identifies "an ambiguous use" of the interrogative word "Why?" as a source for the confusion between reasons and causes of actions. The following passage contains the gamut of Wittgenstein's *Blue Book* remarks on the matter:

> The proposition that your action has such and such a cause, is a hypothesis. The hypothesis is well founded if one has had a number of experiences which, roughly speaking, agree in showing that your action is the regular sequel of certain conditions which we then call causes of the action.

> In order to know the reasons which you had for making a certain statement, for acting in a particular way, etc., no number of agreeing experiences is necessary, and the statement of your reason is not a hypothesis. The difference between the grammars of "reason" and "cause" is quite similar to that between the grammars of "motive" and "cause". Of the cause one can say that one can't know it but can only conjecture it. On the other hand one often says: "Surely I must know why I did it" talking of the motive. When I say: "we can only conjecture the cause but we know the motive" this statement will be seen later on to be a grammatical one. The "can" refers to a logical possibility.

> The double use of the word "why", asking for the cause and asking for the motive, together with the idea that we can know, and not only conjecture, our motives, gives rise to the confusion that a motive is a cause of which we are immediately aware, a cause 'seen from the inside', or a cause experienced. – Giving a reason is like giving a calculation by which you have arrived at a certain result.[8]

A look at the respective grammars of reasons and causes is in order. Wittgenstein does not provide a full characterization of these notions. However, from his above remarks one might glean, it seems, the following: that causes are conjectured or known only through empirical evidence, and knowledge of them is fallible; that reasons, on the other hand, are known and known without evidence, and come with an air of certainty. In "I must know why I did it", this "must" (to give it a Wittgensteinian gloss) refers to a logical necessity.[9]

---

8 BBB, p. 15.

9 This kind of attribution of knowledge and the use of the concept of knowledge is not generally representative of the later Wittgenstein. On the contrary, what has since been lamented even by sympathizers as "peculiar obsessive theoretic tics" (Thompson 2011, p. 198) includes his ruling that "It can't be said of me at all (except perhaps as a joke) that I *know* I'm in

Apart from trying to delineate the grammars of reasons and causes, Wittgenstein apparently regards causality pertaining to human agency to be dealt with by psychologists rather than by philosophers.[10] He questions conceptions of "mental causes" being identified in the context of a philosophical account, remarking, for example, in the *Brown Book* that "[t]here is a kind of general disease of thinking which always looks for (and finds) what would be called a mental state from which all our acts spring as from a reservoir".[11] Other passages ridicule the idea of one's reason being "a cause 'seen from the inside'",[12] the idea of the agent watching her causes directly, as it were, or of her reasons being causes experienced.

In the philosophy of action up until the early 1960s, one finds a number of little red, and other, books which, paying heed to the above observations, contribute to the said Wittgensteinian current. And this is the current Davidson undertakes to respond to. Now what does Davidson argue? Chiefly, he argues that reason-explanation – which he calls "rationalization" – is a species of causal explanation, and that the primary reason of an action – 'the reason why' – is its cause.[13] For Davidson the primary reason of an action is a compound of a belief and a desire (or other pro-attitude), which he understands as the cause of that action. The definite article is important here: an agent may be credited with different beliefs and pro-attitudes; the primary reason for an action, however, is the reason why she acted as she did, hence the belief-cum-pro-attitude compound which caused her action – and which rationalizes it. So, when providing the primary reasons one provides the cause of the action for which it is the primary reason, and action explanation, drawing as it does on primary reasons, is thus a species of causal explanation.

---

pain. What is it supposed to mean – except perhaps that I *am* in pain?" (PIr § 246). According to Wittgenstein, this cannot be said (except perhaps as a joke) for the opposite ("I don't know I'm in pain") either. The point made here would arguably apply, *mutatis mutandis*, to that of knowledge of one's reason or motive, and so, according to the rationale of the *Philosophical Investigations*, these would be excluded from the scope of possible knowledge proper.

10 See, for example, the *Brown Book* remark: "If you ask 'why', do you ask for the cause or for the reason? If for the cause, it is easy enough to think up a physiological or psychological hypothesis which explains this choice under the given conditions. It is the task of the experimental sciences to test such hypotheses." (BBB, p. 88)

11 BBB, p. 143. This is not to deny Wittgenstein's attention to the conception of "mental cause" such as discussed, for example, by Anscombe 1963, § 10; see PIr § 476.

12 BBB, p. 15.

13 Davidson 1963, pp. 4–5.

Of particular interest in the present context are Davidson's arguments against Wittgenstein and the view of Wittgensteinianism they depict. Davidson's 1963 paper is the focal point for his criticism of Wittgensteinian conceptions of action, addressing Wittgenstein himself but also authors in his wake.[14] Davidson agrees with much of what the Wittgensteinian current seems to be able to offer:

> When we learn his reason, we have an interpretation, a new description of what he did, which fits it into a familiar picture. The picture includes some of the agent's beliefs and attitudes; perhaps also goals, ends, principles, general character traits, virtues or vices. Beyond this, the redescription of an action afforded by a reason may place the action in a wider social, economic, linguistic, or evaluative context. To learn, through learning the reason, that the agent conceived his action as a lie, a repayment of a debt, an insult, the fulfilment of an avuncular obligation, or a knight's gambit is to grasp the point of the action in its setting of rules, practices, conventions, and expectations.[15]

Beyond that and ignoring the Wittgensteinian ridicule, however, Davidson argues that the characteristics which Wittgenstein provides, the apparent peculiarity of the grammar of reasons and of the agent's knowledge thereof, furnishes no cogent argument against the assumption that such reasons can also be causally efficacious.[16] In the same vein, and apparently providing the most enticing ground against a Wittgensteinian approach, and for a Davidsonian one, he argues that his framework helps explain, in a way continuous with other kinds of scientific explanations, why an agent acted. Wittgenstein's understanding of reasons and his distinction between reasons and causes of action apparently leave an explanatory gap between an agent's reasons and her actual actions. According to Davidson, if one leaves open a gap between reasons and causes of actions,

> something essential has certainly been left out, for a person can have a reason for an action, and perform the action, and yet this reason not be the reason why he did it. Central to the

---

14 Notably Melden 1961, which is advanced as a Wittgensteinian account, though important arguments of Melden's which are criticized by Davidson do not trace back to Wittgenstein (thus, for example, the notorious logical-connection argument does not find its origin in Wittgenstein; see thereon also n. 15 *infra*). Ryle 1949 should be named independently as a target text of Davidson's criticism.
15 Davidson 1963, p. 10.
16 See Davidson 1963, pp. 13–15. In this course he also dismantles arguments such as Melden's so-called "logical connection" argument against a Humean conception of causation being relevant for the explanation of action (because of its requirement for logical distinctness of cause and effect).

relation between a reason and an action it explains is the idea that the agent performed the action because he had the reason.[17]

By giving this "because ..." (and so by giving the reason) a causal construal, he proposes to close the gap he complains remains open on the Wittgensteinian account.

In the Davidsonian conception, all genuine reasons for action are potentially causes, that is: everything that qualifies as a primary reason qualifies as the cause of an action.[18] For Wittgenstein, on the other hand, one seems committed to holding that reasons, by virtue of their grammars, are generally distinct from causes. To get clear about the exact locus of disagreement between Davidson and Wittgenstein on this matter, it will be necessary to examine Wittgenstein's remarks on causality more closely. It is not the case that Wittgenstein would generally shun causality in the context of reasons or reason-explanation. Such an all-out separation between the grammars of reasons and causes (which a quick reading of the *Blue Book* passage might suggest) would be baffling, if only on the grounds that agents seem to come to terms with causality via actions and causality-imbibed causative verbs which, as action verbs, naturally invite corresponding reasons for action.[19]

2 Wittgenstein on Reasons and Causality

In the *Brown Book*, Wittgenstein considers, whilst discussing imaginary tribes and their supposed betting practices, a possible distinction between causes and reasons of action. In one case, bettors place bets on fighters simply upon observation of certain regularities, yet their language does not comprise a language-game of giving reasons. I "can understand 'why' they [i.e. the bets] were thus placed", for "observation has taught me certain causes for their placing their bets as they do, but that the bettors used no reasons for acting as they did".[20] In another, the tribe has "a language which comprises 'giving reasons'. Now this game of giving the reason why one acts in a particular way does not

---

17 Davidson 1963, p. 10.
18 This is not to say, of course, that every genuine reason is ipso facto causally efficacious. Many a reason may cause nothing, notably if outdone by a salient reason for a conflicting action.
19 See Anscombe 1971, p. 137, on causative verbs such as "scrape", "push", "wet", "carry", and the like, which capture actions that can be done for reasons.
20 BBB, p. 110.

involve finding the causes of one's actions (by frequent observations of the conditions under which they arise)".[21] Reasons are given, for example, by pointing at features of the fighters (size, biceps, etc.) which justifies the bettors' actions without adverting to such regularities. Albeit a bettor, when providing a reason for a bet by pointing to the biceps of a favoured fighter, adverts to something causally relevant, this does not elucidate a causal relation to the bettor's action. A fighter's biceps might be causally efficacious of the other fighter's defeat, but not of the bettor's betting action.

What is of importance in these cases? Wittgenstein argues that the provision of a reason need not involve recourse to the causes of one's having a reason, nor need it draw on the obtaining of relevant causal relations. The tribe member need not provide a cause for their betting on one fighter rather than another, nor a cause or a *reason* for favouring one, nor need the reason they provide for favouring a particular fighter advert to the existence of causal relations.[22] At the same time, Wittgenstein clearly does not prohibit causes or causal regularities being adverted to by the reasons provided. The reason provided by pointing to a fighter's biceps does just advert to a fighter's causal powers.

In his 1938 "Lectures on Aesthetics", Wittgenstein speaks of three different uses of the notion of cause:

> 'Cause' is used in very many different ways, e.g.
> (1) "What is the cause of unemployment?" "What is the cause of this expression?"
> (2) "What was the cause of your jumping?" "That noise."
> (3) "What was the cause of that wheel going round?" You trace a mechanism".[23]

Wittgenstein relates the first notion of cause to that of experiment and statistics; the second to reasons; the third to mechanisms.[24] He thus again admits a conceptual connection between the notions of cause and reason, albeit he clearly does not provide a causal rendering of reasons (of reasons being, at the bottom, causes of actions).[25]

---

21 Ibid.
22 See ibid., p. 111.
23 LC, p. 13.
24 See ibid., n. 4. (Taylor).
25 These remarks clearly invite further investigation. Thus the association of reasons and causes in (2) ought to be examined along the lines of the above lamented confusion of reasons and causes invited by the interrogative word "Why" and the different kinds of responses to it. Likewise, the notion of "cause" – as opposed to those of object, target, but also reason – deserves further investigation. On these distinctions, see PIr § 476 and Anscombe 1963, p. 16, § 10. Obviously (2) can be given a genuine-reason reading, however, for example, in the case

Yet, despite the fact that such conceptual connections between reasons and causes can thus be established, the initially supposed grammatical implications of reasons and causes, respectively, seem to stand against their being connected. To repeat, agential knowledge regarding one's reasons seemed to involve certainty, whereas knowledge about causes seemed to retain hypothetical or conjectural status. Such a construal is contradicted, for example, in Wittgenstein's 1937 lectures on "Cause and Effect: Intuitive Awareness", which are inter alia a response to Russell's 1936 "The Limits of Empiricism". In these lectures, he explores a language-game and basic schema of cause and effect that expressly rule out doubt. Lacking doubt, the language-game is a more primitive yet also more fundamental one; a language-game that is the basis for more sophisticated language-games.

> I want to say: it is characteristic of our language that the foundation on which it grows consists in steady ways of living, regular ways of acting.
> Its function is determined above all by action, which it accompanies.
> We have an idea of which ways of living are primitive, and which could only have developed out of these. We believe that the simplest plough existed before the complicated one.[26]

In this vein, doubt only enters the stage in a non-primitive setting, as a refinement or qualification of the initial setting:

> First there must be firm, hard stone for building, and the bricks are laid rough-hewn one on another. Afterwards it's certainly important that the stone can be trimmed, that it's not too hard.
> The primitive form of the language game is certainty, not uncertainty. For uncertainty could never lead to action.[27]

Wittgenstein does not confine such certainty to causality at large (*viz.* to certainty about causality being operative in the world), but relates it to individual causes and effects. Certainty thus pertains to the determination of a given cause:

> The simple form (and that is the prototype) of the cause-effect game is determining the cause, not doubting.
> The basic form of the game must be one in which we act.

---

where I jump because I hear a noise, where that noise gives me reason to jump (you shout "Jump!"). Thanks to Lucy Campbell for the pointer.

26 CE, p. 397.

27 Ibid.

> How could the concept of 'cause' be set up if we were always doubting?[28]

This kind of certainty is itself intimately wedded to action, with practically engaging with the world rather than speculating about it.

> The essence of the language game is a practical method (a way of acting) – not speculation, not chatter.[29]

Contrary to the supposed *Blue Book* notion of causality according to which one "can only conjecture the cause" and respective propositions remain at best well-founded hypotheses,[30] Wittgenstein ought to be taken to employ "a more flexible notion of causality".[31] Likewise the features of certainty and immediacy cannot be maintained as criteria for distinguishing reasons from causes of action.[32] In this vein, then, also the above *Blue Book* ridicule of the supposed certainty "about causes of which we are immediately aware" should be reconsidered: It should be read not as questioning the applicability of certainty to causes generally, but the view that reasons or motives be among such causes.[33]

Consequently, the presumed general distinctness of the grammars of reasons and causes cannot be established by recourse to certainty as a criterion for the former. In conjunction with the above outline of relations of reasons

---

28 Ibid.

29 CE, p. 399. Wittgenstein's *On Certainty* would be an obvious source for further discussions and corroboration of his concerning notions of certainty as pertaining to causal relations. As the present essay is concerned with Wittgenstein's early investigations, however, *On Certainty* is not adduced in the present context.

30 BBB, p. 15.

31 Schroeder 2001, p. 158.

32 See ibid., pp. 158–159, on a related discussion regarding immediate awareness of certain causes. Schroeder associates certainty about causes with what Anscombe terms "mental causes" (see Anscombe 1963, pp. 15–16, §§ 9–10). While this is certainly a plausible candidate family of cases of certainty about causes or causal relations (and apt for the example Schroeder cites), Wittgenstein's own general discussion in "Cause and Effect" does not suggest him speaking of certainty about "mental causes" only.

33 Concerning the applicability of certainty regarding causes and reasons, caution is advised with regard to the notion of certainty as discussed by Wittgenstein, as one may understand him to employ different uses of it for reasons and causes respectively, and of cognate terms such as that of prediction, or explanation. There is a point to assuming, for example, a different direction of fit with regard to certainty about causes on the one hand, and one's reasons or motives on the other. (For a source for the distinction of directions of fit already in Wittgenstein, see, for example, his discussion of different conceptions of prediction in PIr §§ 629–31; compare this to the *locus classicus* of the distinction in Anscombe 1963, § 32).

and causality, the initial *prima facie* construal of the *Blue Book* passage seems to require thorough reconsideration. This is not to suggest a construal of Wittgenstein as claiming a general likeness of reasons and causes of action, though. On the contrary: What Wittgenstein generally reminds us of in these passages is an unfortunate state of confusion – motivated, for example, by the interrogative word "Why?" – where distinctions ought to be recognized after all. The locus of disagreement with Davidson, notably the question of reasons being the causes of action, remains unaffected. A few remarks on different conceptions of kinds of reasons will help to specify and locate this disagreement further in that context.

3 Wittgensteinian vs. Davidsonian Kinds of Reasons

According to a standard distinction of kinds of reasons, on the one hand there are normative reasons which are the kind of reasons that are for something, that speak in favour of it and can be provided for guidance, advice, or justification. These are usually taken to be facts. On the other hand, there are motivating reasons, that is to say, the things that actually motivate agents and thus have some bearing on their motivational state. These are usually taken to be mental states.[34] The reasons figuring in Davidson's above reading of "because" would count as a typical motivating reason – albeit a rather rational variant thereof (and hence normative in aspiration, insofar as it also rationalizes the action it explains).[35] It is a compound of mental states – or the onslaught of such – which is taken to be causally efficacious.[36]

---

34 Where the notion of "state" is used in an indiscriminate fashion, disregarding possible distinctions of states as opposed, for example, to processes. A third kind – that of "explanatory reasons", i.e. reasons that are regarded thus only for figuring in causal explanations, but are by nature "brute causes" (such as the implosion of one's lungs being the explanatory reason for their collapse) – shall be noted only in passing for it would be confusing in the present context (as Davidson speaks of explanatory reasons when having in mind causally efficacious motivating reasons). See, for example, Alvarez 2009 for discussion of the distinction.
35 Thus inherent potential to figure as normative reasons: the content of the respective belief is one which supposedly speaks in favour of the action and potentially justifies it.
36 The question whether states themselves or their onslaught ought to be taken to be causally efficacious is related to Davidson's general understanding of action in terms of event-causation, where only the onslaught of mental states, but not the states themselves, are allowed the status of event. See Davidson 1963, p. 12.

What about Wittgenstein's account of reasons in this regard? In virtue of his contrast of reasons with causes, and the conception of causal efficacy resounding in the notion of motivating reason, one might *prima facie* take Wittgenstein, in the passages quoted, to be speaking of normative rather than motivating reasons. At the same time, one might glean from a proximate *Blue Book* passage (in which Wittgenstein distinguishes reasons from justifications *post hoc*) that motivating reasons alone are to be recognized as genuine reasons. Insofar as the latter are to be regarded as mere justifications (as opposed to reasons proper), only motivating reasons would be recognized as reasons (proper).

Both readings, however, are unsatisfactory. The former view, according to which Wittgenstein shows his disregard of motivating reasons, would just beg the question against Wittgenstein. This is because it would presuppose motivating reasons to be conceived as causes. It is not at all clear, though, that motivational reason needs to be construed in such a causalist fashion (albeit, post-Davidson, one may be inclined to think of mental causation when speaking of motivating reasons).[37] Wittgenstein's association of reasons with motives – regardless of the underlying "hypothetical" motivational structure – arguably lends support to the inclusion of motivating reasons of some kind or other.[38] The task of coming to terms with Wittgenstein's distinction between grammars of reasons and causes and of providing a viable Wittgensteinian account of reasons for action includes then the provision of a viable Wittgensteinian account of motivating reasons, since these seem to be a fundamental kind of reason yet one apparently wedded to causalist accounts.[39]

Likewise, the latter reading of Wittgenstein, in which he recognizes only motivating reasons based upon the distinction between reasons and justifications, is untenable. The thrust of the distinction remains somewhat open in the *Blue Book*, yet the *Investigations* make clear that it is not to be read as a distinction between genuine (motivating) reasons and apparent reasons (mere justifications). As Wittgenstein remarks in PIr § 479,

> [t]he question 'For what reasons do you believe this?' might mean: 'From what reasons are you now deriving it (have you just derived it)?' But it might also mean: 'With hindsight, what reasons can you give me for this supposition?'

---

37 For one standard alternative, of all reasons being facts, see, for example, Alvarez 2009 and 2010.

38 Wittgenstein does not give many hints as to the respective specificities and differences of the notions of reason and motive; see, for example, LC, pp. 21–23, 26–27; PPF §§ 333–337 (discussions of motives).

39 The task will be taken up again in the following section.

Although "one could actually take 'reasons' for a belief to mean only what a person had said to himself before he arrived at the belief – the calculation that he actually carried out",[40] there is no inherent need to take that route, nor to read Wittgenstein as endorsing it. This is corroborated also, for example, by his 1938 "Lectures on Aesthetics":

> Giving a reason sometimes means "I actually went this way", sometimes "I could have gone this way", i.e. sometimes what we say acts as a justification, not as a report of what was done, e.g. I remember the answer to a question; when asked why I give this answer, I gave a process leading to it, though I didn't go through this process.[41]

Rhees's corresponding notes read as follows:

> Thus 'reason' does not always mean the same thing. And similarly with 'motive'. 'Why did you do it?' One sometimes answers: 'Well, I said to myself: "I must see him because he is ill."' – actually remembering having said things to oneself. Or again, in many cases the motive is the justification we give on being asked – just that.[42]

In the relevant *Blue Book* passage,[43] Wittgenstein does not say that "giving a reason is giving a calculation" or that "giving a reason is giving the calculation", but "giving a reason is like giving a calculation by which you have arrived at a certain result." The calculation may actually have been carried out and the reason been adverted to in the course of action. All the same, the calculation would apply – or would have applied – counterfactually, even when the relevant reason had not been adverted to in the course of, or prior to, the action. When comparing a reason to a calculation, Wittgenstein is likening it to a pattern, a signpost or rule, not to any (mental) event or process of its application. What is dispensed with then, with justifications *post hoc*, is the alleged general requirement for reasons to have been adverted to in the course of action. What is dispensed with more generally is the assumption that reasons are referring expressions where the referent is a mental state. There are no grounds, consequently, to take Wittgenstein to confine his understanding of reasons to only some of their kinds.

---

40 PIr § 480.
41 LC, p. 22.
42 Ibid.
43 BBB, p. 15.

Where Wittgenstein makes reasons similar to signposts or rules, for Davidson they are akin to mental batteries. Agents run on these batteries, and do so
in relatively rational manners which can yet be fully accounted for in a causally-
explanatory way, which apparently allows one to bridge an explanatory gap
between agents' reasons and their actions.[44] This, as suggested earlier, may be
the cardinal feature which allowed Davidson to effectively deflect the Wittgensteinian current in the philosophy of action in favour of his own. In the light of
numerous problems with Davidson's account which do not affect Wittgenstein,
this is surprising. Thus Davidson's account leads to a strong inflation of the
notion of reason insofar as, according to it, intentional action generally means
action for (primary) reasons.[45] In the case of someone acting "for no (particular)
reason", for Davidson this must be paraphrased as "for no further reason" – apart
from some basic primary reason which is required by his theory as only such
a reason renders the action intentional. Wittgenstein, on the other hand, does
not face any particular problem with the idea of someone acting for no reason
(acting without adverting to anything like a signpost, rule, or the like).[46] Another
problem that is as germane to the Davidsonian account as it is irrelevant to the
Wittgensteinian one is the problem of "deviant (or 'wayward') causal chains" –
the problem that conditions for an action to be intentional may be satisfied (for
a causally efficacious belief-desire compound can be identified) yet without it
intuitively appearing to be an intentional action.[47] The consequential demand
that with intentional actions, primary reasons cause actions "in the right way"
has been given little credit even by Davidson himself.[48] This calls into question

---

44 See supra n. 15.

45 For Davidson, it should be remembered, actions are events that are intentional under
some description. They are intentional for involving reasons (causally efficacious belief-desire
compounds). See, for example, Davidson 1963, p. 6; Davidson 1971, pp. 46–47.

46 See, for example, BBB, p. 15: "If on the other hand you realize that the chain of actual
reasons has a beginning, you will no longer be revolted by the idea of a case in which there is
no reason for the way you obey the order." See also, for example, his remarks on the "chain
of reasons" coming to an end at some point, which is a recurrent theme in his works (see,
for example, PG, p. 97; BBB, pp. 14–15, 143; PIr § 326). Likewise: "Once I have exhausted the
justifications, I have reached bedrock, and my spade is turned. Then I am inclined to say: 'This
is simply what I do.'" (PIr § 217)

47 See Davidson's own climber example: "A climber might want to rid himself of the weight
and danger of holding another man on a rope, and he might know that by loosening his hold on
the rope he could rid himself of the weight and danger. This belief and want might so unnerve
him as to cause him to loosen his hold, and yet it might be the case that he never chose to
loosen his hold, nor did he do it intentionally." (Davidson 1973, p. 79)

48 See Davidson 1973, pp. 79–81; for further dissatisfaction with the response, see, for

his suggestion that a causalist construal is the most satisfactory reading of the "because" connecting the agent's reasons and her actions.[49]

Returning to the gap which apparently remains open if the "because" is not given a causal reading, the problems inherent in Davidson's conception of reasons suggest that his solution does not fare well. Yet does Wittgenstein's fare any better? Or does he even notice a gap here? To begin with, Wittgenstein is alive to an *apparent* gap. In the *Investigations* he writes: "Can one ask: 'How do you know that you do it because of this, or not because of this?' And is the answer perhaps: 'I feel it'?"[50] Likewise he asks in § 631 – and echoing the quoted passages from the *Blue Book* – whether one might "see the causal connection from inside"?[51]

Why does he refrain from bridging the gap? The response is that in Wittgenstein's view there is no gap to be bridged, and notably not in causal terms. For Wittgenstein it would be confused to claim that reasons function as causes of actions in the precise way Davidson advances the suggestion. In this vein, one might equally well invert the dialectic between Wittgenstein and Davidson so as to read the former as criticizing the latter for taking mental concepts (such as want, desire, belief or intention) to refer to corresponding mental states that underlie the language of reasons and reason-explanation just as they underlie intentional agency. Such attempts at sublimation[52] are criticized frequently in the *Investigations*, notably in the examples of such cognate concepts such as *intention* or *understanding*.[53]

---

example, Schroeder 2001, pp. 152–153.

49 Further lines of criticism of Davidson's account include, for example, his focus on actions understood as already complete(d) event particulars, which prevents him from apprehending first-personal knowledge of one's present (yet unfolding) actions (see Thompson 2011); or the differential analysis he is forced to apply to actions that are mere bodily movements, on the one hand, and actions which are causes of other events, on the other (see Hornsby 2011).
50 PIr § 487.
51 See similarly PIr § 637. An alternative red herring response about ascertaining why one acted is contemplated in PIr § 488: "How do I judge whether it is so? By circumstantial evidence?"
52 See PIr § 38 on corresponding criticisms of certain understandings of language. This notion of sophistication (as opposed to naivety) will be explicated in due course.
53 See, for example, PIr §§ 591ff. on the former, PIr §§ 151ff. on the latter. These are to be read in the context of Wittgenstein's more general critical discussion of associations of language with primitive language-games relating to reification and reference. The connection for the philosophy of action is drawn, for example, by Tanney 2009a, 105, and Hacker 2009.

4 Wittgensteinian Non-Causal Reasons and Reason-Explanations

Wittgenstein does not provide a full characterization of reasons or reason-explanation. Still, he provides sufficient grounds to guide current approaches on the matter, including non-causalist renderings of motivating reasons as well as of reason-explanation.[54] Compared to the focus on the causally efficacious mental life and hard-wiring of agents as is supposedly laid bare by the provision of reasons, a Wittgensteinian approach in this context might proceed quite differently. Generally, it is best committed to paying close attention to actual practices of the supply and demand of reasons, the circumstances and modes of acceptance or refusal of reasons. In this vein, actual use of reasons and their grammar take precedence over philosophical stipulation concerning their use. A Wittgensteinian conception of reasons might then be taken, most generally, to be outward- rather than inward-looking, and overall outlook-oriented. Insofar as causes play a role at all, we should be interested in the final rather than the efficient cause of action.

A general point of departure similar to Wittgenstein's can be found in Anscombe. As Anscombe famously remarks in *Intention*:

> What distinguishes actions which are intentional from those which are not? The answer that I shall suggest is that they are the actions to which a certain sense of the question "Why?" is given application; the sense is of course that in which the answer, if positive, gives a reason for acting. But this is not a sufficient statement, because the question "What is the relevant sense of the question 'Why?'" and "What is meant by 'reason for acting'?" are one and the same.[55]

This is quite clearly owed to Wittgenstein himself in tracing different – and identifying certain – kinds of responses to the notorious "Why?"-question mentioned in the *Blue Book*.

From there, at least two interrelated – equally outlook-oriented – avenues appear promising, where reasons form part of a language-game that sheds (more) light on an agent's circumstances and actions.

---

54 For the traditional Wittgensteinian approaches, see the current of little red books, notably Melden 1961, Anscombe 1963 and Kenny 1963.
55 Anscombe 1963, p. 9, § 5.

Firstly, reasons may be taken to facilitate getting more perspective on the character or outlook of a given agent as displayed by her action, figuring as fractions of her "autobiography".[56] Thereby, they lay bare the agent's viewpoint, and highlight what she finds salient in the context of her action. This conception is shown, for example, in the above *Brown Book* fighters-and-bettors example: where agents provide their reasons for betting on their fighters by pointing at certain of their features (the biceps, the heights, etc.), they provide considerations that are salient for them; for their views of what is at stake. If these are what "made them" place their bets on some fighters rather than others, this is not to say that these salient features thus caused them to act. They are not to be taken to conjecture what causally "made them" act in one way rather than another - they do not register as a cause the biceps, or the content of the belief in the relevance of their size, or the believing it, or whatever - but "speak their minds" on what they took or take, in these circumstances or generally, to be salient. The recognition of such salient features in turn reflects, in a more or less general way, the kind of outlook these agents have of the world. Reasons thus contribute to shedding light on an agent's views and outlook on things, her character and actions alike. Such an understanding is already emphasized by Melden[57] and is partly recognized by Davidson.[58] Davidson's attempt at incorporating it into a causally-explanatory framework, however, undermines this recognition by ignoring such agential grasp and use of reasons in favour of his own – highly theory-laden – conception. For it is not the case – or it is at least clearly unsupported – that when operating with reasons agents employ anything like the Davidsonian conception.

Apart from shedding more light on the agent, reasons may be taken, secondly, to clarify the relevant context and circumstances of a given action; they yield "teleological" characterizations thereof.[59] Thus, for example, Tanney,

---

56 This does imply the attribution of corresponding intentions to an agent to provide such parts of her autobiography when giving her reasons – an agent may not have the slightest intention to relate to herself in any wider sense a reason why she acted in a given case. Still, the agent may effectively do so when providing her reasons (by effectively representing herself as someone who recognizes this-and-that as salient in these circumstances).
57 Melden 1961.
58 See the quotation supra of Davidson 1963, p. 10.
59 See, for example, Hacker 2009, pp. 85–86 on this label (for a standard "teleological" account in current philosophy of action, see, for example, Schueler 2003). The labelling of teleological accounts as opposed to Davidson's own account is somewhat misleading, however, as integral features of his account are best viewed in a teleological light. (See thereon also Thompson 2008, p. 90, n. 9: "The selection of apt belief-desire pairs is evidently controlled by

expressly affiliating herself with a Wittgensteinian faction,[60] advances reason-explanation as non-causal context-placing explanation, whereby an action is redescribed and thereby presented in a "context that is more understandable than a description that leaves this context out".[61] She provides the example of a chemistry teacher who writes "c", "a" and "t" on the blackboard, an action that becomes more intelligible in its larger context – her eventually writing not just "cat" but "catalyst": "The 'because' in 'She wrote the letters "c", "a", and "t" because she was writing "catalyst"', then, signals a different pattern of explanation from the causal pattern in which one event follows another".[62] The pattern is that of elucidation of the agential context of an action as intended by the agent.

A similar chord to Tanney's (which itself is reminiscent of Anscombe's *Intention*) is struck with the "analytic Anscombian Aristotelianism" of Thompson's *Life and Action*, in which he argues for "naïve" as opposed to "sophisticated" action-explanation. Where the latter seeks to explain action by recourse to underlying wants or desires (in a way shunned by Wittgenstein), conceiving it as a "movement from inner to outer, [...] from 'desire' to 'action'",[63] the former explains an action by putting it in the context or wider circumstance of another action, where the agent's want or desire emanates from "the progress of the deed itself".[64] Naïve action explanation, in direct response to a "Why?"-question, then takes the form of "I'm doing A because I'm doing B", rather than "... because I want to do B".[65] Albeit such sophisticated explanations of actions are still available (naïve explanations basically transcribable into them), they do not nourish the urge to identify underlying mental states or frame reasons and actions into causal relations.[66]

---

the intelligibility of a purposive rendering of the rationalization; and we are surely supposed to advert to this form in characterizing a causal relation as non-deviant or rationalization-supporting. His [Davidson's] doctrine is not a rejection of practical teleology, but a theory of it.")
60 Albeit Tanney does apparently understand Wittgensteinianism in the generic way which denotes the current of little red books – and especially Melden 1961 – rather than Wittgenstein's own remarks.
61 Tanney 2009a, p. 99.
62 bid., p. 98.
63 Thompson 2008, p. 90.
64 Ibid. This conception of want or desire, therefore, does not need or wish to refer to mental states (as Davidson's does); see also Ibid., pp. 103–105.
65 Examples of Thompson's include: "I am mixing mortar because I am laying bricks" and "I am laying bricks because I am building a monument to the great works of Frege." (Thompson 2008, p. 87)
66 See Thompson 2008, p. 104; see likewise Hacker 2009, pp. 90–91, on a reading of "want" which dissociates it from mental states.

These two basic options are not only compatible but are indeed closely related to each other.[67] Regardless of their specificities, in the light of such accounts of rationalization it is clearly possible to provide viable non-causal conceptions of reasons, including "motivating reasons".[68] If this latter category is construed in a way which is not question-begging against non-causalist accounts, these may well be given renderings according to the two avenues presented above. Motivating reasons may thus be conceived as salient – motivating – considerations,[69] or as contexts from which an agent's motivation, her wants and desires (which are then, to reiterate, not necessarily conceived as mental states) can be read off. The special character of certainty in the case of reasons accrues from the fact that, as it were, "action and explanation are on the same footing. In both cases the person speaks his mind; and there is no puzzle about our ability to say repeatedly what we think about a subject, being a little more explicit the second time."[70] Thus an agent may act with a given outlook, in given circumstances as they present themselves to her, and let the inquirer know about – a relevant part of – that outlook and circumstances when asked about it.

5 Conclusions

Wittgenstein's remarks on the grammars of reasons and causes of actions have to be treated with due care. Although for Wittgenstein reasons are not to be identified with the causes of actions, there are manifold connections between the grammars of both concepts. The distinctness of reasons and causes of action does not preclude a viable Wittgensteinian conception of reasons in general, or of motivating reasons in particular. On the contrary. His remarks on the matter motivate a conception of reasons which is outlook-oriented; duly reflective of

---

67 Differences of these accounts may be aspectual only: where the first approach highlights more the agent, the second highlights more her action; where the first adverts more to something stable (for example, the agent's character), the second adverts more to something dynamic (the action, for example, as it is unfolding).

68 See, for example, variants of the offerings of Hacker 2009, p. 80. Hacker admits inter alia "facts and values, norms and obligations, backward- and forward-looking reasons [past facts, prospective consequences, purposes and goals]" as candidate classes of reasons.

69 For another such example of a conception of motivating reason which does not understand them as mental states – but as facts (i.e. true propositions) – see, for example, Alvarez 2009 and 2010. (It is unclear why Tanney would want to shun such a conception of facts as plausible candidates for reasons. See Tanney 2009a, p. 104).

70 Schroeder 2001, p. 165.

uses and practices involving the supply and demand, the acceptance and dismissal of reasons. Contrary to the received Davidsonian (causalist) conception of reasons, Wittgenstein's conception does not attempt to identify mental states underlying such reasons or suppose agents to refer to such states when engaging with reasons (or to implicitly acknowledge Davidson's conception of reasons). Insofar as a Wittgensteinian conception can thus be conceived as being directed against the sublimation or sophistication of the use of reasons and reason-explanation, it may well be advanced in response to the received Davidsonian tradition.

Alberto Arruda
Intention in the *Investigations*[1]

1

In PI § 591 Wittgenstein makes the following remark:

> Am I to say that any one who has an intention has an experience of tending towards some-
> thing? That there are particular experiences of "tending"? – Remember this case: if one
> urgently wants to make some remark, some objection in a discussion, it often happens that
> one opens one's mouth, draws a breath and holds it; if one then decides to let the objection
> go, one lets the breath out. The experience of this process is evidently the experience of
> tending towards saying something.

In this first part of his remark, Wittgenstein describes what would be the noticing
of a certain kind of interior process that is characteristic for a certain intention.
One of the interesting aspects of this remark is the example Wittgenstein chose.
He speaks of a tendency to talk, without mentioning what that person would
say. The tendency described by Wittgenstein is rather general, a tendency to talk
rather then a tendency to say_____. Of course, when we finish Wittgenstein's
paragraph we find out that he has less hope for this idea of an interior movement
than this quotation seems to indicate. But this set back, as if his attack on every
description that postulates an interior process throughout the *Investigations* had
gone too far, reveals something important. The example describes someone who
is having a discussion, and is therefore in a particular circumstance. But if that
person is noticing a tendency like the one described by Wittgenstein, then she
has to notice what that tendency to talk is about, in the sequence of *that* discussion. This simply means that the conditions of identity cannot be, for the person
experiencing the tendency, as general as the ones Wittgenstein describes. Wittgenstein's description is a description from the point of view of someone who is
watching this person having this tendency, rather than the person herself. I think
it is important that these two levels get confused in the same example. One also

1 I would like to thank Nuno Venturinha for his comments on this paper and to Professor
Miguel Tamen and Nathan Hauthaler for their discussions, which were of great help for writing
this paper. This is a contribution to the FCT-funded project "Wittgenstein's *Philosophical
Investigations*: Re-Evaluating a Project".

notices that his example of an experience of this particular tendency is a description of physical features. (It is only until some lines later that Wittgenstein's example suffers a turn when he says "Anyone who observes me will know that I wanted to ..."). Partially, this confusion shows us Wittgenstein's position regarding this problem. It seems that he holds a place for the notion of "tendency" but not a private one. This notion of "tendency" is dependent on a particular circumstance, and will serve to highlight an aspect about the latter notion. Of course we can, dismissing my claim that this description fuses two different levels, interpret Wittgenstein as saying that the person that has this tendency could say something like: (1) "I am having the tendency to talk". I think it is rather unlikely that someone utters this sentence just like that. Rather it would be expected that the person in question, when asked about what she was going to say answers: (2) "Well, I was thinking about saying that_____". The interesting aspect about (1) is that it can be the answer to the question, "Were you having a tendency to talk?", but this is a very specialized question (one about something you already knew, unless some doubt prevails over the character of those physical movements). As I have said before, it is unlikely for someone to have this tendency without having the tendency to say anything at all. But the example has another aspect: Wittgenstein's *characteristic* description of someone who just gave up on saying what she was about to say. We do want to say, together with Wittgenstein, that this is a characteristic description, but we do suspect that it will not tell us everything about the meaning of people's intentions. This is only because we know that the total sum of these characteristic descriptions of all sorts of tendencies (physical or not), do not give us the key to what people are intending. But Wittgenstein's example, and his fusing of two perspectives in the same example, gives us an insight into how we understand a certain circumstance. Consider the following example: Imagine I am sitting at a table, and there are several people around me. I try to catch someone's attention by looking at that person. After I do so, I look with an inquiring look at some corner of the room. The person's eyes follow my indications, and she turns around to find out that there is nothing noticeable. All of the time I was doing this with the sole intention of conducting an experiment. I had not myself noticed anything about that specific corner. The person that I fooled in my example did understand the situation *well*: she thought I was indicating something. Of course here "to understand well" has a peculiar sense. What we have in the example is indeed an example of the same family as Wittgenstein's example; it stresses what you get when you try to describe a tendency. We see that, since I have fooled this person, she did not, in a sense, get it right. The tension we have here is similar to the ambiguity of the term 'sign'. As Ockham remarked, in a conventional sense of sign, a spoken word is a natural sign of a thing as the barrel-hoop is a sign of wine in a tavern.

The tension lies precisely in this habitual sense of sign, of which our description seems to be a case, and a sense where these signs are constituents involved in our judgments.

Back to my example, we can say that doubt about my actions might even prevail, and after a while this person might ask me what I was looking at in that manner. She would be looking for an answer like in (2). We could even say something like (1) is obvious to her, but there is yet another possibility. She might, after not noticing anything special in that corner of the room, give up, because anything past that situation would be uninteresting to her, as if her interest in my action had expired its validity date. My example gives us two sets of related concepts. First, the characteristic features of a situation or circumstance do not *necessarily* tell us everything about their meaning. They, nonetheless, contribute to it. The way they contribute will have to be worked out properly. Second, the understanding of a particular circumstance is dependent upon the interest someone shows for that particular circumstance. Both these aspects lead to the thought that the identification of a circumstance or situation is a complex one.

2

When I refer to a particular interest in an occasion, I am referring to a competence that can, although not always, be trained. Interest as an activity will develop within a practice. Thus, the notion of interest that is being sketched has to unfold throughout time in the environment of a certain practice if it is to have any application. However, dependence upon practice will not be fully constitutive of interest since there will be a personal element. This personal element can be explained in terms of the variable capacities people have. It is necessary that we have situations, and therefore people capable of being in a position, where they have to have an inquiring interest that is not merely trivial. Of course, non-trivial interest amounts to nothing more than actively producing judgments about one's surroundings. The idea of interest, as it is being used here, serves only to explain how one actively engages in trying to make sense of others' actions (so the use I am making of this concept is a limited one). One does not have an interest in everyone's actions, and certainly not at all times. If you walk down a crowded street, you do not have more than limited interest in all the people around you (perhaps merely avoiding collision with them). Although you could have such an interest, it would of course be terribly demanding.

So, to understand what the circumstances demand presupposes the ability to understand these as entrapping the necessities of their protagonists. As in Wittgenstein's example, that particular configuration of body movements entrapped the necessity to say something. As noted, in Wittgenstein's example we have a very thin relation between certain muscles moving and the meaning of these movements, and Wittgenstein will indeed on PI § 594 talk about these as an "inclination" rather than a "testimony". But Wittgenstein's description has a rather positive tone to it. Since he, nonetheless, maintains that these movements show us a tendency. It is tempting, in a certain Wittgensteinian fashion, to dismiss this idea of a tendency *tout court* as postulating some indescribable interior process. However, this would be incorrectly spelling out Wittgenstein's project. It would avoid what I think is his (last) reconciliatory step between *our* banal conceptions of inner life and what makes these conceptions possible. Even in the case of faking, these movements show us that this person knows how to *mean something* by acting *somehow*. This is a way of displaying his internal grasp of a certain practice (although in my example it is not a very customary one), that is the kind of grasp that makes it possible for someone to have a motive, and so to behave as I described in the example above. The skill that constitutes *acting somehow* is not merely a deliberate use of the customary sense of sign (physical or spoken); it is a more complex skill that might be the expression of knowing that someone will have interest in such a *somehow*. We make Wittgenstein's example out to be dependent on a certain correlation between these two different things (muscles, meanings), and I think rightly so. Wittgenstein expresses this same idea in a more explicit way (in PI § 580) by mentioning the necessity of outer criteria for the understanding of an inner process. But what he is implying by these outer criteria is something that will be connected with how a particular agent comes to form such an inner process. The sort of things that will contribute to this formation will fall into two distinct categories. The first will have to do with learning and teaching, the second with embeddings in situations that cause these inner processes. The second kind explains such things as expectations[2] that are appropriately caused under the pressure of a particular threatening environment. Nevertheless, Wittgenstein is eager to show us how both categories are interdependent.[3] His argument (which is a familiar one) starts by eliciting the discomfort of treating these inner processes as implying duration in time: "Could someone have a feeling of ardent love or hope for the space of one second" and then more importantly "*no matter what* preceded or

---

2 PI § 582.
3 PI § 583.

followed this second?" The answer is no, and the implication is that what precedes and follows it, a particular phenomenon (this term is Wittgenstein's) of which I am necessarily part, makes it possible for me to have such inner processes. So, as said, there is nothing wrong with having a tendency to say something since having such a tendency is elicited and made possible by my surroundings. But the eliciting I am referring to, and we have to keep in mind that this idea arose in connection with Wittgenstein's impatience towards the *interlocutor's* "But you talk as if I weren't really expecting, hoping, *now*", has to explain the particular reaction to the constraints of the environment, not merely that there are some. So Wittgenstein is not really responding to the interlocutor's *now* (and this is not because it is not important, otherwise Wittgenstein would not have written it). Instead, he tries to direct his attention to how it comes about that what is *happening now in him* means something. This will lead us to the first category mentioned above. The next move has to make apparent, not necessarily, how everything that is *in him* has its possibility conditions outside of him. Rather how what is in him now, is, and probably was since he can remember, directed *to* what lies outside of him. That is, not merely that the environment he lives in constrains his thoughts, as in the deliberately obvious case chosen by Wittgenstein of an expectation about something that is about to blow up, but also, how his thoughts make up the environment he lives in (as Wittgenstein is implying in his "... *what* ... followed this second"). So an example of what pertains to the first category would be, for example, someone learning the expression "seriously *meaning* what one says".[4] It is striking that something like this would have an importance that exceeds the inner space it occupies (at least that is what Wittgenstein wants us to wonder at), that something like this would even demand a gesture, or an utterance that would make it apparent. Wittgenstein goes on to introduce, as an aid to the learning of the meaning of such an expression, the gesture of pointing to one's chest. But this pointing cannot be conceived merely as a kind of iconology. Its purpose is precisely to assure someone of something like the interlocutor's *now* (provided one is elucidated about this assurance having nothing to do, in a specific sense, with time nor with location and so excluding it from the family of feelings and tickles).[5] The pointing at one's chest should be a step towards the final reconciliatory step in the argument of the *Investigations*. That is, because unlike the private linguist, the person who learns to point at her chest learns the importance of what can be located in her inner space and the importance of the thoughts she is able to entertain and

---

4 PI § 590.
5 PI § 588.

sustain. So the mistake of the private linguist was not so much that he could point out what was in him, but solely that he was the only one who could point it out, that the possibility of a discernible semantic content of what was *in him* was possible only for him. I hope that now my example seems less obscure. The interest of the person who asks me about what I was possibly directing my attention to, can be seen as an inquiry into what is *in me* (not that being in me is a sufficient condition). It is obvious that her interest seeks to understand the thoughts I was entertaining, but that these were located in particularly me can play an important role. Her interest, say, she knows me very well, might be an interest in the history of my thoughts, or less pompously, an interest in what I usually think. The habitual sense of the movements of which I was a protagonist (in my example) could be completed by an assurance of the type described by Wittgenstein. But, unfortunately, the inquirer came to understand that there was precisely nothing discernible in me, nothing that she could count as backing up the form of the happening she perceived. Here we can ask, together with Wittgenstein, "How does it come out that he has learnt it" to assure someone that he seriously means something? We can answer: he properly uses these movements, or this utterance, or it shows in what he does. But we can add to these: when he successfully passes the inquiry – an inquiry that is brought about by *his* acting in a specific way and my comparison with what is acting in *such and such* a way. If we go back to Wittgenstein's *before* and *after* we see that the assurance that I *"really mean it"* cannot be independent of the environment in which it is embedded, but neither can we miss that by assuring, I conditionally imply the environment of which I am part. Those who together with me form this environment have an interest in the egocentric[6] character of my assurance, much like they might have in the history of my thoughts. Their interest in this egocentric character will make possible the formation of their confidence in my capabilities to exercise certain competences. For instance: the confidence that *I* am capable of continuing *this* series, that *he* is capable of continuing *this* series (thus the spelling out of the interest of others in this egocentric character of the thoughts I am able to sustain will turn out to be their interest in my exercises of freedom). It may seem that these last remarks are very un-Wittgensteinian in spirit. I think

---

6 I am using this term in the literal sense of arising out of a particular person's experience, and not merely as the capacity to have specific perception about a spatial location of which one is part (as for instance Evans, in some passages, as I understand him), although such information will also be included. This usage is then taking everything that is important for a subject to be capable of being a competent agent. That is, not only the capacity for perception but the capacity for a complex kind of perception. Taking a phrase from Evans, "it is not thoughts about the experience that matter, but thoughts about the world" (Evans 1995, p. 158).

they are not: not merely because Wittgenstein assures us that pointing to one's chest should be seen as "psychologically serious",[7] but also because it avoids a harsh conception of person that Wittgenstein would like to avoid. That is, the importance of the banal idea that our thoughts are located in *us*, and that is so because we are embedded in a certain environment upon which we, by necessity, have to impinge. That this is Wittgensteinian in spirit could be shown by bringing to the discussion Wittgenstein's remark about a person to whom it "comes natural to ... understand our order with our explanation as ...".[8] It is absolutely unnecessary to read too much into this remark, when we can maintain plainly that it is possible to make mistakes and these may impact negatively on the environment of which I am part, and that in turn, will constrain me.

3

Now the second part of PI § 591 reads the following:

> Anyone who observes me will know that I wanted to say something and then thought better of it. In *this* situation, that is. – In a different one he would not so interpret my behaviour, however characteristic of the intention to speak it may be in the present situation.

The most striking thing in this remark is Wittgenstein's confidence in the fact that anyone will recognize that I was about to do some *one* thing. I have claimed before that this confidence relies, partially, on the habitual sense of signs, or in this case, on a particular form of a happening that putatively actualizes the knowledge Wittgenstein is confident about. This is so, given the necessary embedding Wittgenstein describes, the embedding that would make possible, and constrain what I could actually do. These particular forms of happenings which are observed depend on particular *doings* which they are actualizations of. Such forms will constitute the environment in which an agent acts and, reciprocally, the possession of a capacity to individuate such forms implies the knowledge of the agent's use of such forms. The habitual sense mentioned before is therefore habituation to such an environment. However there are cases, as in my example, where these forms are not void, but also not constitutive of the habitual use of such forms: they are not proper actualizations. An example

---

7 PI § 589.
8 PI § 185.

of such a mis-actualization would be the form 'pointing to one's chest' that is a false assur*ing*. Here the capacity for individuation might turn out to be insufficient, but such insufficiency calls in turn for an interest that will not be trivial. This is, a more complex form of judgment will be required. This more complex form ([2] in what follows) will be a reflection about a particular agent and his relation to a particular environment.

It is possible to make a list of such forms (in *Intention* Anscombe presents one in § 47 [although her list has two columns that differ significantly, we are interested here in the one on the right]), this list would fulfil the Wittgensteinian project[9] of attempting at a natural history of men (the forerunner of Anscombe's list). It will suffice for us to say the items that would figure in this list would all have the general form: f-ing. This general form could be explained by noticing that these forms of happenings are indispensable in judging and making sense of the doings of which they are actualizations. Otherwise, these doings could not be *positively signified*.[10] This bit of Kantian terminology serves only to bring out the difficulty that arises out of trying to describe, or refer to, a particular doing without referring to it in a physical space and time. Kant's argument, although focusing on a different matter[11] implies a preoccupation with the conception of an object of judgment. Our problem reflects the same issue. Namely, that our object of judgment is a complex one. This is so because an action as a happening will necessarily imply a deictic element in one's judgment: it will occur in a certain place at a certain time by a certain person in a certain environment in a certain way, perhaps reconcilable with other things this person has done, or perhaps in a contrasting way. The impossibility of such separation is in fact the point of Wittgenstein's idea of a natural history of men.[12] The force of his claim arises out of the lack of criteria, given by him, for the inclusion in such a history. His idea is that these items – commanding, questioning, storytelling, chatting – would figure in the same history along with eating, sleeping and so on. But we are able to discern a fundamental difference between these. This difference is acknowledged by Wittgenstein in his "however characteristic of the intention to speak it may be in the present situation". This remark is a consequence of the different interest we have in some of the doings that are part of this list. It is also worth noticing that in his remark, Wittgenstein uses the demonstrative *this* to

---

9 PI § 25.
10 Kant 1974, B311,312/A256. It seems that Kant is concerned here with bringing out the idleness of certain theoretical excesses.
11 The split Noumena/Phaenomena and the characterization of the former as a *Grenzbegriff*.
12 PI § 25.

refer to a situation. This demonstrative has, in this usage, the situation in which the happening is embedded as its object, and it contributes to the differential judgment about the doing in question. We can comment on this more complex interest by considering the following distinction:

(1) S's doing *such and such* movements during t is φ-ing

(2) S's φ-ing during t is *in this situation* ξ-ing

What we have been calling *habitual* is what figures in (1), where a certain string of movements by a subject are identified with a particular form. This type of identification will form the ability to refer to actions; it will be constitutive of the positive signification mentioned before. Of course, this is not saying much yet, and this idea appears in Wittgenstein's argument so that we can be properly warned in what follows. The forms of happenings have certain habitual movements associated to them just in the sense that some of these are merely the form of a physical limit of our bodies. That is, these are no more than a certain way of doing a certain thing we do – so for instance walking implies moving one's legs (unless you are performing the trick of walking on your hands). (2) will be required to accommodate the function the demonstrative is performing in the example. It does no more than to elicit the deictic dependence of these movements on a particular embedding. What it elicits will motivate the idea of interest previously sketched, and it can furthermore include the kind of interest *in* what was described as the egocentric character of thoughts. That is, to take interest in a particular agent as responsible and to which, in turn, his environment responds with particular constrains. These responses take his acting, *in principle*, as a deliberate meaningful participation. To construct such an agent as the possessor of certain thoughts *now*, or at given point in time, will be compulsory to form appropriate responses, be these corrections or further co-operation. In both of these cases, the happenings brought about by an agent and the putative actualizations of which the first are forms, will only be possible if our judgments include in their content the agent as an individual. This was stressed earlier by Wittgenstein in his indication of the impossibility to even hold thoughts in isolation of what can constrain these. This point was made by questioning the interlocutor about the origin of his intentional state, which in turn brought out the important contribution to our judgments about actions of something like: "how does *he* respond to" or "*he* knows about that". That is, these constrains will not be limited to threats of the physical world, but also normative ones. Wittgenstein's 'before and after' is, in part, a continuation of the theme of normativity developed in earlier stages of the *Investigations*, a theme that results from the necessary impinging of agents upon their atmosphere and each other.

The manner of inquiring so far explored is then the obvious reply to the threat of behaviourism (as we find it in PI § 307), since the answer is not to give enface to the unreliability about perceiving certain forms of happening or behaviour and how this throws us off balance. The reply is rather to explain how we recover such balance and how, curiously enough, the perceived forms might be an aid to such recovery.[13] The movement of thought we find in this paragraph is simply an indication of how human cognition of actions proceeds by a specific kind of comparison. This is, how the sensible capacities and the power to act are tightly interwoven and how derivation of knowledge by perceiving some forms of happenings implies estimation regarding what is being done – or interest in this particular agent.[14] This form of judgment (2) will accommodate what Wittgenstein described as the dependence upon the before and after in the sense that the perceived form might be inchoate, a judgment of its full significance might not be possible just by trivial identification. So, the deictic function will accommodate, into one's judgments about S's actions, the changes impinged on his environment throughout time (the background against which one is judging). The importance of the actual movements that one can observe, play an important practical role in our understanding of action. As in the case where two people are having an argument about what exactly one of them did on a particular day: was he simply distracted, or was he avoiding the other person. Such a discussion might be a discussion about the actual movements: "You did turn your face when I entered the room". There are more cases where the actual movements are used to state standards of correctness of a given practice, as in the case of sports.

So our interest to continue one's inquiry about S's action will also lead to judgments of the form (2) in cases where one will have been able to individuate, say, S's omissions, or where we accommodate the significance of this particular

---

13 Wittgenstein's position in PI § 307 is a difficult one. The grammatical fiction he wants to talk about excludes the possibility that he is endorsing a behaviourist position, in the characterization offered by him, which would imply interiority as fiction. But on the other hand, we have his peculiar position that made the threat of such an accusation possible in the first place – is insistence in calling descriptions of certain forms of behaviour *characteristic*. Of course, PI § 591 and the idea about a characteristic description could be read just as paying lip service to a bad piece of argument. But what follows, the advertence that follows, only qualifies the previous assumption. It does no drop it.

14 Wittgenstein is furthermore interested in trying to accommodate the possibility that agents are not omniscient of all the implications of their doings, which only stresses the necessity of appropriate responses by others. PI § 659 is a good example.

φ-ing by S in his personal history. Our interest will also accommodate rectifying *post eventum* judgments as in:

(3) S *was* φ-ing, at t_i, t_i before t_{now} [15]

The spelling out of Wittgenstein's example would then amount to say how the notions that seemed to be untreatable, because they seemed to be doomed to assimilation to interior processes, will be necessary in any positive signification of actions and intentions. This is a move towards Wittgenstein's project: the idea that judgments about others would be embedded in particular situations and times. Given these limitations, the judgments we talked about would have to be extended to judgments about the success of such actions, things like: S has φ-ed.

As a conclusion one could look at Wittgenstein's thought experiment in PI § 420. This thought experiment, constructed to be unsuccessful,[16] is meant to show the unavoidable character of the embeddings, which he will talk about later. This is so because it seems, at first, that you could picture everyone around you as being an automaton. These machines would still be acting, they would still be walking, looking, etc., and the trick would be to lead us to think that the mere possibility of such an image is showing something essential to us about action. (Nevertheless, Wittgenstein is unable to imagine them without a fixed look as in a trance, which is to say, as if something was wrong with them. Perhaps he could say something like: "He is walking" but say if this thing bumped into another, he could not say, "he reacted badly" or "he was exceptionally nice about it"). It has to be noticed that the thought experiment concludes with an illustration of a reduction: to see the cross-pieces of a window as a swastika/to see people as automatons. This critical remark should remind us of the earlier discussion regarding tendencies and also that there have to be subjects in the embeddings that turned out to be so important. That one could attempt to make such a reduction will lead to the excesses Wittgenstein famously described in PI § 621 (excesses that Kant was also worried about: the positive and negative

---

15 (3) will differ from (1) and (2) since it cannot be used in a demonstrative act of reference, because of its time restrictions. Of course what matters her is not the capacity for mere recollection, but rather the judgment about the significance of a past event.

16 The thought experiment concludes with and idea about a limit case *(Grenzfall)*. That is, an idea about a certain movement of thought that transfigures, somehow, the object that it takes at first in. The analogy with perception is of course an indication of the importance of the perceived object in the accumulation of knowledge about it. After all, in a way, whatever limit you decide to establish it has to play, partially, along with the possibilities set by the objected being limited.

variety of signification). The question he asks, "what is left if I subtract the fact that my arm goes up from the fact that I raise my arm?", does not have to be answered. The thought experiment of PI § 420 is in this way a description of such an attempt, an attempt that will not answer the question but instead reduce it to something else that is not our subject. Now, forms of happenings cannot be reduced to tendencies and vice versa. The subtlety of Wittgenstein's example was that no reduction will be philosophically profitable – try to describe the one and you will see the other. However, sometimes our interest in others will reveal mis-actualizations to us. These will be dependent precisely on the things we could observe, and in referring to such mis-actualizations we shall be referring to whatever the agent in question is doing.

Emiliano La Licata
Propagating Meaning. Kauffman Reads Wittgenstein: A New Interpretative Paradigm?

1 Wittgenstein, Complexity Theorists and Meaning as Use

The work I have developed over the last few years partly belongs to the field of studies dealing with the reception of Wittgenstein's philosophy and in part tries to develop insights belonging to complexity theorists regarding the Austrian philosopher. Some of these theorists readily refer to Wittgenstein. This is not just by chance, or even because of his reputation, but because they have strong empathy with the Viennese philosopher for deep theoretical reasons I would like to discuss here.

The first mention of Wittgenstein is made by Prigogine and Stengers:

> Dans son introduction à la Critique de la raison pure, Kant dénonçait l'illusion de l'idéa-lisme platonicien: de même que la colombe, sentant la résistance que l'air oppose à son vol, pourrait s'imaginer qu'elle volerait mieux dans la vide, Platon crut, quittant le monde sensible et les obstacles qu'oppose ce monde à l'entendement, pouvoir se risquer, sur les ailes des idées, dans le vide de l'entendement pur. De manière quelque peu similaire, Wit-tgenstein dénonça, dans *Philosophical Investigations*, l'illusion sur laquelle fut construit son *Tractatus*: celle d'un rapport univoque entre l'essence, logique, du langage, et l'ordre a priori du monde. Le présupposé selon lequel la langage répond à la pureté cristalline de la logique nous situe sur une surface glacée "où il n'y pas de friction, et où les conditions sont donc, en un certain sens, idéales, mais où, justement pour cette raison, nous sommes aussi incapables de marcher. Nous voulons marcher: aussi avons-nous besoin de la friction. Revenons au sol rugueux! (*Philosophical Investigations*, § 107)".[1]

It is a fleeting mention, not fully reasoned but suggests that the two great complexity theorists attribute a dynamic view of semantics to the *Philosophical Investigations*. They cite § 107 in which Wittgenstein criticizes the idea of an ideal language with the help of a metaphor: the crystalline purity of an ideal

---

1 Prigogine & Stengers 1988, p. 177.

language lacks movement. He makes it clear that, on the contrary, he wants to move through the language and the activities which are interwoven within it:

> We have got on to slippery ice where there is no friction, and so, in a certain sense, the conditions are ideal; but also, just because of that, we are unable to walk. We want to walk: so we need friction. Back to the rough ground![2]

Reading Prigogine and Stengers, one realizes that, starting from their dynamic and evolutive philosophy of nature, they believe that the semantics of the *Philosophical Investigations* do not interpret meaning as a static object but as a dynamic process. It seems they affirm that, according to Wittgenstein, meaning is neither a material nor immaterial object that lies in reality or in an internal psychological and private world, but is a constructive and often creative process that takes place within the language game.

As is known, according to analytically orientated interpretations, Wittgenstein's philosophy struggles to be associated with a philosophy of the dynamics of meaning, and never with concepts such as evolution and history. According to analytical interpretation, it would be a hermeneutic heresy to associate Wittgenstein's philosophy with some theories of becoming. Indeed, the most authoritative interpretations of Wittgenstein's *Philosophical Investigations* make the Austrian either a philosopher of common sense[3] or a sceptical philosopher.[4]

Yet when Prigogine and Stengers interpret Wittgenstein's later philosophy, on the basis of a simple mention in the *Philosophical Investigations*, they tend towards the idea that the semantics of the language game have dynamic characteristics.

Indeed, what can we intuitively understand from the now abused quotation *The meaning of a word is its use in the language*?[5] Without further analysis, it tells us that:

Meaning is not an object but a process.[6]

Meaning is not an object or material - a thing in the world – or immaterial – a psychological or platonic entity.

---

2 PIr § 107.
3 Kenny 1973.
4 Cavell 1979; Kripke 1982.
5 PIr § 43.
6 On "process", see PIr § 7.

This view of meaning is not without consequences. With this theoretical shift, from objects to processes, it reveals a dynamic contingent and relational dimension of semantics which therefore has two faces:

> The face of social connection. In fact, only social dynamics develop meaning. Within a language game, speakers work together to build meaningful linguistic forms.

> The face of linguistic contingency. Because meaning is a performative gesture, it lives in the linguistic contingency of the event. Meaning is no longer a substance but an event of reality.

To summarize, meaning is not a *thing* that can be found somewhere, it is not a concept, thought, or definition, not an object of the senses, psychology or reality, it is not an *object*. With a spontaneous and peremptory gesture, Wittgenstein's definition of meaning moves the level of semantics from the world of *objects* into the world of *processes* and *actions*, and into the busy arena of *relations*. Meaning is a *movement* that connects and involves people and things in a contingent situation. In my opinion this is why Prigogine and Stengers are interested in the semantics of Wittgenstein's late philosophy.

It seems that Wittgenstein, with his strange definition of meaning, wants to suggest that obviously thought and reference to reality and psychological processes are involved in the process of meaning. However, beyond all this, there is a higher level of semantics which includes these elements and which has inherently relational and dynamic characteristics. By linking use to meaning, Wittgenstein seems to want to emphasize the dynamic relationship above anything else. In fact, language use requires a *context*, a *situation*, a more or less declared purpose, and one or more speakers in a given spatial-temporal location which are linked to a semantic relationship. In a language game, there is a semantic organization related to meaning-use which includes many elements which must interact together during a series of events.

According to Kauffman, this semantic organization produces linguistic creativity. Let us see what it is.

2 Kauffman's Nature Philosophy

Stuart Kauffmann is the complexity theorist who is most inspired by Wittgenstein's later philosophy. The title of Kauffman's book *Investigations* is, on Kauffman's own admission, a reference to Wittgenstein's *Philosophical Investigations*.[7] He does this for many reasons and from different viewpoints that I wish to expose and, if possible, extend in order to build a bridge between Kauffman's science of complexity and Wittgenstein's philosophical reflections on meaning.

In the preface to *Investigations*, Kauffman immediately cites Wittgenstein in an attempt to mirror the Viennese philosopher. Just as Wittgenstein in the *Philosophical Investigations* breaks with the philosophical tradition of logical atomism which he had learned in his youth, so Kauffman wants to trace the line of a philosophy/science of life in order to surpass forms of thought which explain the phenomenon of life in atomistic and reductionist terms.

Kauffman's creative and radical constructivism is a philosophy of autonomous agents which, performing thermodynamic cycles, produce work that propagates itself. They manipulate the world to their own advantage and construct constraints to exploit energy for self-reproduction. They measure and seek new sources of energy; they create constraints to channel energy and make it useful for the propagation of more work.

From the thermodynamic point of view, autonomous agents produce organization using low entropy (raw material) energy sources. This energy is converted into useful *work* that generates further work and further organization, then it dissipates irreversibly and becomes high entropy (dissipating energy which is no longer usable) once it has been used and transformed into propagating work.

The concept of entropy is fundamental to understand Kauffman's reinterpretation of the *Philosophical Investigations*, so let us give it a basic definition. What is entropy? Entropy is a measure of disorder within a given system: that is, of how much energy is *disorganized* or in a chaotic form. For example, the entropy of a room is said to increase if furniture is set alight and the energy is transformed into heat and dispersed by combustion. Entropy is the measure of the second law of thermodynamics, which states that the energy disorder of any closed system tends to increase and point to a uniform equilibrium.

Everything moves towards entropy eventually. So, low entropy means forms of energy that can be used to construct propagating work. High entropy means forms of energy which are dissipated and no longer usable.

---

7 Kauffman 2000, p. ix.

In short, Kauffman's idea is that autonomous agents seek and transform energy sources into propagating work with the purpose of self-reproduction and prospering in the world. They construct an organization of life following this circular pattern:

Low Entropy
↓
Creative Work
↓
High Entropy

Since they produce differing forms of life, autonomous agents are constantly creative. They work inventively to reproduce themselves and create innovative forms of existence that stimulate further organization which expands and propagates in an unpredictable way, not predictable a priori. The autonomous agents modify the environment to their own advantage creating unpredictable forms of life, and also creating the conditions to release new forms of energy which diversify the biosphere.

> We cannot predefine the configuration space, variables, laws, initial and boundary conditions of a biosphere.[8]

Not being able to predefine configuration space in the biosphere, the working process of autonomous agents is inherently creative because it leads to something new and unexpected.

Proof of the inherent unpredictability of the creativity of autonomous agents and of the biosphere is testified by Darwinian pre-adaptations which found a function in contextual and contingent conditions which are no longer repeatable.

> By "preadapted" Darwin did not mean that some intelligence crafted the preadaptation. He simply meant that an incidental feature with no selective significance in one environment might turn out to have selective significance in another environment.
> Preadaptations are abundant in biological evolution. When one occurs, typically, *a novel functionality comes into existence in the biosphere* – and thus in the universe. [...] Now I come to my radical question. Do you think you could say ahead of time, or finitely prestate, all possible Darwinian preadaptations of all species alive today? Or could you prestate all possible human preadaptations?
> I have found no one who believes the answer is yes. Well all appear to believe the answer is no.[9]

---

8 Kauffman 2000, p. 22.
9 Kauffman 2008, p. 132.

3 Kauffmenstein: Wittgenstein as a Philosopher of Semantic Emergentism

Referring to Wittgenstein, Kauffman writes:

> Indeed, part of why I have so blatantly borrowed Wittgenstein's title, without my presumption to similar intellectual stature, is that there is a parallel between Wittgenstein's abandonment of the Tractatus and my growing awareness of knowing as living a language game [...]. Life and language-games seem persistently open to radical innovations that cannot be deduced from previous categories and concepts.[10]

And he continues:

> Wittgenstein invented the concept of a "language game", a co-defined cluster of concepts that carve up the world in some new way [...]. Wittgenstein's point is that one cannot, in general, reduce statements at a higher level to a finitely specified set of necessary and sufficient statements at a lower level. Instead, the concepts at the higher level are co-defined. We understand "guilty of murder" within the legal language game and thus in terms of a co-defining cluster of concepts concerning the features noted above - law, legal responsibility, evidence, trial, jury. Useful new concepts arise in co-defining clusters. [...]; hence, the web of concepts touches, articulates, discriminates, and categorizes the world.[11]

Kauffman interprets Wittgenstein as a philosopher of semantic emergentism. He argues that:

> *Within a language game, speakers creatively produce concepts that cannot be reduced to a set of statements that are out of the language game.*

> *Every linguistic act, every statement, every naming act is a creative act because it constructs semantic forms, puts parts together and produces something potentially new which is propagated within the game.*

> *The language game is the place where creative semantic gestures produce connections constituting a semantic embroidery, a semantic pattern that develops in this co-defining and environment manipulating cluster called Sprachspiel.*

---

10 Kauffman 2000, p. 50.
11 Ibid., p. 52.

Now, let us read some paragraphs of the *Philosophical Investigations*, remembering the general pattern noted above in order to understand how the semantic creative process discussed by Kauffman works:

> *Semantic Entropy*
> ↕ ↕
> *Creative Work*

4 Philosophical Investigations §§ 49 and 6: Semantic Entropy

Let us see first of all what semantic entropy can mean in the *Philosophical Investigations*. Let us remember that semantic entropy is semantic disorder, something that has little or no meaning.

In §49, Wittgenstein criticizes the idea that the meaning of a word is an object in the world, and also the idea that, by naming a thing, we have given meaning to a word:

> Naming is not yet a move in the language-game - any more than putting a piece in its place on the board is a move in chess. One may say: with the mere naming of a thing, nothing has yet been done. Nor has it a name except in a game.[12]

Naming a thing does not produce any meaning, because it lacks use of the name in the language game that attributes a meaning to the statement.

So, let us imagine having a list of names denoting things. From a semantic point of view, what are we going to do with this list out of the language game and out of the linguistic work that happens in language-games?

> With the mere naming of a thing, nothing has yet been done [*Mit dem Benennen eines Dings ist noch nichts getan*].[13]

Nichts, Nothing. In thermodynamic terms, we only have low entropy – semantic raw material – that must be used and manipulated creatively in language-games. Indeed, what is a list of names out of the language game? It is only *semantic*

---

12 PIr § 49.
13 Ibid.

entropy (semantic disorder) that must be used in the game. Out of the language game, names and statements are linguistic forms that must be used and worked to acquire a meaning.

Following this interpretative line, let us read § 6 of the *Philosophical Investigations*. What is an ostensive expression *without* the contextual use that takes place within language-games?

> It may be anything, or nothing [*Kann alles Mögliche sein, oder nichts*].[14]

Again, *nichts, nothing*: semantic entropy. Ostensive expressions out of the language game that manipulates them are only low entropy, semantic disorder waiting to become linguistic work, linguistic propagating work that is connected to other semantic gestures within a language game.

5 Philosophical Investigations § 47: Linguistic Work

Now let us see what happens within a language game. Starting from semantic entropy, what is the linguistic work that speakers do?

> If I tell someone without any further explanation, "What I see before me now is composite", he will legitimately ask, "What do you mean by 'composite'? For there are all sorts of things it may mean" – the question "Is what you see composite?" makes good sense if it has already established what kind of compositeness - that is, which particular use of this word is in question.[15]

What does the word "composite" mean in a language game? I must have a regulated use of the word "composite" to give it sense, or I have to immediately invent a use of the word so that it makes sense to my interlocutor.

In thermodynamic terms, I have to immediately construct a new semantic form with defining work. Otherwise I have to show a semantic form already known via linguistic work. This is in order to connect with my interlocutor to create a semantic pattern in the middle of a semantic organization, and thus

---

14 PIr § 6.
15 PIr § 47.

avoid semantic work collapsing into entropic forms: nonsense, misunderstandings, confused communication.

In a language game, autonomous agents, the speakers, construct propagating semantic organization: semantic webs that arise via semantic work using the linguistic material available. The thermodynamics of the speakers is soon clear in the *Philosophical Investigations*: there is a flexibly regulated language game that takes part in this. Taking part in a language game means:

working semantically, producing collective linguistic creativity;

producing statements linking up to the general context to construct a semantic pattern;

using known ad hoc semantic forms and already regulated uses;

constructing new semantic forms from scratch, defining and redefining them and thus the concepts and the linguistic uses that are helpful within language-games.

6 Philosophical Investigations §§ 29 and 50: Linguistic Creativity

As seen, linguistic work is also *potentially creative*. Within language-games the speaker's activity produces continually creative acts that arise within the relationships established when we are playing. Let us see some examples of this linguistic creativity.

In §29 of the *Philosophical Investigations*, there is a fine example of this emerging linguistic creativity. What is the ultimate definition of the word "two"? We could say, for example, that "this number is called two" is a correct definition because by introducing the word "number" to define "two", we are able to assign a place in language to the word "two". However, Wittgenstein argues that by doing so we have not really solved anything; on the contrary, our problems have only just begun.

We must define the word "number" to give a sense to the statement "this number is called 'two'", and we must define it with other words that must in turn be defined with further words. So theoretically we can spend our entire existence

looking for ultimate definitions (a boring job for someone like Wittgenstein).[16]
All of this makes no sense to Wittgenstein in his later years. He explains:

> Whether the word "number" is necessary in an ostensive definition of "two" depends on whether without this word the other person takes the definition other than I wish.
> And that will depend on the circumstances under which it is given, and on the person I give it to. And how he 'takes' the explanation shows itself in how he uses the word explained.[17]

When do we use the word "number" to define "two"? When we have to construct a semantic pattern that we need to make a move within the language game, for example, when we have to explain to our interlocutor what we mean.

In that situation, after listening to the interlocutor, we begin to elaborate a strategy of semantic cooperation suitable to construct a structure with contextual sense. This is done to reach a precise goal in *that* game, with *that* person, in *that* space-time that is *here and now*. This strategy is useful to avoid entropic forms such as misunderstandings or confusion. Depending on the situation and on the interlocutor, our linguistic creativity is exercised in constructing semantic forms appropriate to contexts and audience. These semantic forms that we create are:

> *not predictable a priori because the situations and the contexts change continually and we cannot specify all of these in advance;*

> *linguistic use is thus bound to a set of variables that cannot be pre-defined and that allow the creative skills of the speaker to express themselves in an improvised manner.*

In § 50 of the *Philosophical Investigations*, we can find another example of radical linguistic creativity starting from semantic entropy. In this paragraph, Wittgenstein argues that by naming something we set a linguistic paradigm which we use within a language game.

By naming a thing, we construct a semantic object in virtual time (whose existence is not material because it exists in the language) and real (because it is part of this socially shared reality). We use this semantic paradigm to achieve something within a language game. So, the standard metre measurement kept in Paris, *das Urmeter*, is a semantic invention, at the same time virtual and real, with which and via which we play our game of measuring. Constructing the Paris

---

16 Monk 1990.
17 PIr § 29.

standard metre and naming it, we have constructed an artificial object and we have brought it into language.

Doing so, according to Wittgenstein, we have carried out a *constructive and creative process* because with that artificial and semantic object, we play our language game concerning the human practice of measuring.[18]

Linguistic practices and language-games, reality and language are linked in this form of radical and creative constructivism of our form of life that manipulates the so-called reality with the purpose of making something out of it and whose actions are manifested in language-games, within which we construct virtual and real semantic objects that are needed to carry out typically human practices, practices of our form of life.

7 Conclusions

By introducing the notion of language game, Wittgenstein abandons the philosophy of logical atomism. A statement is co-defined in a language game, its meaning is determined in a language game. There are a lot of concepts that construct a context defining the meaning of the statements. These mutually defining concepts, interdependent on one another, are fundamental to give a semantic frame to the meaning of the statement. Besides, we cannot translate out of a language game any necessary and sufficient set of statements about simple atomic elements (logical atomism).

Therefore, Wittgenstein's emergentist philosophy is explained in these two points:

> *(1) The meaning of a statement is co-defined in a language game: rules and praxis give a semantic frame to the statement.*

> *(2) The language game manipulates environment and constructs, invents a ritual reality, a semantic and systemic praxis characterizing the human form of life.*

Point (2) is very innovative and interesting. Let us say something more about it. Meaning is an emerging relational web, collective and alchemical (it binds and transforms semantic objects), which the speakers construct and reconstruct in

---

18 Plr § 50.

language-games. This is Kauffman's interpretation of the later Wittgenstein. By working collectively, speakers put semantic parts together, connect them and create new patterns in a semantic plot which intertwines, splits off and reconnects in a different way every time. Talking is performing creative acts in a common praxis (language game); we have just seen at least three creative acts in the above-mentioned paragraph of the *Philosophical Investigations*:

> *first creative act: from semantic entropy, we invent a virtual and real object that we name;*[19]

> *second creative act: we use that virtual and real object to play a language game and, moreover, we put it in relation with other objects which speakers bring into the game;*[20]

> *third creative act: we build semantic and contextual objects while we play, to harmonize and propagate semantic organization and thus avoid semantic entropy.*[21]

Maybe Kauffman opens the way for a new interpretative paradigm that interprets Wittgenstein as an emergentist philosopher. According to this interpretation:

> *There is a semantic pattern that the speakers build creatively in a language game. Every time this is different and with new, innovative and unpredictable outcomes.*

> *This semantic pattern that emerges from the speaker's collective work is an expanding pattern, circularly defined, re-defined, co-defined and subject to entropy.*

It is a *propagating semantic organization*, constantly creative and subject to entropy. Playing is performing constantly creative acts, collectively constructing a semantic pattern against the background of semantic entropy in a different way each time.

---

19 PIr § 50.
20 PIr §§ 47–49.
21 PIr § 29.

Constantine Sandis
Understanding the Lion for Real

"Narnia, Narnia, Narnia, awake. Love. Think. Speak. Be walking trees. Be talking beasts. Be divine waters."
It was of course the Lion's voice. The children had long felt sure that he could speak: yet it was a lovely and terrible shock when it did.

C.S. Lewis, The Magician's Nephew, 1955

We gazed at each other his implacable yellow eye in the red halo of fur
Waxed rheumy on my own but he stopped roaring and bared a fang greeting.
I turned my back and cooked broccoli for super on an iron gas stove

Allen Ginsberg, "The Lion for Real", 1958

1 Introduction

Is it an accident that one of the most quoted remarks by Wittgenstein is also one of the least understood? I do not propose to answer this question by conducting an investigation into our reasons for quoting,[1] though such a study would not be irrelevant to certain aspects of the one below. My focus shall instead be on the contrast between the original philosophical context of § 327 of the typescript previously known as "Part II" of *Philosophical Investigations* (from here onwards PPF § 327) and some of the conditions surrounding its incredibly muddled reception.

The published version of the remark in question is:

Wenn ein Löwe sprechen könnte, wir könnten ihn nicht verstehn.[2]

In her otherwise influential English translation of what became known as *Philosophical Investigations* (parts I and II), Elizabeth Anscombe renders the claim as follows:

---

1 For socio-historical explanations see Finnegan 2011.
2 PI, p. 223/PPF § 327.

If a lion could talk, we could not understand him.[3]

On the face of it the remark seems absurd and commentators have obligingly voiced numerous complaints against it. These frequently revolve around the thought that Wittgenstein did not know the first thing about animals:

> Wittgenstein once claimed, "If a lion could talk, we would not understand him." He seemed to assume that because the lion's consciousness is so different from ours, even if there were a spoken lion language, it would be too alien for us to understand. However, lions and many other animals do indeed communicate in their own ways, and if we make an effort to understand their communications, we can learn much about what they are saying. If Wittgenstein had gotten off his couch and actually watched animals, he might agree.[4]

> "If a lion could talk, we could not understand him," the philosopher Ludwig Wittgenstein once said. "It's clear that Wittgenstein hadn't spent much time with lions", commented the gambler and conservationist John Aspinall.[5]

> Wittgenstein's too-often quoted aphorism [...] is implausible because lions, after all, are social mammals, predators, cousins of the familiar cat who has no difficulty speaking to us and being understood. Another remark of Wittgenstein's is more apposite: "what is the natural expression of an intention? – Look at a cat when it stalks a bird, or a beast when it wants to escape" [PI § 647]. If Wittgenstein could not understand that cat, how could he interpret it as "stalking"?[6]

But things are not so simple. One question is whether "talk" is the correct rendering of "sprechen", or whether Wittgenstein might have had something like "speak" in mind. It is difficult to ascertain if his decision not to use the more colloquial "reden" instead was more stylistic than semantic, the two German terms being closer in meaning than the English ones. At any rate, the issue cannot be

---

3 PI, p. 223e. All other quotations from the *Investigations* are from the revised 4th edition, unless otherwise noted.

4 Bekoff 2000, p. 38.

5 Gray 2002, pp. 52–53.

6 Clark 1997, pp. 145–146; cf. Clark 1991, p. 92. But see also Anscombe (1963, p. 5), in which she writes: "Intention appears to be something that we can express, but which brutes (which, e.g. do not give orders) can *have, though lacking any distinct expression of intention. For a cat's* movements in stalking a bird are hardly to be called an expression of intention. One might as well call a car's stalling the *expression of its being about to stop. Intention is unlike* emotion in this respect, that the expression of it is purely conventional; we might say linguistic if we will allow certain bodily movements with a conventional meaning to be included in language. Wittgenstein seems to me to have gone wrong in speaking of the 'natural expression of an intention'." (Emphasis in original; for critical exegesis see Moran and Stone 2009, esp. p. 135.)

settled in advance, without philosophical prodding. Another question is what the exact referent of "we" is here, assuming there is one at all. I shall be attending to these in due course. I wish to begin, however, with a comment on two alternative translations of "könnten...nicht".

A surprising number of writers (approximately three-hundred and fifty of them) attribute to Wittgenstein the considerably weaker assertion that if a lion could talk or speak we *would not* understand him or it.[7] These include Annette C. Baier, Marc Bekoff, Margaret Boden, Stephan Budiansky, Marcia Cavell, Stephen R. Clark, John Dupré, Douglas R. Hofstadter, Brian McGuinness, Iris Murdoch, D. Z. Philips, and D. J. Richter.[8] In addition, H. O. Mounce, Roger Scruton, A. N. Wilson, and more than fifty others opt for the more formal, but otherwise identical, "should not".[9] Both sets largely believe themselves to be quoting directly from Anscombe's translation,[10] a fact which points towards a potential case of collective misremembering.

There are two obvious factors which may (together or alone) help to explain this selective amnesia, though no doubt there are other contenders:

(i) The claim has been taken out of context.
(ii) Even in its weaker guise, the remark is frequently mocked and rejected as outright false.

I shall be arguing that these two factors go hand in hand since the remark is only rendered implausible if taken to be a statement about either (a) lions specifically or (b) wild animals in general, and such mis-readings ignore the philosophical context in which the remark occurs. It is worth pointing out, at this point, that none of this is being offered as a defence of Anscombe. In fact, to anticipate, I later make a case for the revisions recently made to her translation by Joachim

---

7 Google searches reveal that over two-hundred and twenty books, one-hundred and thirty different papers, and countless blogs etc. (totalling at approximately five percent of the total number of quotations) have "would not" or "wouldn't". One out of four would-notters mistakenly (and tellingly) also translate "ihn" as "it" rather than "him", in contrast to only one out of fifty-five could-notters (though part of the explanation for the latter statistic will be that many of these are quoting Anscombe accurately).
8 Baier 1985, p. 14, Bekoff 2007, p. 38, Boden 1981, Budiansky 1998, Cavell 1996, p. 129, Clark 1991, p. 92, Dupré 2002, p. 232, Hofstadter 1979, McGuinness 2002, p. 221, Murdoch 1993, Philips 2004, p. 135, and Richter 2004.
9 Mounce 1989, p. 159, Scruton 1976, p. 94, and Wilson 2004, p. 152.
10 The few which omit to reference it offer no explicit challenge to it either.

Schulte and Peter Hacker. First, however, we must determine what the remark is actually about.

Consider Thomas Nagel's justification for choosing bats as the stars of his famous paper "What is it like to be a bat?":

> I have chosen bats instead of wasps or flounders because if one travels too far down the phylogenetic tree, people gradually shed their faith that there is experience there at all. Bats, although more closely related to us than those other species, nevertheless present a range of activity and a sensory apparatus so different from ours that the problem I want to pose is exceptionally vivid (though it certainly could be raised with other species). Even without the benefit of philosophical reflection, anyone who has spent some time in an enclosed space with an excited bat knows what it is to encounter a fundamentally *alien* form of life.[11]

The criteria for a being counting as alien here are primarily *behavioural* in a superficial sense unconnected with ethology or physiological studies. Similarly, the earliest occurrence of the lion remark in Wittgenstein's *Nachlass* is followed by the words "It is puzzling to us due to a certain behaviour",[12] and there is no reason to think that "Er" does not refer to the lion here.

It need not be pointed out that Nagel's paper is not a paper about bats but about the nature of consciousness. Similarly, I wish to suggest, Wittgenstein's remark is not about lions (or wild animals in general) but about the nature of *understanding*, and its relation to the behaviour of those we understand. Wittgenstein, on this account, takes himself to be presenting us with a case in which understanding would no longer be present, despite certain superficial behavioural similarities to cases in which understanding is not in doubt (the lion speaks, or at the very least talks). *Prima facie*, the lion seems like a good contender of an "alien form of life" for such a role. It is not as close to the average human as, say, a cat or a dog. *Pari passu*, it is not as "easy" to understand it. But nor is the lion so far removed from us so as to justify the suspicion that there might not be anything there at all for us to understand, as would be the case with a beetle or a fly. It is hardly surprising, then, that animal lovers confronted with the remark find it less persuasive than do those whose experience with animals is limited.[13] Hence also the sarcastic retort of the lion tamer who already presumes to understand the lion: "you mean I would cease to understand him?"[14]

---

11 Nagel 1974, p. 435, emphasis in the original.
12 MS 167, pp. 12v-13r.
13 See also Beardsmore 1996, p. 41, Gaita 2002, pp.18–20, and Osborne 2007, p. 70.
14 Of course the lion's sudden use of language could shock the puzzled trainer into losing his or her previous understanding of it.

The extent to which the knowledge and abilities of experts is relevant to Wittgenstein's remark partly depends on whether "we" here refers to all members of the human race or, as I implied above and shall soon present some evidence for, to the average person who is not an animal trainer or behavioural scientist. It equally depends on whether Wittgenstein is claiming that the "we" in question could never understand the talking lion, or merely that they would not understand it but *could*, should they undertake the relevant training. Either way – even if the very claim that Wittgenstein intended to make turns out to be factually false – this would not detract from what he is trying to do. Just as the force of Nagel's argument regarding the nature of consciousness does not rest on any empirical findings relating to bat experience, so Wittgenstein's point about the limits of understanding does not stand or fall with any ethological facts about lion behaviour.[15] In both examples, the form of life in question can easily be replaced with a 'higher' or "lower' one until we are happy with the claim that the chosen animal's way of life is sufficiently alien to ours.

More tentatively, there are plausible literary causes of the lion remark. One is the spectacled yawning Lion in Lewis Carroll's *Through the Looking Glass*, depicted by John Tenniel as standing on two feet. He asks Alice if she is animal – or vegetable – or mineral, insists on a fair portion of plum cake, and calls the Unicorn whom he fights for the King's crown a "chicken". Another is L. Frank Baum's turn of the century fairy-tale *The Wonderful Wizard of Oz*, featuring a cowardly lion who converses in English with various beings including humans, a tin woodman, and a scarecrow.[16] In William W. Denslow's accompanying illustrations the lion looks ordinary, but it is anthropomorphized in the 1939 musical film.[17] The final possible influence, of course, is C. S Lewis' *The Lion, the Witch and the Wardrobe*. Like the cowardly lion of Oz, Lewis' lion, Aslan is presented to us as a normal English speaker (albeit one whose style is highfalutin) and depicted – in the accompanying illustrations by Pauline Baynes – as an animal.

---

15 Similarly, the ethical lessons of ancient and monastic tales about intelligent beasts do not hang upon the scientific accuracy of the stories (see Osborne 2007, pp. 138 and 149).

16 A key theme of the book is that the lion is cowardly even though he regularly acts in the face of fear, the tin woodman is tender yet has no heart, and the scarecrow wise but literally brainless. Baum's writing chimes nicely with the thought of the later Wittgenstein, who saw thought and feeling as abilities that were conceptually independent of the possession of any material states. In the sequel, *Ozma of Oz*, Dorothy also comes across a mechanical man called "Tik-Tok" who "Thinks, Speaks, Acts, and Does Everything but Live" (Baum 1907, p. 43; cf. PIr § 281 and Matthews 1977).

17 The lion retains this form in the recent West End musical, in contrast to the dog who (as in the book) only tries to communicate with Dorothy by barking.

Though not published until 1950, it was written between 1939 and 1949, thus overlapping with the 1946–1949 period in which "Part II" of the *Investigations* was written). Wittgenstein's lion remark was first recorded in November 1948.[18]

It is likely that Wittgenstein found the very supposition of these English-speaking lions one could converse with as akin to the sort of nonsense we find in Edward Lear's poetry, various fairy tales, as well as other parts of the work of Carroll, Baum, and Lewis:

> "But in a fairy tale a pot too can see and hear!" (Certainly; but it *can* also talk).
> "But a fairy tale only invents what is not the case; it does not talk *nonsense*, does it?" — It's not as simple as that. Is it untrue or nonsensical to say that a pot talks? Does one have a clear idea of the circumstances in which we'd say of a pot that it talked? (Even a nonsense poem is not nonsense in the same way as the babble of a baby.)[19]

Whether or not any particular utterance about a speaking lion is nonsensical depends on the context in which it is uttered and Wittgenstein's remark is perhaps best interpreted as the conceptual or "grammatical" claim that there is no such thing as a speaking lion which "we" could or could not understand.[20] On such an outlook, our failure to understand the speaking lion would not be on a par with that of a Greek person's failure to understand an Austrian. To give just one anticipatory example, we might fail to understand the lion because do not even recognize that it has a language. As we shall see, this may be so even if the lion is speaking in words, as opposed to roars and growls.

---

18 Some months before, on 2 February, Anscombe had debated Lewis on the subject of miracles at the Oxford Socratic Club. For accounts of this encounter and its aftermath see Reppert 2005 and Wolfe 2011.

19 PIr § 282, emphasis in the original.

20 If it is nonsense to say that we could understand a speaking lion then it is arguably also nonsense to deny it (see Baker and Hacker 2009).

2 If a Lion Could Speak, Would It Sound like Liam Neeson?

Baker and Hacker claim that a speaking creature with the appearance of a lion would not be a lion at all. The point is reminiscent of Erich Fried's poem, *Definition*:

> A dog
> that dies
> and knows
> that it dies
> like a dog
>
> and who can say
> that it knows
> that it dies
> like a dog
>
> is a man.[21]

On this view, to imagine a lion *speaking* is to imagine a human being which is merely shaped like a wild animal:

> Of course, in a fairy tale a lion may speak. But then, as in *The Wizard of Oz*, the Lion is really a human being "in the shape of a lion" (imagine the famous film, but with a real lion in the role of the Lion).[22]

In the case of *Narnia*, imagining a real lion in such a role is exactly what the film-makers have done,[23] thus keeping more closer to the vision of the original

---

21 Fried 1964. The translation is Georg Rapp's, as quoted by Hacker (1996, pp. 413–414) in relation to PIr § 650.

22 Baker and Hacker 2009, pp. 173, n. 1. The first edition (1985, p. 186, n. 1) adds the following thought: "Or, as in the *Tales of Narnia*, God is a lion. But *that* is no stranger than God's being an old man with a long white beard!" Perhaps this was removed because it is stranger, for it is essential to the Christian religion that humans – but not lions – were made in the image of God and, consequently, that Jesus (who Aslan is intended to be allegory of) is the word made *human* flesh. As such he can be joyful, sad, depressed, and so on; this is indeed no ordinary lion.

23 In the BBC television series the animal speaks in perfect English with the voice of Ronald Pickup and in cinema films with that of Liam Neeson.

illustrations than the musical film version of *The Wizard of Oz* did. Are we to say that what is being imagined here is a human being (or whatever other English-speaking person we can allow ourselves to imagine) which does not only look like a lion but has taken its actual form? Is it integral to the stories that we entertain the false supposition that it is a creature with lion vision, neurology, vocal chords, etc. which speaks English?

Daniel Dennett certainly thinks of Wittgenstein's lion in this way, though his precise objection alters across a series of books:

> Wittgenstein once said, "If a lion could talk, we could not understand him" (1958, p. 223). I think, on the contrary, that if a lion could talk, that lion would have a mind so different from the general run of lion minds, that although we could understand him just fine, we would learn little about ordinary lions from him.[24]

> Ludwig Wittgenstein famously said, "if a lion could talk, we could not understand him." That's one possibility, no doubt, but it diverts our attention from another possibility: if a lion could talk, we could understand him just fine – with the usual sorts of effort required for translation between different languages – but our conversations with him would tell us next to nothing about the minds of ordinary lions, since his language-equipped mind would be so different. It *might* be that adding a language to a lion's "mind" would be *giving* him a mind for the first time! Or it might not. In either case, we should investigate the prospect and not just assume, with tradition, that the minds of non-speaking animals are really like ours.[25]

> Wittgenstein once said "If a lion could speak, we could not understand him". I disagree. If a monkey could speak – really speak a language – we could understand him just fine because, if a monkey could speak, his way of life would have to be very much more like ours than it is.[26]

A similar sort of worry has been raised by Budiansky:

> The philosopher Ludwig Wittgenstein made the famous observation, "If a lion could talk, we would not understand him." But that begs the question [sic]: if a lion could talk, we probably could understand him. He just would not be a lion any more; or rather, his mind would no longer be a lion's mind.[27]

---

24 Dennett 1991, p. 447.
25 Dennett 1996, p. 18.
26 Dennett 1998, p. 306. Note the change here from "talk" to "speak".
27 Budiansky 1998, p. xxi.

Insofar as a creature might be said to communicate in roars and growls, these claims are questionable. It is certainly more natural to conceive of many animals as talking (but not speaking) to each other,[28] and such outlooks are far from obviously false (a fact which in itself lends support to those who translate "sprechen" as "speak", for the hypothetical form of the remark reveals that Wittgenstein takes it as a given that lions are not able to do this). More importantly, we should in any case be wary of taking *per impossibile* claims at face value. One might as well claim that if walls had ears they would not hear a thing because the ears would be made of brick or plaster, or deny this on the grounds that if they had ears they would be *human* walls, made of flesh and blood.[29] Claims such as "if a pot could talk it would have a mouth" are best seen as conceptual ones, not empirical statements to which one could respond with questions about the acoustics of porcelain.[30]

With this in mind, let me focus more closely on the question of what Wittgenstein means by "sprechen". Hans-Johann Glock offers two possible readings, suggesting that the second lends more plausibility to PPF § 327:

> On one reading, this means that we could not understand a lion who utters English sentences like "I'm not interested in you, I've just eaten an antelope", which is obviously false (although one might, following Austin, question whether such a talkative creature could count as a lion). On a charitable reading, it means that if lions had a *feline* language of complex growls, roars, etc., we could never come to *learn* it. Why? Because their form of life, and their behavioural repertoire are so alien to us. We could not make head or tail of their facial expressions, gestures and demeanour. Moreover, our ability to interact even with a tame lion is strictly limited.[31]

Glock presents us with a false dilemma here. For the question is not whether the lion would talk in growls or words (including ones that sound just like German or English) but whether its lifeworld overlaps with that of the humans in a way

---

28 This can be readily confirmed by a quick Google search (approximately 108,000 hits for the first and 17,200 for the second). It is also worth noting that "talk" may also imply two-way communication (compare "we had a talk" and "it's good to talk" with "he gave a speech" or "he spoke to me"). So if a lion could talk, it could not talk with us, even if its talking were to take the form of speech.

29 Many thanks to Max de Gaynesford for drawing my attention to this figurative aspect of Wittgenstein's remark.

30 See PIr § 282, quoted further below. This is not to deny that fantastical hypotheticals can reflect empirical facts. Hence the joke: if a dog could play poker it would lose, because its tail would wag whenever it had a good hand.

31 Glock 1996a, p. 166; see also 1996b, p. 128.

which allows for a sufficient degree of shared concepts which would make it possible for us to come to learn its language. A language that is *private to lions* need not have feline *syntax*, nor an accessible lionese take the form of words or humanlike gestures. How can we be sure that a speaking lion *would* say things like "I've just eaten an antelope", even if it did utter propositions? Unlike the talking animals in Hollywood films and cartoons, or the talking car in *Knight Rider*, real animals do not share most of our concepts, if they share any of them at all. It is consequently wrong to suppose, as Blaise Pascal did, that animals instinctively find the world to be as we conceptualize it:

> If an animal did with a mind what it does by instinct, and if it spoke with a mind what it speaks by instinct in hunting and in warning its mates that the prey is found or lost, it would certainly also speak about things that affect it more, as for example, "Gnaw on this chord that is hurting me and [which] I cannot reach".[32]

It begs the question to assume that if a lion could think and speak it would say things like "gnaw me this chord" and "fetch me an antelope", as opposed to "milk my sugar" or whatever. For to know what sorts of things the lion would say if it could speak is to already understand it. Another thing worth observing is that if the feline language reading is combined with the "would not" translation, the entire remark becomes trivially true, whereas this is not true of Glock's (preferable) translation. What about the first reading? Notwithstanding the parenthesis on the concept of a lion,[33] is it as obviously true as Glock deems it to be that we *would* understand a speaking lion-like creature? Here we need to at the very least distinguish between understanding what the lion *says* and understanding the lion *itself*, for do we not often understand the words people say while failing to understand why on earth they should say such things, or at any rate have the thoughts they are expressing?

The question is only partly rhetorical, since what we make of it depends on whether we are talking about expression, utterance, or speaker meaning (to say nothing of communicative intention). If expression meaning, we need to further distinguish between what the expression "I'm not interested in you, I've just eaten an antelope" would in this context mean in (human) English and what it might mean in lionese. Would we obviously understand the latter version of the expression? And how could we tell if the lion was joking, or being ironic, sarcas-

---

32 Pascal 1670/2005, L 105 (S 137), p. 30. I owe this reference to Søren Landkildehus.
33 We have already seen that Wittgenstein is not interested in lions per se.

tic, metaphorical, etc. unless we can also understand the practices which give meaning to its behaviour (including tone and gesture)?[34]

It is tempting to think that we could perhaps at least understand *what* the lion means to say without understanding *why* it is saying it, though this would admittedly not yet amount to understanding the lion itself. But Anscombe (1963) was right to argue that one cannot fully understand what someone did without understanding why she did it, for the latter can always feature in an informative re-description of the former. The same holds true of the things we say and why we say them.[35] This might have been what the young Wittgenstein had in mind, for example, when at the end of his 1929 PhD Viva in Cambridge he allegedly told Bertrand Russell and G. E. Moore that they had failed to understand anything he had written in his *Tractatus*, a suspicion which became increasingly more general as his work became more popular. This lead him to announce in the Preface to the *Investigations* that he "could not help noticing that the results of [his own] work [...] were [...] frequently misunderstood",[36] and he has also been quoted as having said that Ryle was one of just two philosophers who understood his work.[37]

In what way might the inability to understand a speaking lion differ from the inability to understand Wittgenstein when he speaks? Understanding comes in degrees, but we should not discount the possibility that Wittgenstein is working with a relatively demanding notion of understanding. This is evidenced not only by his incredibly high personal standards for every aspect of life,[38] as well as remarks such as the following:

---

34 Wittgenstein himself acknowledges this in connection with questions about understanding others that were troubling him as early as 1914. I return to these in § 3, in relation to the accusation that PPF § 327 is anthropocentrist.
35 I am thus in sympathy with traditional interpretations (e.g. Pitcher 1964, p. 243) insofar as they claim that we are not able to understand the lion's speaker meaning (let alone his communicative intention) because our forms of life are sufficiently different to render the lion's reasons opaque. This view has been criticized by von Savigny (1991, pp. 111–112) for taking the lion remark out of context, but this is not so if Wittgenstein's intended it to contrast with the remarks which precede it (see § 3 below).
36 If understanding the expression meaning of what anybody says was always sufficient for understanding them, there would be far less need for exegesis. Would our failure to understand the speaking lion also be a case of *mis*undersanding? Insofar as there is something there to be understood, that would depend on whether we think we understand it.
37 Monk (1990, p. 436). For whether or not Wittgenstein was merely being polite to Ryle's cousin see Tanney (2009b, n. 1).
38 See Monk 1990.

It's important for our approach, that someone may feel concerning certain people, that he will never know what goes on inside them. He will never understand them. (Englishwomen for Europeans.)[39]

Of course feeling that we will never understand some people is compatible with in principle being able to do so (even if we never come to manage it). A philosophy professor recently confessed to me that Russell does not *speak* to him.[40] He did not mean by this that he could not understand any individual sentence but, rather, that he cannot find his feet with what Russell is generally getting it, because he does not share a certain philosophical outlook. Such reactions need not be negative ones:

I could only stare in wonder at Shakespeare; never do anything with him.[41]

Would a speaking lion speak *to* us, or would we only stare in wonder at it?

In his book *Radical Hope: Ethics in the Face of Cultural Devastation* Jonathan Lear describes the reluctance of Frank B. Linderman to say that he knows much about "the Indian" despite the fact that he had "studied him" for more than forty years and had been told by his own subject that he had "felt his heart".[42] Lear's book centres around the possibility that when Indian chief Plenty Coups stated that "nothing happened" after the buffalo went away he meant this in a literal way that we (non Indians) cannot begin to comprehend. Lear himself writes: "I cannot pretend to say with confidence what Plenty Coups really meant. His remark is enigmatic in part because it is compatible with so many different interpretations. Some of them are superficial; others delve to the heart of the human condition."[43] He might as well have been talking about Wittgenstein's remark, or indeed the talking lion itself.

An even more radical example may be found in Matt Groening's *Futurama*. Two aliens from the planet Omicron Persei 8 watch an episode of the human television series *Friends*, laughing at all the jokes. When it is over, one of them says to the other, in English: "Why does Ross, the largest friend, not simply eat the other five?" Understanding a creature is not just a matter of being able to

---

39 CV, p. 84e (9 July 1948).
40 Similarly, when Anscombe (1963) writes "I do what happens" I do not fully understand what she is thinking and at times believe that I may never be able to.
41 CV, p. 95e (1950).
42 Lear 2006, p. 2. I owe this reference to Roger Teichmann.
43 Ibid, p. 5.

translate individual sentences it utters. This is why, jokes aside, talking animals in books and films typically possess a full gamma of human concepts which cannot be acquired independently of knowledge about a range of habits, values, feelings, and motivations.

Given their reaction to television comedy, we can barely imagine what the Omicronians would make of something like the Eucharist. They have obviously not understood the first thing about humans, despite the stipulation that they nonetheless (*per impossibile*) understand one or more human languages. One cannot understand a language whilst lacking any clear notion of the practices in which it is embedded. How do humans fair with regard to lions, in this respect? Being in possession of relatively sound knowledge of their eating habits, most are unlikely to fail to understand them in the above sort of way described, though other gaps of understanding could in principle be equally radical.

3 Cultures and Values

There are cultural complications relating to what we are disposed to understand when spoken to as illustrated in the following passages from a humorous article in *The Economist* which demonstrates that "a literal understanding of what someone says is often a world away from real understanding":[44]

> [...] when a Briton says "I hear what you say", the foreign listener may understand: "He accepts my point of view." In fact, the British speaker means: "I disagree and I do not want to discuss it any further." Similarly the phrase "with the greatest respect" when used by an Englishman is recognisable to a compatriot as an icy put-down, correctly translated by the guide as meaning "I think you are wrong, or a fool." [...] when a Briton says "by the way/incidentally", he is usually understood by foreigners as meaning "this is not very important", whereas in fact he means, "The primary purpose of our discussion is..." On the other hand, the phrase "I'll bear it in mind" means "I'll do nothing about it"; while "Correct me if I'm wrong" means "I'm right, please don't contradict me."As the Brits see things, a Frenchman who says "*je serai clair*" (which literally means "I will be clear") should be understood as meaning: "I will be rude".[45]

44 Charlemagne 2004.
45 Ibid. For further discussion see http://www.thepoke.co.uk/2011/05/17/anglo-eu-translation-guide/ and http://itre.cis.upenn.edu/~myl/languagelog/archives/001781.html

Clearly our failure to understand the lion is more radical than the French person's failure to understand the Brit. There is a world of difference between a person from a different culture and a creature from a different species. But is it a difference in degree or in kind? The English-speaking French person does not understand the Brit but surely he is *able to*. It can take years to overcome the cultural differences, but it only takes seconds to explain how each phrase is to be "really" understood.[46] We, by contrast, are not even able to understand the lion. But what kind of impossibility is this?

Anscombe's translation of "könnten…nicht" as "could not" is both accurate and true to the aesthetic of Wittgenstein's remark. It also retains an important ambiguity in how we are to understand the modality in question, namely that of whether Wittgenstein is marking a *logical possibility or* simply noting a general *lack of ability*. Indeed, we may distinguish between the following three modalites:

i) Having an ability (but not being able to exercise it)
ii) Lacking an ability (that one can nonetheless acquire)
iii) The impossibility of even acquiring an ability[47]

In their revised translation Hacker and Schulte explicitly opt for the middle modality, rendering the remark as follows:

If a lion could talk, we *wouldn't be able* to understand it.[48]

This is an interpretive translation (as opposed to one which seeks to preserve the ambiguities of the original), but a very convincing one. For short of attributing lions with a language private to themselves (as Bekoff seems to accuse Wittgenstein of doing in the passage quoted in § 1) there is no reason to think that a human could not in principle *acquire* the ability in question e.g. by immersing herself in the form of life of another creature, perhaps from early childhood like Mowgli or Tarzan. Unlike the lion tamer, such a human might even come to

---

46 Shakespeare would need to spend some time in our world in order to be able to understand people who say things like "yr fbk account haz bin hacked bro" or "wicked - text me if U R comin 2 bbq chav, laters", but he *could* come to understand the relevant concepts without the acquisition of an overarching any new ability. The point about the lion, by contrast, is not just about the ever-changing, contextualist, nature of language.
47 For a rewarding discussion of the relation between abilities and their exercise see Kenny 1993, p. 156, and 2002, p. 59.
48 PPF § 327, my emphasis.

resemble a lion in any number of ways, though this would undoubtedly involve *learning* to behave in ways that come naturally to other creatures. The extent to which such abilities may be acquired is an empirical question which Wittgenstein does not seemed troubled by, presumably because he takes its answer to be irrelevant to the insight he is trying to convey.[49]

Most commentators also assume that "we" refers to all *humans*, but it is clear from Wittgenstein's other writings that he believes there are groups of people that "we" are not able to understand, be it because we lack the ability to do so, or are prevented from exercising it:

> We tend to take the speech of a Chinese for inarticulate gurgling. Someone who understands Chinese will recognize *language* in what he hears. Similarly I often cannot discern the *humanity* in a man.[50]

> We don't understand Chinese gestures any more than Chinese sentences.[51]

Wittgenstein singles out Chinese speech because it appears less *human-like* to "us", or at least to him. As the narrator puts it in Lewis' *The Magician's Nephew*, "what you see and hear depends a good deal on where you are standing; it also depends on what sort of person you are".[52] When Aslan and the other Talking Beasts begin to speak they are understood not only by the Witch but also several humans, to their own amazement. The sole exception is uncle Andrew who "tried to make himself believe that he could hear nothing but roaring" and soon "couldn't had heard anything else even if he'd wanted to", hearing "only barkings, growlings, bayings, and howlings" when the Beasts spoke in answer.[53]

---

49 Shweder (1991), Prinz (2012), and Haidt (2012) all argue that it is in our human nature to be culturally malleable. This multiplicity may well extend to our understanding of conceptions held by non-human animals. Might any other animals share this malleability with us or is it unique to our (human) nature? This too is an empirical question.
50 CV, p. 1 (thanks to Yuuki Ohta for drawing this remark to my attention). We may, conversely, mistake decorative pseudo-inscriptions for the real thing.
51 Z § 219. Cf. LW II, p. 89: "I wouldn't know, for instance, what genuine gladness looks like with the Chinese." At the time in which the former remark was written (1914) Wittgenstein was far more sympathetic to solipsism than when he wrote the latter, and the following remark from the same early period betrays an acceptance of Russell's argument from analogy which he would later explicitly reject: "Only remember that the spirit of the snake, of the lion, is *your* spirit. For it is only from yourself that you are acquainted with spirit at all" (NB, p. 85e, 20/10/16).
52 Lewis 1955, Ch. 10, p. 116.
53 Ibid., p. 117.

Stephen H. Webb has argued that "when uncle Andrew hears the animals speak, he can't understand them because he doesn't recognise them as belonging to the same community as his own [...] even when they are given the gift of human-like speech. Likewise, they can't understand him."[54]

This may be true in Narnia,[55] but while one may undoubtedly fail to recognize sounds as speech, in the real world it is community belonging itself – along with all that it entails – which makes the crucial difference, not one's recognition of it.

Wittgenstein seems comfortable talking of a "we" which presumably excludes Western scholars of Chinese language and which, *mutatis mutandis*, would also exclude lion ethologists, Mowgli, and so on.[56] Moreover, as Richard Beardsmore has noted, Wittgenstein is also happy to group human and animals in the same cognitive and behavioural groups:

> Imagine a human being, or one of Köhler's monkeys, who wants to get a banana from the ceiling, but can't reach it, and thinking about ways and means finally puts two sticks together etc.[57]

Beardsmore claims further that Wittgenstein aims to "draw an analogy between communication between human beings of different groups and any hypothetical communication between humans and animals".[58] But it is evident from the passages which immediately precede the lion remark that Wittgenstein *does* see a radical break occurring between the intra-human scenarios and those that cut across species:

> We also say of a person that he is transparent to us. It is, however, important as regards our considerations that one human being can be a complete enigma to another. We learn this when we come into a strange country with entirely strange traditions; and what is more, even given a mastery of the country's language. We do not *understand* the people. (And not

---

54 Webb 2005, p. 11. The absence of any reference to Wittgenstein throughout this article is conspicuous.

55 For the view that his recognitional failure is the result of intellectual vice see Kinghorn 2005. It is likely that Lewis borrowed this idea from ancient and monastic stories about beasts whose intelligence humans fail to perceive because of their false preconceptions (see Osborne 2007, pp. 152–153 and n. 15 above).

56 See also notes 46 and 71; cf. Beardsmore 1996, p. 46

57 RPP II § 224.

58 Beardsmore 1996, p. 42). His view is elaborated upon by Sharpe 2005, pp. 170ff.

because of not knowing what they are saying to themselves.) We cannot find our feet with them. [Wir können uns nicht in sie finden.⁵⁹]

"I can't know [Ich kann nicht wissen] what is going on in him" is, above all, *a picture*. It is the convincing expression of a conviction. It does not give reasons for the conviction. *They* are not obvious.⁶⁰

Simon Glendinning argues that Wittgenstein is here stressing a difference of *order* rather than one of mere degree.⁶¹ It would seem that whilst we *cannot* (are not able to) understand the lion, it is only true that we *do not* understand the people, but could in principle manage were we to live with them for long enough. Understanding the human strangers does not require us to acquire a new ability; we may currently lack their ways and concepts but already possess the ability to master them. By contrast, this is exactly what would need to happen for us to understand the lion, at least according to Wittgenstein's demanding criteria for understanding. The contrast is missed by those who take Wittgenstein to be claiming that we "would not" understand the lion.⁶² We do not understand the humans in the sense that we *cannot* find our feet with them, though presumably we *could* do so. The language suggests a failure to exercise an ability we already have by nature. By contrast we must try and *acquire* the ability to find or feet with the speaking lion. This predicament is similar to the one we face when we encounter the non-humanlike tribe in *Zettel*:

Imagine that the people of a tribe were brought up from early youth to give no expression of feeling *of any kind*. [...] an education quite different from ours might also be the foundation for quite different concepts. [...] What interests us would not interest *them*. [...] 'These men would have nothing human about them.' Why? We could not possibly make ourselves understood to them. Not even as we can to a dog. We could not [könnten] find our feet with them. And yet there surely could be such beings, who in other respects were human.⁶³

59 See von Savigny (1991, p. 110) for why the phrase does not just mean that we cannot "get along" with them but, rather, that we are constantly surprised by their behaviour to the point of alienation.
60 PPF §§ 325–326, emphasis in the original. Note that the "kann nicht" of § 326 is but the expression of a conviction whose reasons are not at hand.
61 Glendinning 1998, p. 71.
62 It is worth noting here that understanding the people in this context is not shorthand for understanding what they say when they speak. For the study of contrasts to work we must take it that (as I have been arguing above) the same holds true of the lion remark.
63 Z §§ 383–390.

The mention of the dog makes it clear that Wittgenstein does *not* have a human-animal divide in mind. So what is the distinguishing factor between this sort of case – in which "we could not possibly" understand or be understood – and that of the strange people which "we do not *understand*"? Catherine Osborne alludes to the lion remark in describing the bad temptation to think that "there is a radical difference between the world experienced by a language user and that of any other". On such an outlook, it is a mistake to assume that if a lion could talk it could give expression to the sorts of things we would understand because the world of the lion would be so different from ours. This linguistic reason is not to be confused with the "form of life" of the argument offered against Pascal in § 2. At its most extreme the linguistic view leads to the controversial claim that the lion has no world, because it has no concepts and all thought and perception is conceptual.[64]

We have already seen that there is little in Wittgenstein to suggest that what he has in mind is an unbridgeable gulf between the experience of language-users and that of other creatures. Accordingly, Osborne allows "for more fruitful analyses of Wittgenstein's remark"[65], listing as an example John Dupré's claims that the lion remark "develops the intuition that language is deeply integrated with non-linguistic practices and behaviour" and that "'[s]ince lions, and other animals, lead wholly different lives, their hypothetical language could make no sense to us".[66] Dupré adds:

> Suppose [...] that our lion found its voice and said something that we were (somehow) inclined to translate as "I am in pain". What might we not be right in the translation, and thus understand the lion? One might imagine a Wittgensteinian answering that the role that such an utterance could, imaginably, play in the life of lions, and its relation to the natural leonine expressions of pain, would be different from the equivalent role of the English utterance in the life of humans. If this seems wholly implausible, it is perhaps because the behaviour associated with pain is so primitive that it really does extend to many non-human species without serious alteration.[67]

---

64 Dennett 1979, 1995 and 1996, Davidson 1984, McDowell 1996. For criticisms of this outlook see Beardsmore 1996, p. 56, Glock 2000 and 2006, Sandis 2006, p. 13 and 2010, pp. 30ff., and Blassime et al. 2012. I tried to show in § 2 that Dennett's concerns were, in any case, a red herring.

65 Osborne 2007, pp. 65 and 67.

66 Dupré 2002, p. 232. Osborne also refers to Beardsmore (1996), discussed elsewhere in this essay.

67 Dupré 2002, p. 233. This is not intended to show that Wittgenstein chose the wrong species for his example (see § 1 above), for presumably the talking lion would not only talk of pain and may, in any case, have very different speech-behaviour associated with it (our behaviour is

In MS 137, the lion remark is preceded by the note "Zu S. 742 Tscr". This refers to remarks now published as RPP II, §§ 566–569, which include the following thought experiment:

> But imagine people whose upbringing is directed toward suppressing the expression of emotion in their faces and gestures; and suppose these people make themselves inaccessible to me by thinking aloud in a language I don't understand. Now I say "I have no idea what is going on inside them".[68]

The key to understanding creatures, on this outlook, is behaviour. This may, but need not, be linguistic. The important thing, it would appear, is that it is an expression of "the inner". But is this not exactly what both Chinese gestures and lion roars are? It would seem that "we" can only find our feet with certain forms of behaviour.

4 Alien Patterns of Behaviour

It is tempting to think that whereas the difference between the Chinese and the English person is a cultural one, the one between humans and lions is biological. On this view, the difference of order which Wittgenstein seeks to mark is a biological difference, one which even the most knowledgeable ethologist could never overcome. But this view seems to implausibly commit him to the view that while no *individual* creature can have a language private to itself, it is not incoherent to suppose that any given *species* could have a language which is *in principle* inaccessible to members of certain other species.[69]

Wittgenstein famously does not think it conceivable that an individual can have a private language of his or her own.[70] Whether a species could, for biological reasons, have a language that is in principle private to itself is a somewhat

---

more likely to overlap at the more primitive level of groaning).

68 RPP II § 568. Joachim Schulte, who brought the note in question to my attention, pointed out to me that this version omits the phrase "Welcher Fremde empfindet nicht so, wenn er nach England kommt?" ["Which foreigner doesn't feel that way when he comes to England?"], connected to PPF § 325. See TS 232/MS 135–137, 1947–1948.

69 See, for example, the sort of neo-behaviourism defended by Galen Strawson (2010, pp. 251ff.).

70 See Mulhall 2007 for related difficulties about whether we can even say what a private language is meant to be (cf. Pears 2006).

different question,[71] as is that of whether lions might be such a species. This is not to say that Wittgenstein would have answered either positively, let alone that he would have been right to do so. On the contrary, he would maintain that this use of the concept of language would at best be a secondary one.[72] Moreover, there is no evidence whatsoever to suggest that PPF § 327 is motivated by empirical data about the *purely* biological obstacles of this sort. Moreover, Wittgenstein denies that we would conceive alien behaviour as being linguistic unless we could recognize some kind of pattern:

> Let's imagine that the people in that country carried on usual human activities and in the course of them employed, apparently, an articulate language. If we watch their activities, we find them intelligible, they seem 'logical'. But when we try to learn their language, we find it impossible to do so. For there is no regular connection between what they say, the sounds they make, and their activities; but still these sounds are not superfluous, for if, for example, we gag one of these people, this has the same consequences as with us: without those sounds their actions fall into confusion – as I feel like putting it. Are we to say that these people have a language: orders, reports, and so on?
> There is not enough regularity for us to call it "language".[73]

In MS 124 (pp. 208ff.), in a passage just before that which occurs in §206 he writes:

> I come to an alien people and someone apparently gives an order in a language which I do not know; his gestures, voice and the situation suggest to me that it is an order. I hear these sounds or words from different people in different circumstances expressed in the same tone of voice, But I see no regularity in the reactions of the other to whom the words are directed. Would I call these orders?
> In the reactions to an order there must be uniformity.[74]

---

71 According to Bernard Williams, Wittgenstein is nonetheless committed to "a transcendental idealism of the first person plural" (Williams 1973, p. 161). On this view, Wittgenstein's use of the term "we" is primarily aimed not at privileging one human group over others or even humanity over other language-using creatures, but "the plural descendent of the idealist I who also was not one item rather than another in the world" (Ibid., p. 160). Cf. Malcolm 1982, Moore 1985, Hutto 1996 and Dilman 2002.

72 See PIr § 282.

73 PIr § 207.

74 Translation taken from Baker and Hacker 2009, p. 176; cf. Baker and Hacker 1985, p. 190, which also includes the original German.

We know something is happening here, but we do not know what it is. The activities we perceive do not seem to be governed by any rules. Nor do they form evidence for the existence of a language which is private to the alien people, for we would only be inclined to attribute them with language to the extent that their behaviour contains observable regularities. It is possible, of course, for these to occur in a fashion which renders them unperceivable to us (due to speed, pitch, or whatever), but the only evidence for this would be of a kind that was contingently inaccessible to us.

It is wrong, then, to think that we are forced to choose between a difference that is *purely* biological and one that is *merely* cultural or ethnological. The criteria for the possibility of understanding are behavioural:

> [...] he [the explorer in the foreign land] can come to understand it [the foreign language] only through its connections with the rest of the life of the natives. What we call 'instructions', for example, or 'orders', 'questions', 'answers', 'describing', etc. is all bound up with very specific human actions and an order is only distinguishable as an order by means of the circumstances preceding or following // accompanying it //.[75]

> Suppose you came as an explorer to an unknown country with a language quite unknown to you. In what circumstances would you say that the people there gave orders, understood them, obeyed them, rebelled against them, and so on? Shared human behaviour [Die gemeinsame menschliche Handlungsweise[76]] is the system of reference by means of which we interpret an unknown language.[77]

All this includes both natural and nurtured behaviour. Moreover, as Baker & Hacker and Glock have argued, even the cultural-specific is ultimately rooted in biology:

> [...] understanding an alien language presupposes convergence not of beliefs, but of patterns of behaviour, which presuppose common perceptual capacities, needs and emotions [...] we "could not find our feet" with a community of human beings who give no expression or feeling of any kind, and we would presumably be at a loss with spherical Martians.[78]

> Shared human behaviour provides the essential leverage for understanding mankind. This "shared behaviour" is not only the common behaviour of mankind which manifests our animal nature, our natural needs for food, drink, warmth, our sexual drives, our physi-

---

75 MS 165, pp. 97ff. in Baker and Hacker 2009, p. 177, and 1985, p. 191.
76 See von Savigny (1991, pp. 113–14) for an account of why Anscombe's rendition of this phrase as "the common behaviour of mankind" is problematic.
77 PIr § 206.
78 Glock 1996b, p. 128.

cal vulnerability, etc. It also includes the culturally specific forms of behaviour shared by members of the tribe – their specific forms of social behaviour – observation of which and interaction with which enables us to interpret their language.[79]

[...] any "form of life" accessible to lions, given their natural repertoire of behaviour and their behavioural dispositions, is too far removed from ours for any noises they might emit to count as speech.[80]

In what manner does human behaviour aid us in interpreting an unknown language? It enables us to establish regular connections between the sounds they make and actions. For if such regularities are discernible, then it is plausible to see what is said as providing a reason for what is done. This provides us with the leverage for interpreting their words. But in the absence of any such discernible regularity (even though the noises they make do not seem superfluous) we shall not say these alien people speak a language.[81]

"Leverage" is the key term here, and what it requires is uniformity between the noises they make and their behaviour. *Pace* von Savigny,[82] the latter need not be behaviour that is common with that of humans, let alone shared, so long as it is public, in Wittgenstein's sense of the term.[83] That is to say, the behaviour must be observable and thus in principle shareable viz. identifiable by others under the correct description. As Baker and Hacker put it, "the publicity requirement on rules is that it be *intelligible* that another (the anthropologist) should learn the aliens' (or alien's rule) rule",[84] i.e. that they can in principle come to learn it. The problem, however, is not merely that feline noises do not count as speech but that even if lions did speak (in words, or whatever) we would not be able to understand them.

---

79 Baker and Hacker 2009, p. 173. In this revised version of Baker and Hacker 1985, pp. 186–187), "shared behaviour" has substituted what was previously "common behaviour" throughout, thereby making it clearer that the common behaviour of *humanity* does not completely exhaust our shared behaviour, the latter also including behaviour that is "culturally specific" (the term helpfully replaces what was previously described as "the diverse species-specific forms which such behaviour may naturally take for human beings").
80 Baker and Hacker 2009, p. 173, n. 1; cf. Baker and Hacker 1985, p. 186, n. 1. See also Baker and Hacker 1985, pp. 328ff, and 2009, pp. 218ff.
81 Baker and Hacker (2009: 176; cf. 1985:189–190).
82 von Savigny 1991.
83 This remains compatible with something's being contingently hidden: "If I were to talk to myself out loud in a language not understood by those present my thoughts would be hidden from them." (PPF § 317)
84 Baker and Hacker 2009, p. 177; cf. Baker and Hacker 1985, p. 190.

Shareability is a necessary but insufficient condition for understanding a creature. As we have already seen, it is all too easy to systematically misidentify behaviour, linguistic or otherwise. *Pari passu*, recognizing that someone has a language is not *ipso facto* understanding that language. But Wittgenstein is not presenting us with a theory of understanding which specifies necessary *and* sufficient conditions for its existence, nor is he analysing the concept of understanding by breaking it down to its most basic constituents. Rather, he is probing for *limiting cases* of resemblances associated with knowledge and understanding.[85] Are we able to understand Wittgenstein when he says that if a lion could talk we would not be able to understand it? Are we meant to have a clear and specific vision of the scenario he speaks of, or is the supposed lion intended to be as nonsensical as a private language?[86]

Lions are hardly spherical Martians and Wittgenstein is not claiming that it is logically or metaphysically impossible to understand them. Nor does he have any interest in whether or not it is empirically impossible for even Mowgli to do so. Perhaps lions and humans can both learn (or be trained) to display behaviour that is not just shareable but actually shared. By and large, however, it does not come to them naturally[87] (with some aforementioned exceptions such as that of pain behaviour) and we should consequently wonder whether any learned shared behaviour makes the same kind of sense to each party.[88]

We may never fully understand Wittgenstein himself, but his lion has taught us much about understanding. Even if the latter could speak in words, it is conceptually problematic to assume that the average human being would be able to converse with it. Wittgenstein's behavioural approach may be contrasted to the following speculation by Deryck Cooke, whose 1959 book *The Language of Music* attempted to demonstrate that it is possible to decode the musical "phrases" through which composers throughout history have expressed their emotions:

> Perhaps one day, after intensive research into the various aspects of the art – acoustical, physiological, psychological, and simply musical – it may be possible, by correlating many findings, to discover exactly what it is that music expresses, and exactly how it expresses it; but if the attempt is made, it will have to be guided by the most meticulous regard for absolute truth, especially in the psychological field, where the answer is likely to be found. [...] [I]t seems likely that the fundamental (i.e. psychological) "content" of some musical

---

85 See PIr § 41.
86 See note 70.
87 The problem is magnified when it comes to making inferences about human motivation from experiments conducted on lab rats.
88 A similar point is expressed through the train game example in PIr § 282.

masterpieces may be quite appalling and even horrifying; and when the language of music is finally deciphered, some terrible secrets may be revealed, not only about the particular composer, but about humanity at large.[89]

Here the prospect of understanding is a nightmarish one. Cooke's proposition is unsettling, but there is something amiss in the suggestion that we might only be able to uncover what music expresses by conducting an interdisciplinary investigation across psychology and neighbouring fields. As with philosophers, any given piece of music may or may not speak to us, but there is nothing (human, lionese, musical, or otherwise) which cannot in principle be understood by one who is able to live with – as opposed to alongside – it.[90] Regardless of whether the lion communicates via roars or words, then, we could in principle acquire the ability to understand it. But such things do not come naturally or effortlessly.

---

89 Cooke 1959, p. 273. I owe this reference to Michael Proudfoot.

90 For extremely helpful comments, discussions, and suggestions I would like to thank Max de Gaynesford, David Dolby, Simon Glendinning, Peter Hacker, Søren Landkildehus, Erasmus Mayr, Katherine Morris, Luke Mulhall, Yuuki Ohta, Michael Proudfoot, Catherine Rowett, Elizabeth Sandis, Severin Schroeder, Joachim Schulte, Tom Tyler, and Nuno Venturinha. An earlier version of this paper was presented at the *Oxford Forum for European Philosophy* on 4 November 2011. Thanks to Roxana Baiasu and Pamela Sue Anderson for organising the event, and to members of the audience for helpful questions.

Maria Filomena Molder
The Difference between Drawing a Conclusion and Saying: It is like this!

In philosophy no inferences [Schlüsse] are drawn. "But it must be like this!" is not a philosophical proposition. Philosophy only states what everyone concedes to it.

PIr § 599

1 A Science that Might Abandon Us

Wisdom does not inspect, but behold. We must look a long time before we can see. Slow are
the beginnings of philosophy.[1]

It is this that can be perceived in Wittgenstein, the slowness that has to do with
a concern about premature choices, with the suspending of what is established.
Repeatedly, Wittgenstein makes this gesture, this act of taking his time ("time" is
what two philosophers should wish each other when they meet), always running
the risk of losing their understanding, of being abandoned by science, as Plato
says in *Symposium*:

And there is yet a stranger fact [than the constant changing of our bodies and our states of
soul]: with regard to the possessions of knowledge, not merely do some of them grow and
others perish in us, so that neither in what we know are we ever the same persons; but a like
fate attends each single sort of knowledge. What we call *conning/studying* [*meletaw*] implies
that our knowledge [*episteme*] is departing [...].[2]

In Wittgenstein we find an acute awareness of the state of risk into which study-
ing philosophy pushes us. In some passages of *Denkbewegungen* this awareness,
which forms part of the "work on itself" of which philosophy consists, is very
clear, as in 26.4.30:

---

1 H. D. Thoreau, 11 October 1840 (Thoreau 1853).
2 Plato 1991, 207e-208a.

It is always a terrible thing for me to think that my vocation depends on a gift that could be taken away from me at any moment.[3]

At any moment what was given to us could be taken away and it is often the case that the person who possessed the gifts – simply the tranquillity of the working of the body – did not know that he possessed them. One example of the unstable nature of philosophical knowledge, reported by Wittgenstein himself, refers to his inability to establish the specific difficulties of philosophy when he was preparing his lectures for the autumn term at Cambridge in 1930:

Three weeks have passed since I last thought about philosophy, but any thought about it is as alien to me as if I had not thought anything for years. I want to talk about the specific difficulties of philosophy in my first lecture and I feel: how can I say something about it if I no longer know what it is.[4]

On several occasions he refers to his great susceptibility (being the sort of person who does not break as a result of "weakness", a reflection of his highly paradoxical nature) as well as the fragility of his understanding, which he comes to depict as a glass rod which, bearing the weight that it does, could break at any moment,[5] and even the fear and acceptance of going mad: "you should live in such a way that, when madness appears, it turns out well for you".[6] But besides these diaristic notes, in Wittgenstein's various texts that state of risk is present and penetrating in the comments that he writes for future books, particularly those in which, time and time again, he struggles with what he wants to understand and once more hammers the iron that is sometimes still hot, sometimes already cool, talking to himself: "this is poorly expressed" or "I cannot say that yet", as the case may be, which is not the same as going around in circles, in which someone, he, goes deep into the dense forest of problems towards the open space, the sunlit clearing, but instead remains stuck on winding, zigzagging paths that take him further away from the clearing.[7]

---

3 DB, 26.4.1930 (the translations from this work are my own).
4 DB, 8.10.1930.
5 Cf. DB, 28.1.1932.
6 DB, 20.2.1937.
7 Cf. CV, MS 138, 8a, 22.1.1949.

And that is not all, since the threat of losing what has already been possessed knows yet another form of fertility, in taking the form of a change of direction, a new orientation in the movement of his thought, a change in which he no longer perceives what used to be inherent in his former point of view and wonders: "what could that mean? It sounds like something that I'm no longer doing, that is, the *Tractatus*".[8]

2 Questions of Temperature

> We *feel* that even if all *possible* scientific questions are answered *our problem is still not touched at all*. Of course in that case there are no questions any more, and that is the answer.[9]

This juvenile conviction, namely, that his desires are not satisfied by science, which in this diary is related to a tendency towards the mystical, remains with Wittgenstein in his mature years. It reappears, on the one hand, in the *Tractatus*,[10] in which the reference to the mystical element is maintained; and, on the other hand, this element having been abandoned, in several paragraphs of *Investigations* as well as in *Culture and Value* or even in "Remarks on Frazer's *Golden Bough*". Its most eloquent expression, and perhaps the last one, is found among the notes for *Vermischte Bemerkungen* [*Culture and Value*]:

> Scientific questions may interest me, but they never really grip/intrigue me [*fesseln/intriguieren*]. Only *conceptual & aesthetic* questions have that effect on me. At bottom it leaves me cold whether scientific problems are solved; but not those other questions.[11]

On each reading of the text, it is always perplexing to find that "&" between conceptual and aesthetic; it is in this "&" that the unique character of Wittgenstein's reasoning lies. Namely, it is not merely a matter of an association between two types of questions, the conceptual and the aesthetic, but also of their insepara-

---

8 "Isn't what I am saying: any empirical proposition can be transformed into a postulate – and then becomes a norm of description. But I am suspicious even of this. The sentence is too general. One almost wants to say 'any empirical proposition can, theoretically, be transformed ...', but what does 'theoretically' means here? It sounds all too reminiscent of the *Tractatus*." (OC § 131)
9 NB, 25.5.15.
10 Cf. TLP 6.52, 6.521, 6.522.
11 CV, MS 138, 5b, 21.1.1949.

bility: these are questions of a logical and stylistic nature but also questions in which the logical aspect triggers an undeniable affinity with the aesthetic.[12]

Wittgenstein is not captivated by scientific questions. In other words, although he might still be interested in them, this interest does not affect him or move him; it leaves him cold, which is why he is indifferent to them. By contrast, the same cannot be said of conceptual & aesthetic questions, which are neither empirical nor causal, neither the results of induction nor demonstrated by deduction nor hypotheses subject to the verdict of experimentation, all of which are cases that can be transformed into theories: rather, it is a question of leaving everything as it is.

3 Leaving Everything as It Is, in this Place, before Our Eyes

I see the difference between drawing conclusions/making inferences and saying: it is like this! in the framework of the distinction established by Wittgenstein between science and philosophy. No scientific investigation could help to clarify any philosophical problem, which is why he is genuinely interested only in "conceptual & aesthetic questions", those that can be recognized in everyday language: any sentence in our language "is in order just as it is"; in other words, he does not aspire to any ideal.[13]

When he compares language to a city, he evokes the image of the labyrinth, "a maze of little streets and squares, of old and new houses, of houses with extensions from various periods", which attempts to do justice to the way in which the city's older neighbourhoods formed the heart of the city, so to speak. While the image of the labyrinth is used to highlight the multiple uses of everyday language, its own life (which certainly includes poetry), the image of the grid design detectable in the new avenues of the suburbs serves to elucidate the way in which scientific concepts are incorporated into our language, "for these are, so to speak, suburbs of our language".[14]

---

12 "The queer resemblance between a philosophical investigation (perhaps specially in mathematics) and one in aesthetics. (E.g. what is bad about this garment, how it should be, etc.)" (CV, MS 116, 56, 1937) The determination "queer" will progressively disappear.
13 Cf. PIr §98.
14 Cf. PIr §18.

> It was correct that our considerations must not be scientific ones [...] And we may not advance any kind of theory. There must not be anything hypothetical in our consideration. All *explanation* [*Erklärung*] must disappear, and description alone must take its place. And this description gets its light – that is to say, its purpose [*Zweck*]– from the philosophical problems. These are, of course, not empirical problems; but they are solved through an insight [*Einsicht*] in the workings of our language, and that in such a way that these workings are recognized – *despite* an urge to misunderstanding them. The problems are solved, not by coming up to new discoveries, but by assembling what we have long been familiar with. Philosophy is a struggle against the bewitchment of our understanding by the resources of our language.[15]

> One is often bewitched by a word. For example, by the word "know" [*Wissen*].[16]

Let us highlight the relevant aspects: his reflections are not of a scientific nature; he is not proposing that any theory should be advanced; in other words, no hypothesis exists that is awaiting proof, or that can be replaced by another if it turns out to be false;[17] any attempts to explain must be avoided and replaced by description; the description receives its light, which he defines as its purpose [*Zweck*], from philosophical problems. What is a philosophical problem? Wittgenstein does not respond immediately, but we know that it is not scientific, that is, it is not an empirical, experimental, or causal problem (the problems of science in general, with the exception of mathematics), nor a problem that belongs to the relationship between certain principles and their derivatives. However, an answer is given which, while appearing to be indirect, goes right to the heart of the matter, namely, to its solution; philosophical problems are solved by intuitive understanding, insight, in the way that language works, so that this being-in-action can be recognized. Therefore, in philosophy it is not a question of arriving at new discoveries but of bringing together that with which we are familiar, in spite of our tendency not to look at what is familiar to us, i.e., everyday language, to which we do not pay attention, an oversight that gives rise to misunderstandings and prejudices, which are not *stupid*, he says in § 340, although they prevent us from understanding the way that language works.

Moreover, it is in this way that we finally become aware of which philosophical problems he wishes to dissolve: those which arise from "the bewitchment of our understanding by the resources of our language", and the bewitchment

---

15 PIr § 109.
16 Cf. OC § 435.
17 OC § 402.

to which philosophers can be particularly prone is that provoked by the word knowledge. The passage below could not be more elucidative:

> Compare *knowing* and *saying*:
> how many metres high Mont Blanc is –
> how the word "game" is used –
> how a clarinet sounds.
>
> Someone who is surprised that one can know something and not be able to say it is perhaps thinking of a case like the first. Certainly not of one of the third.[18]

In fact, philosophy appears here to Wittgenstein (in a manner that keeps faith with his youthful thinking, albeit under other expressions) as a fight against philosophical problems (through their clarification/dissolution) and the philosopher's task is therefore presented as that of leaving everything as it is, a bringing together, an ordering of memories for a particular purpose: that of coming to see clearly, not affecting the real use of language, which cannot be substantiated. No scientific discovery (he mentions mathematics, but we feel authorized to make this extension) will cause philosophy to progress. It could even be said that philosophy is the sort of activity that precedes all new discoveries and inventions.[19]

What Wittgenstein does in philosophy could be described as "observations" ("The best I could write would never be more than philosophical remarks"),[20] a fact related to a way of abstaining from the pretensions characteristic of most modern philosophers, namely, the determination of principles from which consequences are deduced, the establishment of a method, the demand for universality: "[...] [Pretentions are a mortgage, which burdens a philosopher's capacity to think]".[21] As is clear, this abstention is tendential and can never be assumed to be satisfied. For example, in *On Certainty* he can be seen to be making an effort, which never stabilizes into a thesis, not to allow himself to be bewitched by the word knowledge.[22]

---

18 PIr §78.
19 Cf. PIr §§127, 124, and 126.
20 PIr, "Preface".
21 OC §549.
22 See, among others, OC §378: "Knowledge [Das Wissen] is in the end based on acknowledgement", and OC §308: "'Knowledge' and 'certainty' belong to different categories. They are not two 'mental states' like, say, 'surmising' and 'being sure'. (Here I assume that is meaningful for me to say 'I know what (e.g.) the word "doubt" means' and that this sentence indicates that the word 'doubt' has a logical role). What interests us now is not being sure but knowledge. That is, we are interested in the fact that about certain empirical propositions no

This method, if any such thing can be found in Wittgenstein, is closer to what he calls *Gedankenbewegung* and *Denkbewegung* in the *Tagebücher* of 1936–37: the expression of his own individuality, which is very difficult at a time when philosophy has lost its aura [nimbus], as he declared to his students in his first lecture of the autumn term of 1930 (the one for which his preparations met with so many obstacles):

> The nimbus of philosophy has been lost. For we now have a method of doing philosophy, and can speak of *skilful* philosophers [...] But once a method has been found, the opportunities for the expression of personality are correspondingly restricted. The tendency of our age is to restrict such opportunities; this is a characteristic of an age of declining culture or without culture. A great man need be no less great in such periods, but philosophy is now being reduced to a matter of skill and the philosopher's nimbus is disappearing [...] This activity of clearing up is philosophy. We will therefore follow our instinct to clarify, and leave aside our initial question, What is philosophy?[23]

It is not just a question of the contrast between establishing and following a method and expressing one's individuality (which allows the philosopher's activity to be imbued with an aura, and prevents him from being confused with a specialist), but of the restrictions that are engendered by the production of the method, involving a corresponding disappearance of the philosopher's aura. This loss is seen as a symptom of the decadence of culture and even of its nullification. One cannot fail to see in this "nimbus" an early version of the concept of style, which later occupied so much Wittgenstein, finding its supreme formulation in Buffon's declaration that *le style c'est l'homme, l'homme même.*[24]

It is the way in which his observations are presented in lectures and conversations, and set down on paper, jumping (in a manner reminiscent of Hamann, who in his letter to Kant of 27 July 1759, claimed that his method was like that of the grasshopper)[25] around each theme and moving from theme to theme, the "only way of thinking" that is innate to him, in which his method is revealed

---

doubt can exist if making judgements is to be possible at all. Or again: I am inclined to believe that not everything that has the form of an empirical proposition *is* one."

23 Excerpt from a lecture given on 13 October 1930 in Cambridge, LWL apud DB (notes on pp. 47, 120).

24 "'Le style c'est l'homme.' 'Le style c'est l'homme même.' The first expression has cheap epigrammatic brevity. The second, correct, one opens up a quite different perspective. It says that style is the picture [Bild] of the man." (CV, MS 137, 140a, 4.1.1949)

25 "Every creature has its own method of thinking and writing. Some move by leaps and bounds like the grasshopper; others by means of a coherent connection, as a worm follows a furrow in the path." (Hamann 1955–75)

to be a movement that obeys the natural inclination of a traveller, a walker, an explorer climbing a mountain, venturing deep into the forest, someone who invents dramatic scenarios, *Gedankenexperimente,* and produces sketches of these landscapes: his observations give us these sketches[26] and, at the same time, allow us to see Wittgenstein's style.

Philosophy is neither about the search for the essence behind phenomena nor the induction made on the basis of empirical cases. For Wittgenstein, essence is a thing that is exposed to the light of day and can be ordered panoramically; it does not lie under the surface, waiting to be found either by analysis or excavation.[27] This is the most difficult movement: to see with our eyes what lies before them;[28] it is summoned by the visible, which is why one does not turn over what one is looking at with the aim of discovering what is behind, since what is behind, now in the sense of the backdrop – its landscape, what is given to it, the form of its life, the vital element – is only seen if we look for a long time at the foreground:

> Philosophy just puts everything before us, and neither explains nor deduces anything. – Since everything lies open to view, there is nothing to explain. For whatever may be hidden is not of interest to us [...].[29]

Furthermore, one does not take what one is looking at from the place where it is visible, nor is any supplementary tool needed (a ladder, for example) to reach the place where one wants to go: this place must be where one is: "Anything that can be reached with a ladder does not interest me".[30] For this reason, the invisible is not better than the visible; the invisible, like the inexpressible, might be the backdrop against which everything that is visible is seen: for example, prosody, intonation, rhythm, pulsation, the living context of the sentence.

> The inexpressible (what I find enigmatic [*geheimnisvoll*] & cannot express) perhaps provides the background, against which whatever I was able to express acquires meaning.[31]

---

26 Cf. PIr, "Preface".

27 Cf. PIr §§ 92–3.

28 A Goethian motif, commented on several times by Wittgenstein: "What is the hardest thing of all!/ That which seems the easiest:/ For your eyes to see/That which lies before your eyes." (Goethe 1982, vol. 1, *Sprüche in Versen*)

29 PIr § 126.

30 CV, p. 10.

31 CV, MS 112, 1, 5.10.1931.

It is this sort of tension that we come up against in language-games, a tension which causes them to belong to a family, tracing a relationship that points to a living community – landscape, atmosphere, vital element – that is insusceptible, like language-games, to being turned into definition.

4 The House Supports the Foundations

> Our clear and simple language-games are not preliminary studies for a future investigation of language – as it were, first approximations ignoring friction and air resistance. Rather, the language-games stand there as *objects of comparison* which, through similarities and dissimilarities, are meant to throw light on features of our language.[32]

Why is language in action called a game, and why does Wittgenstein opt for that word?[33] The answer seems to have to do with his view of the dramatic structure of life, with the evidence that language is a web of actions and reactions, in which: *In the beginning was the deed.*[34] This is what allows us to see clearer what is at stake in primitive forms of language-games and in any language-game: a deed rather than a process of reasoning or an opinion.[35]

"Objects of comparison" are what Wittgenstein calls the language-games that he catches, unawares and describes. Which means that the activity that he is constantly carrying out in his observations is that of placing examples of language-games alongside each other with the aim of sketching out their panorama in search of intermediary links,[36] touchstones to test his view that the existence

---

32 Plr § 130.

33 Recall that on DB 13.1.32 he wrote about "Bread and Circuses" (a socio-political programme conceived by the Romans during the period of decline of the empire) and adds "but also games in the sense that mathematics, and also physics is a game", and it is all the same whether the game takes place in the laboratory or on the football field.

34 Verse of Goethe's *Faust I*, which Wittgenstein quotes at least twice, once when the line appears in isolation (cf. CV, MS 119, 146, 21.10.1937); and elsewhere (OC § 130) when the previous line is also quoted, and with good reason, since it is precisely about confidence: … und schreib getrost/"Im Anfang war die Tat" [… and write with confidence/"In the beginning was the deed"].

35 One important difference between Frazer and the savages is that he believes "that the characteristic feature of primitive is that he does not act from *opinions* (contrary to Frazer)." (GB, p. 137) This is Frazer's theoretical conviction and it is this that prevents him from clearly seeing what is at stake in the rituals of the savages.

36 Cf. Plr § 122.

of language is admirable.[37] From this comparison, however, no construction of what is common emerges; no conclusion about what a language-game (and therefore language) might be; it cannot be surmised that the thing "must be like this". It can only be said, and this is all, and it is a great deal: language is like this, just as human life is like this:

> You must bear in mind that the language-game is so to say something unpredictable. I mean: It is not based on grounds [*Es ist nicht begründet*].
> It is not reasonable (or unreasonable).
> It is there – like our life.[38]

The fact that the language-game is not set up, that it is there, as unpredictable as our life, is another version of leaving everything as it is, a goal that in the last few years of Wittgenstein's life appears as a tendency to accept life, a prodigious sign of maturity: "My *life* consists in my being content to accept many things".[39] One of the most remarkable applications of the unfounded nature of language-games can be found in *On Certainty*, since our beliefs also lack foundation; however it is not merely that; certainty is not "*merely* a constructed point", an ideal, so to speak, to which some things more or less become closer: "No. Doubt gradually loses its sense. This language-game just *is* like that [So *ist eben dieses Sprachspiel*]".[40]And the question that follows bears the hallmark of the Wittgensteinian shift in thinking: "Do I want to say, then, that certainty resides in the nature [*Natur*] of the language-game?".[41]

In fact, this is what he means, since certainty is seen as an assumption (the image is that of the axle, the hinge) in language-games; in other words, language-games are based on some form of certainty or, even more precisely, a language-game is possible only if we trust in something: "I really want to say that a language-game is only possible if one trusts something (I did not say 'can trust something')".[42]

---

37 Already recognizable in the "Lecture on Ethics", albeit within the framework of the separation between what can and cannot be said: "For all I have said by shifting the expression of the miraculous from expression by *means* of language to the expression *by the existence* of language, all I have said is again that we cannot express what we want to express and that all we say about the absolute miraculous remains nonsense." (PO, p. 44)
38 OC §559.
39 OC §344.
40 OC §56.
41 OC §457, translation changed.
42 OC §509.

It does not appear to be much, it does not taste of much, but the fertility of this abstention from judgement, this abstention from the armour and strategies of theory is undeniable: on the one hand, not deceiving oneself[43] (not hiding the difficulty of understanding the lack of foundation for our beliefs, for example) and, on the other, doing justice to the facts,[44] which, seen in a certain light, cease to be empirical entities and become valuable, thereby becoming more costly;[45] that is, they turn into assumptions and start to be considered from a logico-grammatical point of view: "I am inclined to believe that not everything that has a form of an empirical proposition *is* one".[46] For example, people's linguistic habits, beliefs, or even rituals (surrounding death or fertility, for example). In the weight that the adverb *so* acquires it is possible to see a tendential overcoming, whether of the opposition between the *Wie* and the *Was*, or of the reduction of the *so-sein* to a verification of a state of things, as happened in the *Tractatus*. Now the *Wie* and the *Was* are brought together in the *so-sein*, in a magnetic tension, so to speak, since the *Wie* and the *Was* are what is in front of us, and is always there in one way or another, something which pertains to the description of language-games, that is, to logic, as he asserts twice in *On Certainty*: "[...] And everything descriptive of a language-game is part of logic",[47] and "What counts as an adequate test of a statement belongs to logic – belongs to the description of the language-game".[48]

The recognition that there is a language-game in each language-game has its origin in a glance that asks: how did we learn to speak? This question is not answered by giving explanations: "Nicht *erklären!* – BESCHREIBEN!"[49] rings out like a yell, an injunction, containing a mixture of a demand, a warning, a decision, until the point is reached when it is merely accepted that this is how it is, taking into account the language-game, which clearly has nothing empirical about it (and particularly nothing psychological), although the language-game is also not "reasonable (or unreasonable)".

---

43 "Nothing is so difficult as not deceiving yourself." (CV, MS 120, 283, 7.4.1938)
44 "Nothing is so difficult as doing justice to the facts." (GB, p. 129)
45 "The human gaze has the power of making things precious; though it's true that they become more costly too." (CV, MS 106, 247, 1929)
46 OC § 308.
47 OC § 56.
48 OC § 82.
49 DB, 19.2.1937.

Our mistake is to look for an explanation where we ought to regard the facts as 'proto-phe-nomena' [*Urphänomene*]. That is, where we ought to say: *this is the language-game that is being played.*

The point is not to explain a language-game by means of our experiences, but to take account of a language-game[50]

Let us see. It is not a question of investigating what the essence of the language-game is, trying to establish what is common to these processes that turn them into language or part of language, since what can be seen in games is that they have nothing in common, although they are related. "I want to try to clarify this", says Wittgenstein. Let us turn to Goethian morphology. In *The Metamorphosis of Plants*,[51] the original plant is not found by analogy; it is an image that insepara-bly accompanies all of its variations: at each moment in the plant's growth, the plant is a leaf. Consequently, Goethe sees what is common, but this is the result not of a process of induction but of a comparison that stops at a certain point; the common thereby becomes a shape that is recognized in each variation: in the leaf, at every stage of the plant's growth, and none of them is identical to any other; an image is seen, a primordial phenomenon – which always includes a relation of polarity, a rhythm of forces, of opposed energies: expansion and contraction, in the case of plants; passions and actions of light in the case of colours – just as the language-game is seen in all language-games. The primor-dial phenomenon could never be converted into a general concept, which means that the common element that is characteristic of it is of the order of affinity: one recognises a family likeness.[52] We would be tempted to say that in Goethe it is also a question of a conceptual & aesthetic problem: in each variation a shape, which is a web in a permanent state of being formed (and deformed, as we will see later), is recognised. Instead of a general concept we have an unstable design that is compared to another, to many others, and what do we see? Similarities and dissimilarities:

Besides these similarities, what seems to me to be most striking is the dissimilarity of all these rites. It is a multiplicity of faces with common features, which continually emerges here and there. And we would like to draw lines connecting these common ingredients.[53]

---

50 PIr §§ 654–5.
51 Cf. Goethe 1982, vol. 13.
52 Cf. PIr §§ 65, 66, 67, 72.
53 GB, p. 143.

But it must not be forgotten that those lines that we would like to draw, connecting the multiplicity of faces, are not firm; rather, they look like a swarm of intersecting, overlapping resemblances in which precedence is given to affinity. In fact, a link can be seen between this primacy of affinity and the relationship between conceptual & aesthetic questions, which seems to pertain to the tendency to catch a face unawares on every side – the terms used by Wittgenstein are *Verwandtschaft, Familienähnlichkeit* – and when the physiognomy is an expression, it is not the analogies that prevail but the variations that recall others.[54] Language-games are all variations of a type that has blurred edges, that is to say, a web of actions and reactions that can never be reduced to a well-analysed whole of common determinations.[55]

> He who imitates must be careful to ensure that what he writes is similar but not identical and that the similarity is not like that which exists between a portrait and the portrayed/ his model, in which the greater the similarity, the greater the glory of the artist, but like that which exists between a son and a father. In this case, although there is usually a great diversity of individual features, a certain trace and, as the painters call it, a "likeness" will be recognizable particularly in the face and in the eyes that generates that similarity which calls to mind the father as soon as we see the son, although if the matter were subjected to measurement, everything would be unequal; but perhaps there is something hidden there that has this force.[56]

---

54 "Life's infinite variations are an essential part of life [...]." (CV, MS 137, 67a, 4.7.1948)

55 Furthermore, the choice of the term *Aspekt* sheds light on what is characteristic in Wittgenstein's physiognomic vision. Being a development of "seeing like this", it simultaneously allows him to penetrate what is at stake in "seeing like this", since it belongs to those forms of understanding that lie halfway between perception and concept, which certainly belongs to the realm of "conceptual and aesthetic questions".

56 Thanks to Manuel Rodrigues, who, in the text "Uma Sombra de Semelhança", written for the catalogue *Le Besoin du Noble. Modo Minor. Silvae. João Queiroz,* gave me first access to this passage from a letter from Petrarca to Giovanni Malpaghini, and thanks to José Bogalheiro, who provided me with the complete original source of the passage as well as the corresponding translation (Cf. *Empatia e Alteridade – a Figuração Cinematográfica como Jogo,* doctoral dissertation, 2011). Here is the original text: "curandum imitatori ut quod scribit simile non idem sit, eamque similitudinem talem esse oportore, non qualis est imaginis ad eum cuius imago est, que quo similior eo maior laus artificis, sed qualis filii ad patrem. In quibus cum magna sepe diversitas sit membrorum, umbra quedam et quem pictoris nostri aerem vocant, qui in vulto inque oculis maxime cernitur, similitudinem illam facit, que statim viso filio, patris in memoria nos reducat, cum tamen si res da mensuram redeat, omnia sind diversa; sed est ibi nescio quid occultum quod hanc habeat vim." (Petrarca 2004)

A beautiful concept, this Petrarchan idea of the "trace that generates similarity", which painters call "likeness", and which fits so well with the understanding of "family likeness" [*Familienähnlichkeit*] in Wittgenstein since it goes beyond questions of imitative representation in the framework of the relationship between portrait and portrayed (portrait and model). As the matter is presented, the similarity between games is characterized by affinity rather than representation, of the same kind as that which occurs between members of the same family, in this case, between father and son. And this means that, although they would turn out to be different in every respect if they were subjected to agreed measurement standards, this would not affect the engendering of the similarity by "a certain trace" that "our painters" call a "likeness", which contains a force of evocation that reveals the darkness that falls on the intellect whenever it seeks to justify relations of affinity by using reasons and petty reasoning.

"It is so difficult to find the *beginning*. Or, better: it is difficult to begin at the beginning. And not try to go further back":[57] this observation (which is also a critical confession) is frequently found in *On Certainty*. When this backward step, which does not cease to be generated and threatens to drag us into a vortex, into a sort of intoxication with the origin, is successfully avoided, we are prepared to catch unawares the "tacit assumption", so to speak, a precipitate (in the language of chemistry) of this avoidance:

[...] then playing our language-game always rests on a tacit presupposition.[58]

What has to be accepted, the given, is – one might say – *forms of life*.[59]

In order to get clear about aesthetic words you have to describe ways of living.[60]

There is nothing empirical about the fact; it has already been transformed by the attentive eye and becomes recognizable as an assumption, namely, the form of life. Wittgenstein often calls this presupposition "nature" (as in "natural inclination") and the "natural history" of the human being;[61] but also in the case of man considered as a "being of instincts", an "animal";[62] and even in everything that refers to grace, talent, temperament, and spontaneity.[63]

---

57 OC § 471.
58 PPF, v, § 31.
59 PPF, xi, § 345.
60 LC, i, p. 35.
61 Cf. PIr, "Preface" and § 25.
62 Cf. GB, pp. 137–9; OC § 475.
63 Cf. OC § 505; CV 1931, 1939–1940, 1941. Of all the motifs of Wittgenstein's thought, this is

In *On Certainty*[64] we find the concept of the vital element [*Lebenselement*] associated with that of the system, and *Culture and Value* discusses the concept of atmosphere,[65] which we could consider to be other versions of the "form of life":

> All testing, all confirmation and disconfirmation of a hypothesis takes place already within a system. And this system is not a more or less arbitrary and doubtful point of departure for all our arguments: no, it belongs to the essence of what we call an argument. The system is not so much the point of departure, as the element in which arguments have their life [*Das System is nicht so sehr der Ausganspunkt, als dasLebenselement des Argumente*].

In passing from form to element (and atmosphere) an intensification of intimacy is observed between the presupposition that sustains language-games and language-games themselves, that is, from the activity that sustains language-games, seen as form, outline, design, the primitive pulsation is reached, the living web from which internal/external relations are engendered. As a concept, element is more fluid and more absorbing than form, involving exchanges and pores, a medium, a primary undulation. In any one of these cases, however, it is a question of a condition, that to which we cling, that which can never be an isolated phrase but rather a bundle of phrases.[66]

"I have arrived to the bottom of my convictions" declares Wittgenstein at the start of §248 of *On Certainty*, which refers to the doubt about having two hands, which in fact is unsustainable (not being related in any way to an empirical fact): "What I would believe if I didn't believe that? So far I have no system at all within which doubt might exist".[67] This system, formed by a bundle of phrases, is given a very curious formulation at the end of the same §248 of *On Certainty*, in which he reprieves an image dear to modern philosophers, namely that of the foundations of a house, and inverts it, producing one of his most graceful and precise statements: "And one might almost say that these foundation-walls are carried by the whole house". As we know, a house that is not inhabited for a long time starts to deteriorate and will eventually fall into ruin, leaving only the foundations, if that abandonment persists; in other words, it is the lack of inhabitants, and everything that this implies (in a word, the life of the house), which causes it to collapse and, in this respect, the house carries the foundations.

---

one of the most intriguing and the most worthy of attention.
64 OC §105.
65 MS 125, 58v, 1942.
66 Cf. OC §225.
67 OC §247.

"The word 'language-*game*' is used to emphasise the fact that the *speaking* of language is part of an activity, or a form of life": he examines the great multiplicity of language-games, including: giving orders, and acting on them; forming and testing a hypothesis; presenting the results of an explanation in tables and diagrams; making a story; and reading one; acting in a play; singing rounds; guessing riddles; solving a problem in applied arithmetic; translating from one language to another; requesting, thanking, cursing, greeting, praying.[68]

Although all of these language-games involve a tacit element, a form of life, and take place within a web of actions and reactions, the dramatic nature of this web is accentuated – by characters acting on each other – and even made explicit with particular acuteness in some of them, as in the case not only of "requesting, thanking, cursing, greeting, praying" but also of "singing rounds", "guessing a riddle" and "giving orders and acting on them", which reveal more of attitudes and dispositions[69] than they do of knowledge, which in turn is indispensable, for example to "forming a hypothesis and putting it to the test" or "drawing diagrams" or "solving a problem in applied arithmetic". As is clear, the dramatic nature of "acting in a play" is obvious and it is highly significant that Wittgenstein should have selected it.

It must be stressed that theatrical images have abounded in his texts since the very beginning (since the concept of *Bild* in the *Tractatus*, and particularly its variation as *lebendes Bild*, whose pictorial-dramatic nature, of baroque origin, must not be forgotten),[70] and which are found among the most significant *Gedankenexperimente* to test questions relating to private language, for example: the language-game of pain (feeling compassion in the belief that another person is in pain; how can we have the authority to doubt that another person is in pain? Could he be pretending?) They occur with particular frequency in *Last Writings on the Philosophy of Psychology* where even the technique of the actor is mentioned (although they can also be detected in *Philosophical Investigations*).[71] Besides this, the theatrical form may have taken on a singular expression in Wittgenstein as a unique vision of human life *sub specie aeterni*, a play that no one wrote and that is not represented on any stage: it is a question of being able to see someone's life as if it were a scene from a play, at which point it becomes "God's work of art", thereby becoming supremely worthy of being lived.[72]

---

68 Cf. PIr § 23.
69 Cf. DB.
70 Cf. TLP 4.0312.
71 Cf., for example, PIr §§ 287–288.
72 Cf. CV, MS 109, 28, 22.8.1930.

"Our clear and simple language-games are not preliminary studies for a future investigation of language – as it were, first approximations ignoring friction and air resistance" (thus began the text that served as an epigraph of this section and with these words we are going to end it). Moreover, present life is not a preparation for a future life.[73] And, because of this, the hypothesis that our life is a dream in no way alters the facts at stake. Ultimately, it will always be a question of asking: how do we learn the word 'dream'?[74] At the same time, it is necessary to admit, as Rilke says,[75] that in life there are no classes for beginners. As for air resistance and friction, I will return to them later.

5 Changes in Games

But how many kinds of sentence are there? Say assertion, question and command? – There are *countless* kinds; countless different kinds of use of all the things we call "signs", "words", "sentences". And this diversity is not something fixed, given once for all; but new types of language, new languages-games, as we may say, come into existence and others become obsolete and get forgotten (we can get a *rough picture* of this from the changes in mathematics).[76]

If we imagine the facts otherwise than as they are, certain language-games lose some of their importance while others become important. And in this way there is an alteration – a gradual one – in the use of the vocabulary of a language.

When language-games change, then there is a change in concepts, and with concepts the meanings of the words change.[77]

Wittgenstein's sensibility is finely tuned not only to the multiplicity of language-games (which is why reducing types of sentences to the categories assertion, question and command in no way does justice to their "infinite diversity" or to the various uses, which are also endless, of "signs", "words", "sentences") but also to the metamorphoses to which they are subject: new ones suddenly emerge as others die, without us being aware of it, and others become obsolete

---

73 As Antiphon says: "There are some who do not live the present life, but prepare with great zeal as if to live some other life than the present one; and all the while time slips away unheeded." (Stobaeus 3.16.20 [B53a], in Graham 2010, p. 820)
74 Cf. OC and PIr.
75 Cf. his work *Die Aufzeichnungen des Malte Laurids Brigge* (Rilke 1950).
76 PIr § 23.
77 OC §§ 63, 65.

(the example of these changes in mathematics is highly significant): games are formed and unformed; they wane and disappear.

Other examples can be added, some also provided by Wittgenstein, others by us. Among the former is his observation about Frazer's use of the words "ghost" and "shade" to account for the beliefs of the savages without noticing that his use of these words immediately establishes an affinity with his own cultural context. Moreover, at that time all educated men spoke of the "soul" and the "spirit", which once again brings us closer to the sayings of primitive peoples: "Compared with this that we do not believe that our soul eats and drinks is a trifling matter".[78] However, this is no longer the case, particularly where the word "soul" is concerned, since the ways in which this word is used by most children and young people have become very limited.

Other words which have lost their importance include those relating to the traditional maternity/paternity/parentage language-game: test tube babies, several mothers, surrogate mothers, dead fathers' frozen semen, homosexual marriage, adoption by homosexual couples, involve key conceptual transformations, a change to the language-game and its tacit presupposition.

As for those which have acquired importance, let us recall the game of evaluation, which is revealed in the invasion, across the planet, of agencies of hierarchization and classification of many social activities (the so-called "rating"), from the university to the elected governments of independent nations; or the obsession with security; or the various ways in which each of our deaths is socially occluded, or – to recall a game which Wittgenstein would not have recognised – interplanetary travel.[79]

These shifts that occur in games (which include the emergence of some, the disappearance of others, changes, mergings, transferrals between some and others) lie at the heart of the transformations, gains and losses that take place in the vocabulary of a language; that is to say, concepts and uses of words change, which is a sign that language is an activity interwoven with other activities, and which occurs in multiple functions irreducible to any analytic, semantic, pragmatic or other programme.

---

78 GB, p. 133.
79 Cf. OC §§ 93, 108, 111, 258, 264, 265.

6 A Condition: Learning to Talk

> We do not learn by inference and deduction, and by the application of mathematics to philosophy, but by direct intercourse. It is with science as with ethics – we cannot know truth by method and contrivance – the Baconian is as false as any other method. The most scientific should be the healthiest man.[80]

The direct confrontation to which Thoreau refers cannot be expressed as an experience in the empirical sense but as an exchange, as active attention, as a delay in the glance and a repetition of the glance. Wittgenstein, for whom experience does not allow one to pass beyond it, and behind which it is always possible to retreat, would agree.[81] On the contrary, there is a point behind which one cannot move back, which, not having any origin in experience, runs through it everywhere; it is spelled out in childhood and is called: learning to speak.

He always takes the opportunity to express the bliss of the German verb *kennenzulernen*, in which the temporality of delay, instruction, belief and recognition are woven together: "We got to know [*kennengelernt haben*] the *nature* [*Wesen*] of calculating by learning to calculate".[82]

In order to say something it is necessary to learn to speak. How does someone learn a word? There are two aspects on which to focus: first, learning to speak is a complex activity and there is an infinite multiplicity of primitive language-games; the child does not learn that cupboards exist; the child hides in them: "Children do not learn that books exist, that armchairs exist, etc. etc., – they learn to fetch books, sit in armchairs, etc. etc.";[83] second, learning to speak assumes that one believes and accepts – this is the beginning – and behind this it is not possible to go.[84] However, it is possible to go in front of it, and it is there that knowledge can be embedded: "The child, I should like to say, learns to react in such-and-such way; and in so reacting it doesn't so far know anything. Knowing only begins at a later level".[85]

---

80 Henry David Thoreau, *Journal*, 11 October 1840 (1981, 187, apud Tauber 2009, p. 197).
81 "But isn't it experience that teaches us to judge like *this*, that is to say, that is correct to judge like this? But how does experience *teach* us, then? We may derive it from experience, but experience does not direct us to derive anything from experience. If it is the *ground* of our judging like this, and not just the cause, still we do not have a ground for seeing this in turn as a ground". "No, experience is not the ground for our game of judging. Nor its outstanding success." (OC §§130–131)
82 OC §45.
83 OC §476.
84 Cf. OC §160.
85 OC §538.

What takes hold of my words is what is around them, the living system of which they form part; it is a question of something that we do not learn when we learn to speak: it belongs to the nature of the tacit element, the assumption, which one day we catch unawares if we strive to discover it: the hinge, the axle "around which a body turns", says Wittgenstein. He then makes an observation which is a priceless clarification (belonging to the same family as the "house that sustains the foundations") concerning what is at stake in this axle, in a way that prevents the image from being misinterpreted; in other words, the axle is not fixed, because something is holding it, "but the movement around it determines its immobility".[86] Our beliefs, for example, are not "intrinsically obvious or convincing" in themselves. They are linked to each other, in some cases more firmly, in others less securely; if that movement ceases, beliefs lose their consistency and turn into "rotten mushrooms dissolving in our mouth".[87] Let us imagine that a person standing before us, whom we have recognized since childhood as our friend, refuses to recognize us. Our world could crumble in a moment.[88]

"One can only say something *when one has learnt to speak* [...]".[89] Wittgenstein's examples range from pain to the colour red, as in the phrases "I feel a pain in my chest" or "that dress is red". But he goes further "How do I recognize that this colour is red? – One answer would be: 'I have learnt English'"[90] and "You learned the *concept* 'pain' in learning language".[91] It is this sort of evidence that he wants to tackle, which he strives to clarify, clearing away the obscurities, raising "the fog" which theoretical fixations cause to fall on whatever meaning is, and which are born, let us recall again, from a prejudice that is not *stupid*.

There are two moments: that of saying and that of recognizing: the first is that of learning to speak, which "is not explaining, but training [*abrichten*]";[92] the second is that of learning with the gaze that has devoted itself to the uses of the word, since these uses, this application, cannot be guessed.

---

86 OC § 152; and cf. also OC § 144.
87 Cf. Hofmannsthal 1991.
88 Cf. OC § 613. In many science-fiction television series and novels of the 1950s and 1960s (for example, *Twilight* Zone and Ray Bradbury's *The Martian Chronicles*) we find multiple versions of an aporia affecting recognition, not only between two people (a friend, a relative) but of human beings themselves (as distinguished from extraterrestrials) and we see that when we are unsure whether we are on earth, at home, with this friend, the web in which our life is caught starts to tear as the threads break.
89 LC.
90 PIr § 381.
91 PIr § 384.
92 PIr § 5.

> One cannot guess how a word functions. One has to *look* at its application and learn from that.
> But the difficulty is to remove the prejudice, which stands in the way of doing so. It is not a *stupid* prejudice.[93]

This prejudice is opposed to this second moment of learning (which means that attention is not paid to the first). Wittgenstein's grammatical investigation,[94] which aims to drive away misunderstandings related to the uses of words, belongs precisely to the second moment of learning and can be recognized in the question, which he repeats again: how is it that we learn this word?

> An intelligent way of dividing up a book on philosophy would be into parts of speech, kinds of words. Where in fact you would have to distinguish far more parts of speech than an ordinary grammar does. You would talk for hours and hours on the verbs "seeing", "feeling", etc., verbs describing personal experience. [...] One thing we always do when discussing a word is to ask how we were taught it.[95]

There is learning to speak, learning with the gaze, and another form of learning that certainly has to do with the knowledge (*Wissen*) that he discusses in *On Certainty*. We will stress the second kind of learning. Having an idea about the life of words is not something that occurs through spontaneous generation; it is not enough to have learnt to speak (although nothing would be achieved without that); it is necessary to look at words, to notice them, their depth: learning to look at the use of words until the discovery is made that, beyond the rules, games have a spirit: the life of words.[96]

---

93 PIr § 340.
94 Cf. DB, where the concept of grammar is presented on the basis of Luther's description of theology as the grammar of God.
95 LC, i, §§ 3, 5.
96 Cf. PIr §§ 432, 564. PPF, xi, § 224.

7 The Invention of Esperanto and the Tower of Babel

> Esperanto. Our feeling of disgust, when we utter an *invented* word with invented derivative syllables. The word is cold, has no associations & yet plays at 'language'. A system of purely signs would not disgust us like this.[97]

As Wittgenstein says, Esperanto is the concept of a language consisting of invented words composed of "derived, invented syllables", an abstract, programmatic universal achieved at the cost of eliminating the particularities of each language, suspending the secret by which any language is formed. Esperanto was invented in the late nineteenth-century by Ludwik Zamenhof with benevolent aims: to be an international lingua franca that would make it possible to avoid the harmful consequences of the linguistic particularities that keep people apart. Entirely artificial, constructed from Romance, Germanic and Slavic languages, it is based on very simple rules (for example, in the written form one sound corresponds to each letter and one letter corresponds to each sound). "The word is cold, has no associations & yet plays at 'language'. A system of purely signs would not disgust us like this".

Engendered by construction, ruled by an assembly principle that is so dear to eclecticism, Esperanto is a ghost born of a dream of reason, a forged language that does without any form of life, eliminating any "family likeness", a language that cannot be transmitted by inheritance, free from any dramatic game, in the sense that no child can learn it and no mother can teach it.

In fact, there is a masked relationship between the confusion of languages and the vain hope of replacing the multiplicity of languages by an invented language, which consists of updating the curse of Babel, interrupting translation (one of the language-games listed, and highlighted, in §23 of the *Investigations*) because it dispenses with it, eliminating all tension between one language and another, erasing the maternal language in its original entanglement. If Babel is a curse, Esperanto is an illusory way of seeking freedom from it.

In other words, what Esperanto lacks is that which language knows and we do not; since we know everything about Esperanto, it fulfils that desideratum that Wittgenstein presents with ironic reserve in §475 of *On Certainty*: "Language did not emerge from some kind of ratiocination", which is why it is disgusting. Instead, the language in which we learn to speak always moves ahead of us since

---

97 CV, MS 132, 69, 26.9.1946.

we use many words in relation to which, if we were asked what they are, we would answer as St Augustine did in relation to time: "if you ask me, I do not know".

8 Modesty and Sang-Froid

Let us return to friction and air resistance – which he did not want to leave out of his investigation into language – not because these are physical aspects of life on earth that Wittgenstein studied scientifically but because they provide images into which he can dig, such as those of the toolbox and the engine driver – images of the mechanics and dynamics of our world, sober and daring at the same time, the fecundity of which moves in several directions.[98]

In fact, a great deal of sang-froid is necessary to go no further than "the everyday objects of thought"; not to want to go beyond that which we have and receive, renouncing argumentative subtleties (which he compares, in one of his most extraordinary images, to the gesture of trying to repair a spider's web with one's hands: this is precisely what hands were not made to do.[99] Also, in order for his steps to advance he prefers rough, rugged ground to smooth ground on which, instead of walking, he would slide.[100]

This is why capturing the incomparable essence of language, inventing concepts that sit above our possibilities, super-concepts as he calls them (for example, language or world), linked, so to speak, by a "super-order", correspond to illusory attempts to legislate language, which in fact is a way of burying the problem instead of solving it.[101] To Wittgenstein the goal of hierarchizing the applications/uses of words is a strange one: "if the words 'language', 'experience', 'world' have a use, it must be as humble a one as that of the words 'table', 'lamp', 'door'".[102]

Once again, it is not as if we have to discover new facts. We do not have to learn anything new. We only have to understand what is in front of us, now; after learning what is most difficult, we add what is most modest.

Avoiding definition neither through carelessness nor in the expectation that one day we will be able to achieve it – a positivist expectation, which ends in a

---

98 Cf. PIr §§ 11 and 12.
99 Cf. PIr § 106.
100 Cf. PIr § 107.
101 Cf. PIr § 351.
102 PIr § 97.

gesture of conjuring trick[103]– is therefore a question of modesty and sang-froid that are revealed as love for clarity and the acceptance of unclarity: many and varied are the ways and manners in which language functions; infinite are the variations of life that are essential to life.

9 A Conformity with no Concept of Purpose

Here we can only describe and say: this is what human life is like.

When, for example, he [Frazer] explains to us that the king must be killed in his prime, because the savages believe that otherwise his soul would not be kept fresh, all one can say is: where that practice and these views occur together, the practice does not spring from the view, but they are both just there.

Burning in effigy. Kissing the picture of one's beloved. That is *obviously not* based on the belief that it will have some specific effect on the object, which the picture represents. It aims at satisfaction and achieves it. Or rather: it *aims* nothing at all; we just behave this way [*eben so*] and then we feel satisfied.[104]

Also, the rituals described, being other examples of language-games, have no basis either. Let us go through the cited texts.

1st moment (after freeing oneself from enforced philosophical diets): describing rituals and saying: it is like this.

2nd moment: explanation of the 1st moment: between ritualistic habits/practices and ways of seeing there is no causal relationship; the former are not effects of the latter, that is, practices do not arise from points of view "but they are both just there".

3rd moment: a more complete explanation: ritualistic practices are not based on a belief in their effect on the objects in question; they are not based on anything that resembles an opinion or an inference; the practices aim only at satisfaction; a solution that appears good but will have to be rectified. Rectification: practices do not aim at satisfaction; rather, practices and satisfaction reciprocally accompany each other: "we act in this way and we feel satisfied". The satisfaction cannot be justified; it lacks reason. In ritual, as in language, the expectation and the satisfaction make contact.[105]

---

103 Cf. PIr § 308.
104 GB, pp. 121, 119, 123.
105 Cf. PIr § 445.

In fact, the only thing that we are authorized to say is that things happen at the same time. However, no inference can be drawn from this association; no general concept can be established, no conclusion drawn, no law extracted (something that also repulsed Thoreau: "He has something demonical in him, who can discern a law or couple two facts", also from the diaristic note quoted above).

It is for this reason that the historical point of view and the evolutionary point of view do not provide access to what interests Wittgenstein (which does not mean that he was not aware of the transformations, metamorphoses, and disappearances of language-games, which are as unpredictable as life). We have to jump outside of the historical point of view since it is the view of the simultaneous, of the landscape, that interests him: satisfaction is a colour that tinges the deed, a face that emerges in it.

Contributors

Alberto Arruda, University of Lisbon / New University of Lisbon (Portugal)
João Vergílio Gallerani Cuter, University of S. Paulo (Brazil)
P. M. S. Hacker, St John's College, Oxford (UK)
Nathan Hauthaler, Birkbeck, University of London (UK)
Emiliano La Licata, University of Palermo (Italy)
Nikolay Milkov, University of Paderborn (Germany)
Maria Filomena Molder, New University of Lisbon (Portugal)
Jesús Padilla Gálvez, University of Castilla-La Mancha, Toledo (Spain)
Rui Sampaio da Silva, University of the Azores (Portugal)
Constantine Sandis, Oxford Brookes University (UK)

References

Alvarez, M., 2009, "How Many Kinds of Reasons?", *Philosophical Explorations*, 12, pp. 181–193.

Alvarez, M., 2010, *Kinds of Reasons. An Essay in the Philosophy of Action*, Oxford: Oxford University Press.

Anscombe, G. E. M., 1963, *Intention*, Cambridge, MA: Harvard University Press.

Anscombe, G. E. M., 1971, "Causality and Determination", in *Metaphysics and the Philosophy of Mind. Collected Papers of G. E. M. Anscombe – Vol. 2*, Oxford: Basil Blackwell, 1981, pp. 133–147.

Baier, A. C., 1985, *Postures of the Mind. Essays on Mind and Morals*, Minnesota: University of Minnesota Press.

Baker, G. P., and Hacker, P. M. S., 1985, *Wittgenstein. Rules, Grammar and Necessity* – Vol. 2 of an Analytical Commentary on the *Philosophical Investigations*, Essays and Exegesis of §§ 185–242, Oxford: Blackwell.

Baker, G. P., and Hacker, P. M. S., 2009, *Wittgenstein. Rules, Grammar and Necessity* – Vol 2 of an Analytical Commentary on the *Philosophical Investigations*, Essays and Exegesis of §§ 185–242, 2nd edn by P. M. S. Hacker, Oxford: Wiley-Blackwell.

Bakhtin, M., 1984, *Problems of Dostoevsky's Poetics*, Minneapolis: University of Minnesota Press.

Bassham, G., and Walls, J. L. (eds.), 2005, *The Chronicles of Narnia and Philosophy. The Lion, the Witch, and the Worldview*, Peru, IL: Open Court Press.

Baum, F., 1900, *The Wonderful Wizard of Oz*, illustrated by W. W. Denslow, Chicago, IL: George M. Hill.

Baum, F., 1907, *Ozma of Oz*, illustrated by J. R. Neill, Chicago, IL: Reilly & Britton.

Beardsmore, R. W., 1996, "If a lion could talk ...", in K. S. Johannessen and T. Nordenstam (eds.), *Wittgenstein and the Philosophy of Culture*, Vienna: Hölder-Pickler-Tempsky, pp. 41–59.

Bekoff, M., 2007, *Animals Matter,* Boston: Shambhala.

Bennett, M. R., and Hacker, P. M. S., 2003, *Philosophical Foundations of Neuroscience*, Oxford: Blackwell.

Blassime, A., Sandis, C., and Bortolotti, L., 2012, "Two Approaches to Animal Ethics and the Case of Great Apes", in K. Petrus and M. Wild (eds.), *Philosophical Perspectives on Animals. Mind, Ethics, Morals,* New York: Springer.

Boden, M., 1981, *Artificial Intelligence and Natural Man*, New York: Basic Books.

Braithwaite, R., 1933, "Philosophy", in H. Wright (ed.), *University Studies, Cambridge 1933*, London: Nicholson & Watson, pp. 1–32.

Brandom, R., 1994, *Making It Explicit*, Cambridge, MA: Harvard University Press.

Budiansky, S., 1998, *If A Lion Could Talk. How Animals Think,* London: Weidenfeld & Nicolson.

Caroll, L., 1871, *Through the Looking Glass and What Alice Found There*, illustrated by J. Tenniel, London: Macmillan.

Cavell, M., 1996, *The Psychoanalytic Mind. From Freud to Philosophy*, Boston, MA: Harvard University Press.

Cavell, S., 1979, *Wittgenstein, Skepticism, Morality and Tragedy*, New York: Oxford University Press.

Charlemagne, 2004, "I understand, up to a point: Decoding a Euro-diplomat takes more than a dictionary", *The Economist*, 2 September.

Clark, S. R. L., 1991, *God's World and the Great Awakening,* Oxford: Clarendon Press.

Clark, S. R. L., 1997, *Animals and their Moral Standing,* London: Routledge.

Cooke, D., 1959, *The Language of Music,* Oxford: Clarendon Press.

Crary, A., and Read, R. (eds.), 2000, *The New Wittgenstein,* London: Routledge.

Crick, F., 1995, *The Astonishing Hypothesis,* London: Touchstone.

Davidson, D., 1963, "Actions, Reasons and Causes", in Davidson 2001, pp. 3–19.

Davidson, D., 1971, "Agency", in Davidson 2001, pp. 43–61.

Davidson, D., 1973, "Freedom to Act", in Davidson 2001, pp. 63–81.

Davidson, D., 1976, "Hempel on Explaining Action", in Davidson 2001, pp. 261–275.

Davidson, D., 1984, "Thought and Talk", in *Inquiries into Truth and Interpretation*, Oxford: Clarendon Press, pp. 155–170.

Davidson, D., 2001, *Essays on Actions and Events,* Oxford: Clarendon Press.

Dennett, D. C., 1979, "Intentional systems", in *Brainstorms. Philosophical Essays on Mind and Psychology*, Montgomery, VT: Bradford Books, pp. 3–22.

Dennett, D. C., 1991, *Consciousness Explained,* New York: Little, Brown and Co.

Dennett, D. C., 1995, "Do animals have beliefs?", in H. L. Roitblat and J.-A. Meyer (eds.), *Comparative Approaches to Cognitive Science*, Cambridge, MA: MIT Press, pp. 111–118.

Dennett, D. C., 1996, *Kinds of Minds. Toward An Understanding of Consciousness,* New York: Basic Books.

Dennett, D. C., 1998, *Brainchildren. Essays on Designing Minds,* Boston: MIT Press.

Diamond, C., 2000, "Ethics, Imagination and the Method of Wittgenstein's *Tractatus*", in Crary and Read (eds.), pp. 149–173.

Dilman, I., 2002, *Wittgenstein's Copernican Revolution. The Question of Linguistic Idealism*, Basingstoke: Palgrave Macmillan.

Dummett, M., 1991, *The Logical Basis of Metaphysics*, Cambridge, MA: Harvard University Press.

Dupré, J., 2002, *Humans and Other Animals,* Oxford: Oxford University Press.

Ebbinghaus, H., 1902, *Grundzüge der Psychologie*, Vol. I., Leipzig: Verlag von Vait & Comp.

Evans, G., 1995, *The Varieties of Reference,* Oxford: Oxford University Press.

Finnegan, R., 2011, *Why Do We Quote? The Culture and History of Quotation*, Cambridge: Open Book Publishers.

Ford, A., Hornsby, J., and Stoutland, F. (eds.), 2011, *Essays on Anscombe's* Intention, Cambridge, MA: Harvard University Press.

Frege, G., 1879, *Begriffsschrift*, Halle a.S.: Nebert.

Frege, G., 1966, *Grundgesetze der Arithmetik. Begriffsschriftlich abgeleitet von G. Frege*, Vol. I (1893), Vol. II (1903), Hildesheim: Georg Olms.

Frege, G., 1976, *Wissenschaftlicher Briefwechsel*, Hamburg: Felix Meiner.

Frege, G., 1977, *Die Grundlagen der Arithmetik*, Hildesheim: Georg Olms.

Frege, G., 1984, *Collected Papers*, Oxford: Blackwell.

Fried, E., 1964, *Warngedichte,* Munich: Carl Hanser Verlag.

Gaita, R., 2002, *The Philosopher's Dog*, New York: Routledge.

Geach, P., 1957, *Mental Acts. Their Content and Their Objects.* London: Routledge & Kegan Paul.

Ginsberg, A., 1958, "The Lion for Real", in *Collected Poems 1947–1980*, New York: Harper & Row, 1984, pp. 174–175.

Glendinning, S., 1998, *On Being With Others,* London: Routledge.

Gray, J., 2002, *Straw Dogs,* London: Granta.

Glock, H.-J., 1996a, "On Safari with Wittgenstein, Quine and Davidson", in R. Arrington and H.-J. Glock (eds.), *Wittgenstein and Quine*, London: Routledge, pp. 144–173.

Glock, H.-J., 1996b, *A Wittgenstein Dictionary,* Oxford: Blackwell.

Glock, H.-J., 2000, "Animals, thoughts and concepts", *Synthese*, 123, pp. 35–64.

Glock, H.-J., 2006, "Thought, language and animals", in M. Kobe (ed.), *Deepening our Understanding of Wittgenstein, Grazer Philosophische Studien*, 71, pp. 139–160.

Goethe, J. W. v., 1982, *Werke*, Hamburger Ausgabe, 1948–66, 14 vols., München: C. H. Beck.

Graham, D. W. (ed.), 2010, *The Texts of Early Greek Philosophy. The Complete Fragments and Selected Testimonies of the Major Presocratics*, Part I, Cambridge: Cambridge University Press.

Grayling, A. C., 1988, *Wittgenstein*, Oxford: Oxford University Press.

Hacker, P. M. S., 1993, *Wittgenstein. Meaning and Mind*, pb. ed., Oxford: Blackwell.

Hacker, P. M. S., 1996, *Wittgenstein. Mind and Will* – Vol 4, Part II of an Analytical Commentary on the *Philosophical Investigations*, Exegesis of §§ 428–693, Oxford: Blackwell.

Hacker, P. M. S., 2007, *Human Nature. The Categorial Framework*, Oxford: Blackwell.

Hackerl, P. M. S., 2009, "Agential Reasons and the Explanation of Human Behaviour", in Sandis (ed.), pp. 75–93.

Hacker, P. M. S., forthcoming A, "Kant et Wittgenstein, le problème des arguments transcendantaux", in A. Moreno and A. Soulez (eds.), *Grammatical ou transcendantal, Cahiers de philosophie du langage*, 8, Paris: L'Harmattan.

Hacker, P. M. S., forthcoming B, *The Cognitive and Cogitative Powers: An Essay on Human Nature*.

Haidt, J., 2012, *The Righteous Mind. Why Good People are Divided by Politics and Religion,* London: Allen Lane.

Hamann, J. G., 1955–75, *Briefwechsel*, 8 vols., Frankfurt am Main: Insel Verlag.

Hempel, C. G., 1961, "Rational Action", *Proceedings and Addresses of the American Philosophical Association*, 35, pp. 5–23.

Hintikka, J., and Hintikka, M. B., 1986, "Wittgenstein's *Annus Mirabilis*: 1929", in W. Leinfellner and F. Wuketits (eds.), *The Tasks of Contemporary Philosophy. Proceedings of the 10th International Wittgenstein Symposium*, Vienna: Hölder–Pichler–Tempsky, pp. 437–447.

Hintikka, J., 1993, "The Original *Sinn* of Wittgenstein's Philosophy of Mathematics", in K. Puhl (ed.), *Wittgensteins Philosophie der Mathematik*, Vienna: Hölder–Pichler–Tempsky, pp. 24–51.

Höfler, A., 1897, *Psychologie*. Vienna: Verlag von F. Tempsky.

Hofmannsthal, H. v., 1991, "Ein Brief", in *Sämtliche Werke XXXI. Erfundene Gespräche und Briefe*, ed. E. Ritter, Frankfurt am Main: S. Fischer.

Hofstadter, D. R., 1979, *Gödel, Escher, Bach. An Eternal Golden Braid*, New York: Basic Books.

Hornsby, J., 2011, "Actions in Their Circumstances", in Ford, Hornsby and Stoutland (eds.), pp. 105–127.

Husserl, E., 1968, *Logische Untersuchungen, Untersuchungen zur Phänomenologie und Theorie der Erkenntnis*, II/1, Tübingen: Max Niemeyer Verlag.

Hutto, D., 1996, "With the later Wittgenstein a transcendental idealist?", in P. Coates and D. Hutto (eds.), *Current Issues in Idealism,* London: Continuum, pp. 121–153.

Hyman, J., 2011, "Wittgenstein on Action and the Will", *Grazer Philosophische Studien*, 82, pp. 285–311.

Kant, I., 1974, *Kritik der reinen Vernunft*, Frankfurt am Main: Suhrkamp.

Kant, I., 2002, *Prolegomena to any future metaphysics that will be able to come forward as science*, trans. G. Hatfield, in *Theoretical Philosophy after 1781*, ed. H. Allison and P. Heath, Cambridge: Cambridge University Press.

Kant, I., 2005, *Notes and Fragments*, ed. P. Guyer, trans. C. Bowman, P. Guyer and F. Rauscher, Cambridge: Cambridge University Press.

Kant, I., 2007, *Anthropology from a pragmatic point of view*, trans. R. B. Louden, in *Anthropology, History and Education*, ed. G. Zoller and R. B. Louden, Cambridge: Cambridge University Press.

Kauffman, S. A., 2000, *Investigations*, New York: Oxford University Press.

Kauffman, S. A., 2008, *Reinventing the Sacred. A New View of Science, Reason and Religion*, New York: Basic Books.

Kenny, A. J. P., 1963, *Action, Emotion and Will*, London: Routledge & Kegan Paul.

Kenny, A. J. P., 1973, *Wittgenstein*, Oxford: Basil Blackwell.

Kenny, A. J. P., 1993, *Aquinas on Mind*, London: Routledge.

Kenny, A. J. P., 2002, *The Unknown God. Agnostic Essays*, London: Continuum.

Kienzler, W., 1997, *Wittgensteins Wende zu seiner Spätphilosophie: 1930–1932*, Frankfurt: Suhrkamp.

Kinghorn, K., 2005, "Virtue Epistemology: Why Uncle Andrew Couldn't Hear the Animals Speak", in Bassham and Walls (eds.), pp. 15–26.

Kripke, S., 1982, *Wittgenstein on Rules and Private Language*, Oxford: Basil Blackwell.

Kusch, M., 2006, *A Sceptical Guide to Meaning and Rules. Defending Kripke's Wittgenstein*, Chesham: Acumen.

Lear, J., 2006, *Radical Hope. Ethics in the Face of Cultural Devastation*, Boston, MA: Harvard University Press.

Lewis, C. S., 1950, *The Lion, the Witch and the Wardrobe,* illustrated by P. Baynes, London: Geoffrey Bles.

Lewis, C. S., 1955, *The Magician's Nephew*, illustrated by P. Baynes, London: The Bodley Head.

Malcolm, N., 1982, "Wittgenstein and Idealism", in G. Vesey (ed.), *Idealism: Past and Present*, Cambridge: Cambridge University Press.

Marques, A., and Venturinha, N. (eds.), 2010, *Wittgenstein on Forms of Life and the Nature of Experience*, Bern: Peter Lang,

Matthews, G. B., 1977, "Consciousness and life", *Philosophy*, 52, pp. 13–26.

McDowell, J., 1984, "Wittgenstein on Following a Rule", in McDowell 1998, pp. 221–262.

McDowell, J., 1993, "Meaning and Intentionality in Wittgenstein's Later Philosophy", in McDowell 1998, pp. 263–278.

McDowell, J., 1996, *Mind and World*, Cambridge, MA: Harvard University Press.

McDowell, J., 1998, *Mind, Value and Reality*, Cambridge, MA: Harvard University Press.

McDowell, J., 2002, "How Not to Read *Philosophical Investigations*: Brandom's Wittgenstein", in *The Engaged Intellect*, Cambridge, MA: Harvard University Press, 2009, pp. 96–114.

McGuinness, B., 2002, *Approaches to Wittgenstein. Collected Papers*, London: Routledge.

Medina, J., 2002, *The Unity of Wittgenstein's Philosophy*, Albany, NY: SUNY Press.

Melden, A. I., 1961, *Free Action*, London: Routledge & Kegan Paul.

Milkov, N., 2001, "Tractarian Scaffoldings", *Prima philosophia*, 14, pp. 399–414.

Milkov, N., 2002, "The Joint Philosophical Program of Russell and Wittgenstein (March–November 1912) and Its Downfall", *Contributions of the Austrian Ludwig Wittgenstein Society*, 10, pp. 60–62.

Milkov, N., 2003a, *A Hundred Years of English Philosophy*, Dordrecht: Kluwer.

Milkov, N., 2003b, "Susan Stebbing's Criticism of Wittgenstein's *Tractatus*", *Vienna Circle Institute Yearbook*, 10, pp. 351–363.

Monk, R., 1990, *The Duty of Genius*, New York: Penguin Books.

Moran, R., and Stone, M. J., "Anscombe on the Expression of Intention", in C. Sandis (ed.), pp. 132–168.

Mounce, H. O., 1989,"The Aroma of Coffee", *Philosophy*, 64, pp. 159–173.

Moore, A., 1985, "Transcendental Idealism in Wittgenstein, and Theories of Meaning", *Philosophical Quarterly,* 35, pp. 134–155; reprinted, with corrections and an appendix, in Whiting, D. (ed.), 2010, *The Later Wittgenstein on Language*, Basingstoke: Palgrave Macmillan, pp. 191–212, to which any page numbers refer.

Mulhall, S., 2007, *Wittgenstein's Private Language. Grammar, Nonsense, and Imagination in Philosophical Investigations, §§ 243–315*, Oxford: Clarendon Press.

Murdoch, I., 1993, *Metaphysics as a Guide to Morals*, London: Penguin.

Nagel, T., 1974, "What Is It Like To Be a Bat?", *The Philosophical Review*, 83, pp. 435–450.

Osborne, C., 2007, *Dumb Beasts & Dead Philosophers. Humanity & the Humane in Ancient Philosophy & Literature,* Oxford: Oxford University Press.

Pascal, B., 1670/2005, *Pensées*, trans. R. Ariew, Indianapolis, IN: Hackett.

Pears, D., 1987, *The False Prison*, 2 vols., Oxford: Clarendon Press.

Pears, D., 2006, *Paradox and Platitude in Wittgenstein's Philosophy*, Oxford: Clarendon Press.

Petrarca, F., 2004, *Epystolae Familiares* (1325–1361), *Liber* XXIII, 19, 11–12, Biblioteca Italiana.

Philips, D. Z., 2004, *Religion and Friendly Fire. Examining Assumptions in Contemporary Philosophy of Religion*, London: Ashgate.

Pichler, Alois, 2004, *Wittgensteins "Philosophische Untersuchungen". Vom Buch zum Album*, Amsterdam: Rodopi.

Pichler, Alois, forthcoming, "Reflections on a Prominent Argument in the Wittgenstein Debate", *Philosophy and Literature*.

Pitcher, G., 1964, *The Philosophy of Wittgenstein*, Englewood Cliffs, NJ: Prentice-Hall.

Plato, 1926, *Parmenides,* trans. H. N. Fowler, Cambridge, MA: Harvard University Press.

Plato, 1991, *Lysis. Symposium. Gorgias*, trans. W. R. M. Lamb, Cambridge, MA: Harvard University Press.

Prigogine, I., and Stengers, I., 1988, *Entre le temps et l'éternité*, Paris: Fayard.

Prinz, J., 2012, *Beyond Human Nature,* London: Allen Lane.

Reid, T., 2002, *Essays on the Intellectual Powers of Man*, Edinburgh: Edinburgh University Press.

Reppert, V., 2005, "The Green Witch and the Great Debate: Freeing Narnia from the Spell of the Lewis-Anscombe Legend", in Bassham and Walls (eds.), pp. 260–273.

Richter, D. J., 2004, "Ludwig Wittgenstein", *Internet Encyclopedia of Philosophy*, 30 August 2004: http://www.iep.utm.edu/wittgens; retrieved 6 May 2011.

Rilke, R. M., 1950, "Die Aufzeichnungen des Malte Laurids Brigge", in *Sämtliche Werke*, 7 vols., 1955–1966 & 1997, Frankfurt am Main: Insel Verlag, pp. 707–946.

Russell, B., 1936, "The Limits of Empiricism", *Proceedings of the Aristotelian Society*, 36, pp. 131–150.

Ryle, G., 1949, *The Concept of Mind*, London: Hutchinson.

Sandis, C., 2006, "Animals", in M. Cohen (ed.), *Essentials of Philosophy and Ethics,* London and New York: Hodder Education/Oxford University Press, pp. 11–14.

Sandis, C. (ed.), 2009, *New Essays on the Explanation of Action*, Basingstoke: Palgrave Macmillan.

Sandis, C., 2010, "Animal Ethics", in R. H. Corrigan and M. E. Farrell (eds.), *Ethics. A University Guide*, Gloucester: Progressive Frontiers Press, pp. 21–39.

Schroeder, S., 2001, "Are Reasons Causes? A Wittgensteinian Response to Davidson", in S. Schroeder (ed.), *Wittgenstein and Contemporary Philosophy of Mind*, New York: Palgrave Macmillan, pp. 150–170.

Schueler, G. F., 2003, *Reasons and Purposes. Human Rationality and the Teleological Explanation of Action*, Oxford: Clarendon Press.

Schulte, J., 2005, *Ludwig Wittgenstein*, Frankfurt: Suhrkamp.

Scott, M., 1996, "Wittgenstein's Philosophy of Action", *The Philosophical Quarterly*, 46, pp. 347–363.

Scott, M., 1998, "The Context of Wittgenstein's Philosophy of Action", *Journal of the History of Philosophy*, 36, pp. 595–617.

Scruton, R., 1976, "Self-Knowledge and Intention", *Proceedings of the Aristotelian Society*, New Series, 77, pp. 87–106.

Sharpe, L., 2005, *Creatures Like Us?* Exeter: Imprint Academic.

Shweder, R. A., 1991, *Thinking Through Cultures. Expeditions in Cultural Psychology*, Boston MA: Harvard University Press.

Strawson, G., 2010, *Mental Reality*, 2nd rev. edn, Boston MA: MIT Press.

Strawson, P. F., 1959, *Individuals*, London: Methuen.

Tanney, J., 2009a, "Reasons as Non-causal, Context-placing Explanations", in Sandis (ed.), pp. 94–111.

Tanney, J., 2009b, "Gilbert Ryle", *The Stanford Encyclopedia of Philosophy* (Winter 2009 Edition), ed. Edward N. Zalta, URL http://plato.stanford.edu/archives/win2009/entries/ryle/.

Tauber, A. I., 2009, *Science and the Quest for Meaning*, Waco, Texas: Baylor University Press.

Thompson, M., 2008, *Life and Action. Elementary Structures of Practice and Practical Thought*, Cambridge, MA: Harvard University Press.

Thompson, M., 2011, "Anscombe's Intention and Practical Knowledge", in Ford, Hornsby and Stoutland (eds.), pp. 198–210.

Thoreau, H. D., 1853, *The Writings of H. D. Thoreau*, Riverside Edition, Vol. IX, Boston: Houghton Mifflin.

von Savigny, E., 1991, "Common behaviour of many a kind: *Philosophical Investigations* section 206", in R. Arrington and H.-J. Glock (eds.), *Wittgenstein's Philosophical Investigations*, London: Routledge, pp. 105–119.

Waismann, F., 1967, "Thesen", in *Ludwig Wittgenstein und der Wiener Kreis*, Frankfurt am Main: Suhrkamp, pp. 233–261.

Webb, S. H., 2005, "Aslan's Voice: C. S. Lewis and the Magic of Sound", in Bassham and Walls (eds.), 2005, pp. 3–14.

White, A. R., 1964, *Attention*, Oxford: Blackwell.

Williams, B., 1973, "Wittgenstein and Idealism", in G. Vasey (ed.), *Understanding Wittgenstein*, London: Macmillan, pp. 76–95; reprinted in Williams, B., 1981, *Moral Luck*, Cambridge: Cambridge University Press, pp. 44–63, to which any page numbers refer.

Wilson, A. N., 2004, *My Name is Legion*, London: Hutchinson.

Wisdom, J., 1953, "Philosophical Perplexity", in *Philosophy and Psycho-Analysis*, Oxford: Blackwell, pp. 36–50.

Wolfe, J., (ed.), 2011, *Journal of Inklings Studies – Special Issue on C. S. Lewis and G. E. M. Anscombe*, 1.

Index

www.ingramcontent.com/pod-product-compliance
Lightning Source LLC
Chambersburg PA
CBHW070035100426
42740CB00013B/2696